THE TENTH
GARFIELD TREASURY

THE TENTH
GARFIELD TREASURY

BY: JIM DAVIS

BALLANTINE BOOKS • NEW YORK

A Ballantine Book
Published by The Ballantine Publishing Group

The Sunday strips appearing here in color were previously in black and white in
GARFIELD THROWS HIS WEIGHT AROUND, GARFIELD LIFE TO THE FULLEST, and
GARFIELD FEEDS THE KITTY.

www.randomhouse.com/BB/

Library of Congress Catalog Card Number: 99-90168

ISBN: 0-345-43674-1

First Edition: October 1999

10 9 8 7 6 5 4 3 2 1

THE TENTH
GARFIELD
TREASURY

Work Bytes!

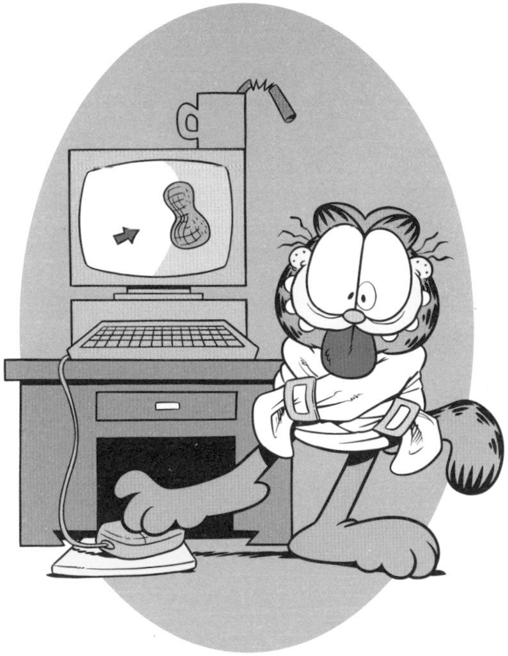

Around here, you gotta be crazy, or you'll go nuts!

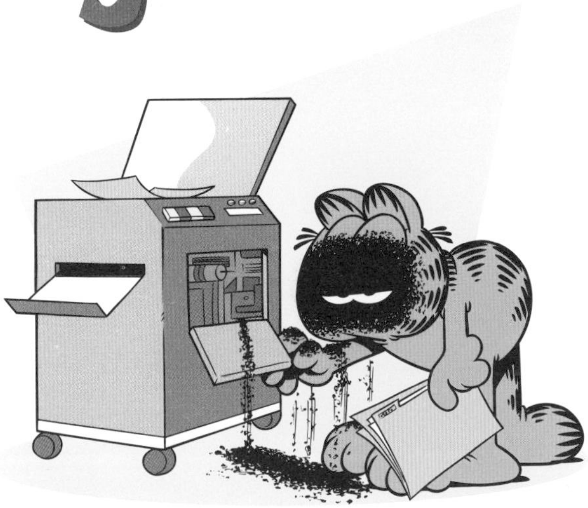

Take life one disaster at a time.

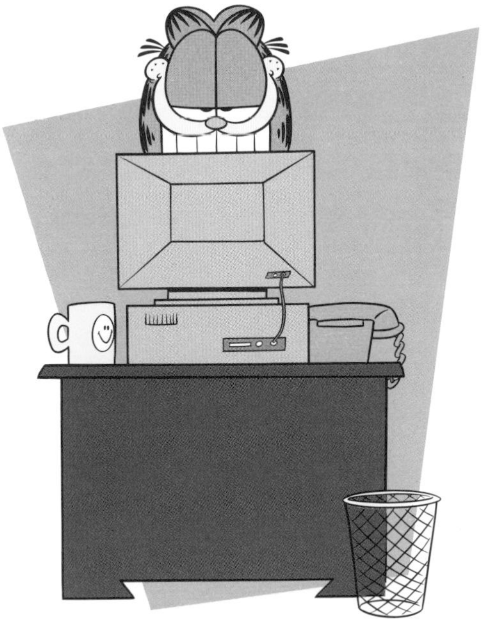

It's not just a job. It's a way to escape my kids.

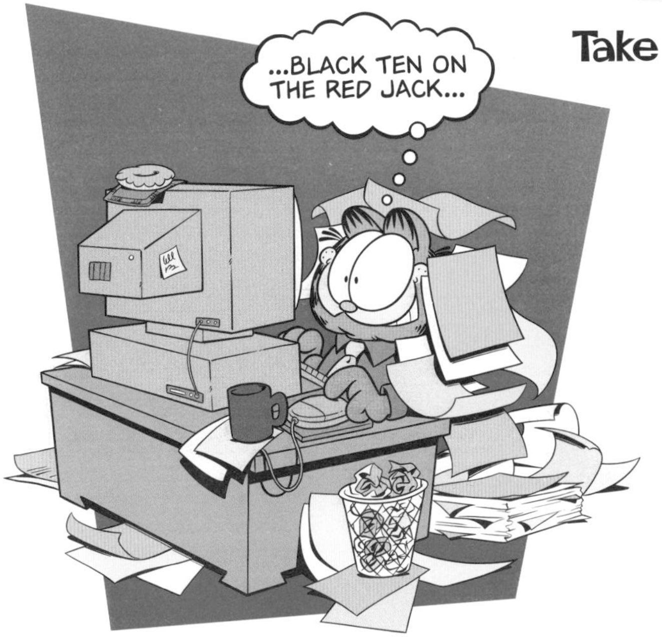
...BLACK TEN ON THE RED JACK...

No problem is too big to be ignored.

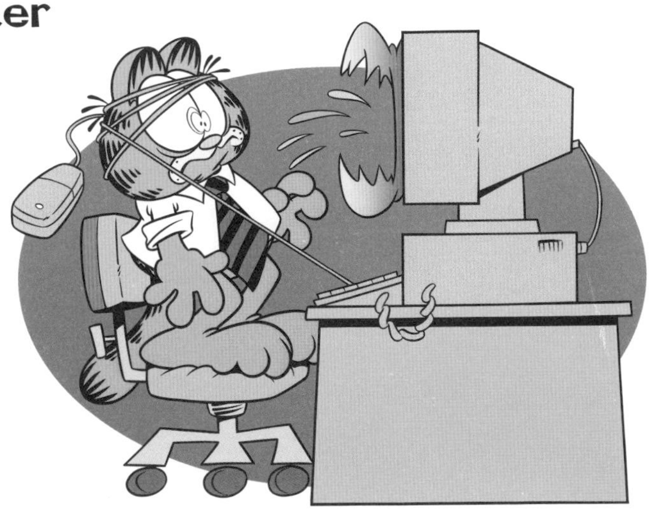

Some days you get the work. Some days the work gets you.

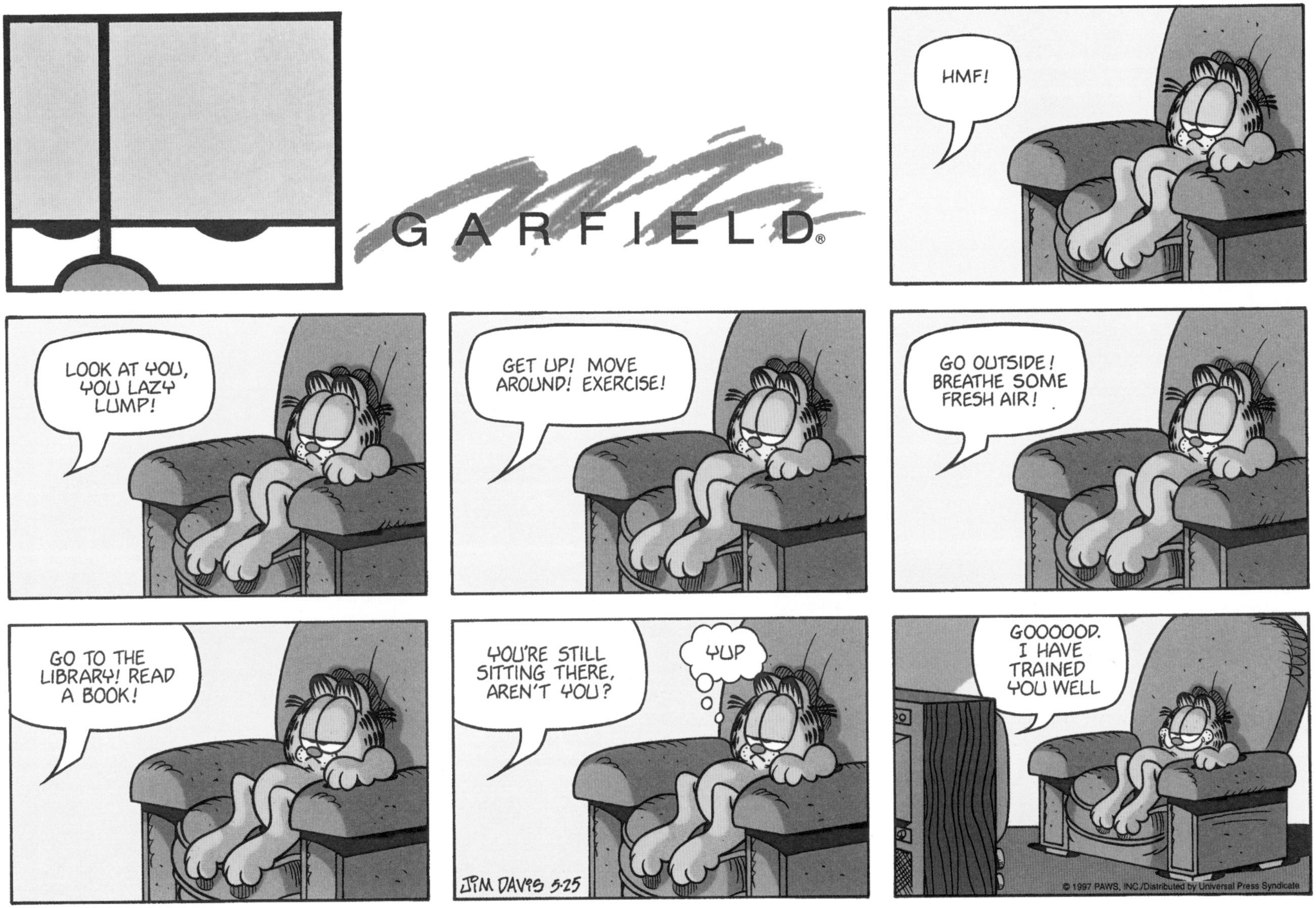
GARFIELD®
HMF!
LOOK AT YOU, YOU LAZY LUMP!
GET UP! MOVE AROUND! EXERCISE!
GO OUTSIDE! BREATHE SOME FRESH AIR!
GO TO THE LIBRARY! READ A BOOK!
YOU'RE STILL SITTING THERE, AREN'T YOU?
YUP
JIM DAVIS 5-25
GOOOOOD. I HAVE TRAINED YOU WELL
© 1997 PAWS, INC./Distributed by Universal Press Syndicate

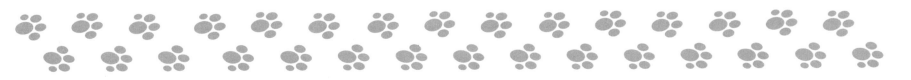

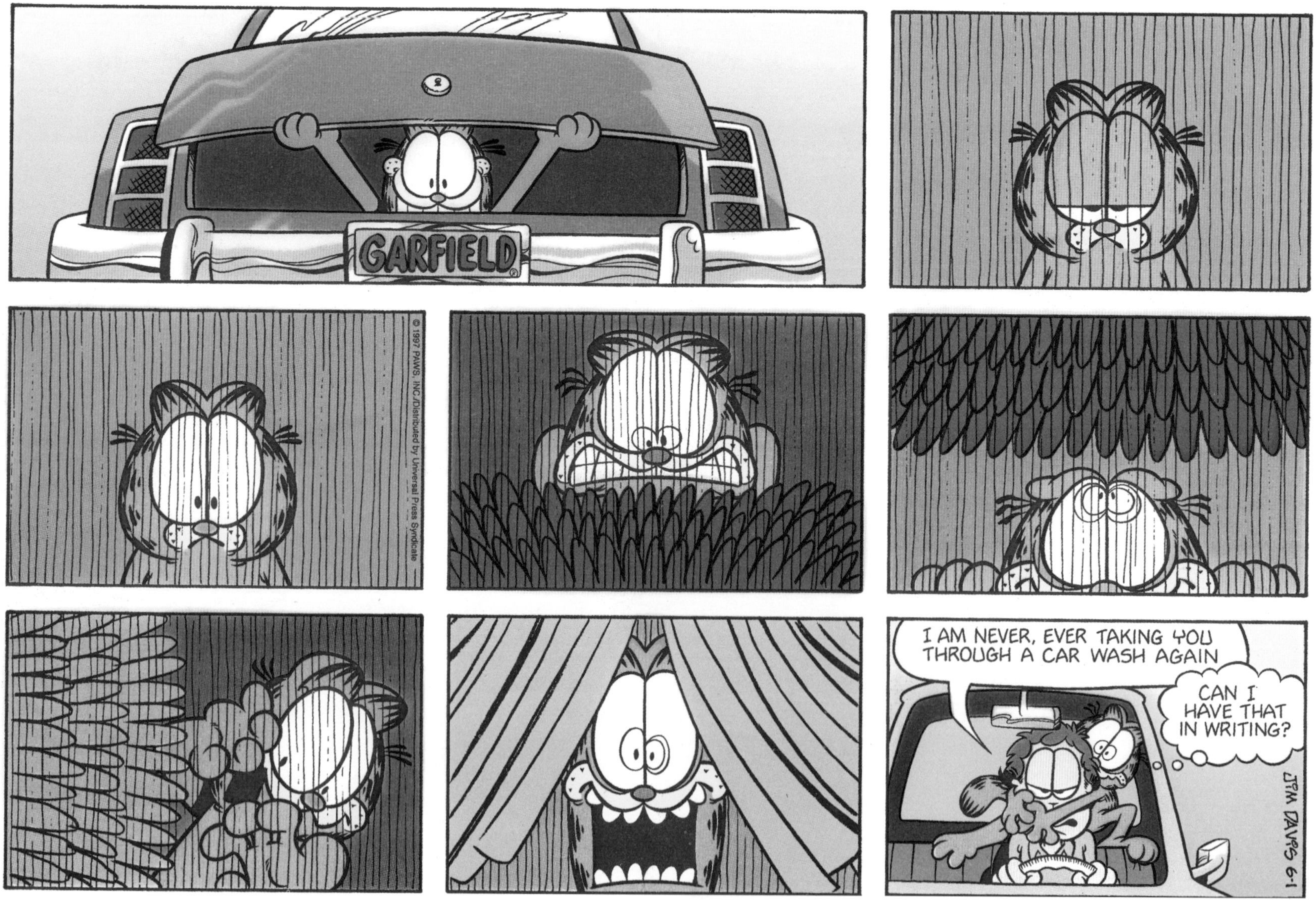
GARFIELD
© 1997 PAWS, INC./Distributed by Universal Press Syndicate
I AM NEVER, EVER TAKING YOU THROUGH A CAR WASH AGAIN
CAN I HAVE THAT IN WRITING?
JIM DAVIS 6-1

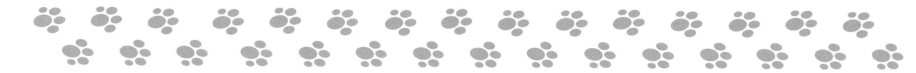

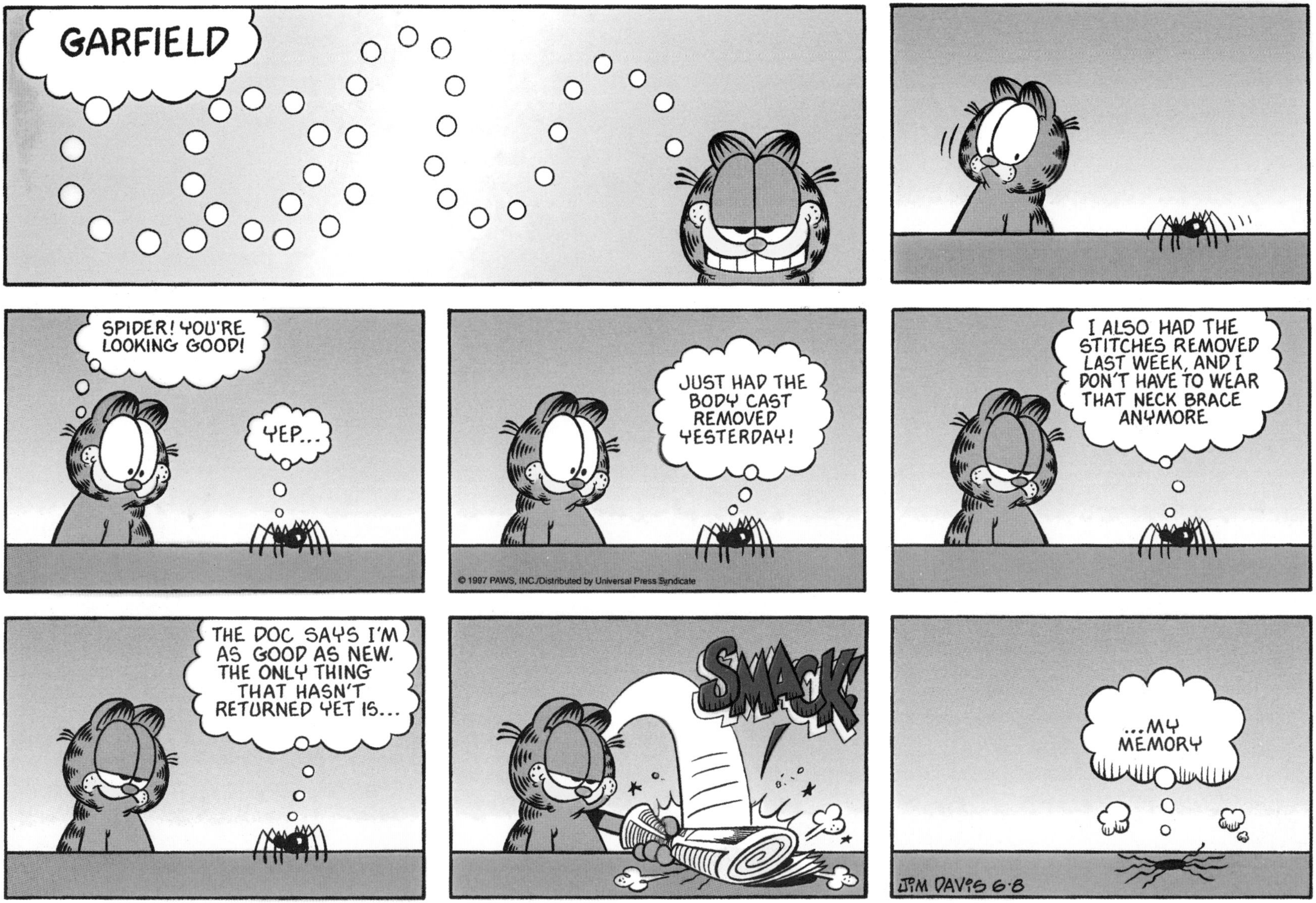
GARFIELD
SPIDER! YOU'RE LOOKING GOOD!
YEP...
JUST HAD THE BODY CAST REMOVED YESTERDAY!
© 1997 PAWS, INC./Distributed by Universal Press Syndicate
I ALSO HAD THE STITCHES REMOVED LAST WEEK, AND I DON'T HAVE TO WEAR THAT NECK BRACE ANYMORE
THE DOC SAYS I'M AS GOOD AS NEW. THE ONLY THING THAT HASN'T RETURNED YET IS...
SMACK!
...MY MEMORY
JIM DAVIS 6-8

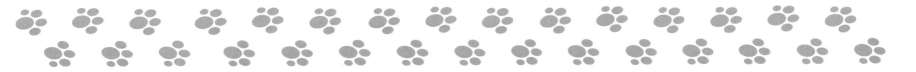

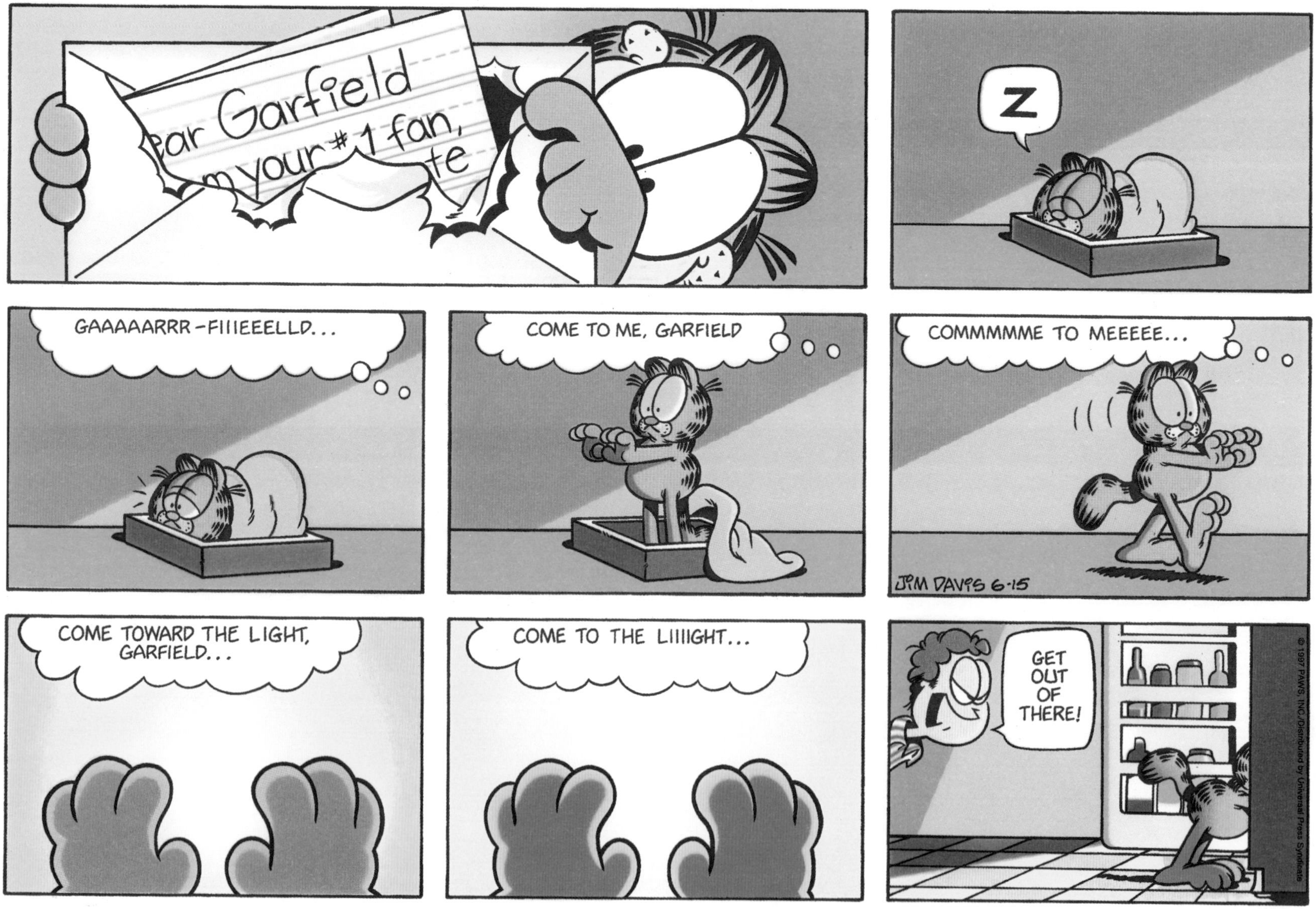
ear Garfield
m your # 1 fan,
te
Z
GAAAAARRR-FIIIEEELLD...
COME TO ME, GARFIELD
COMMMMME TO MEEEEE...
JIM DAVIS 6-15
COME TOWARD THE LIGHT, GARFIELD...
COME TO THE LIIIIGHT...
GET OUT OF THERE!
© 1997 PAWS, INC./Distributed by Universal Press Syndicate

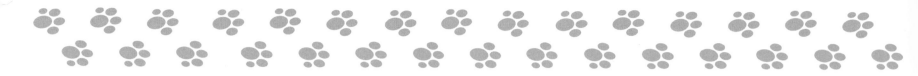

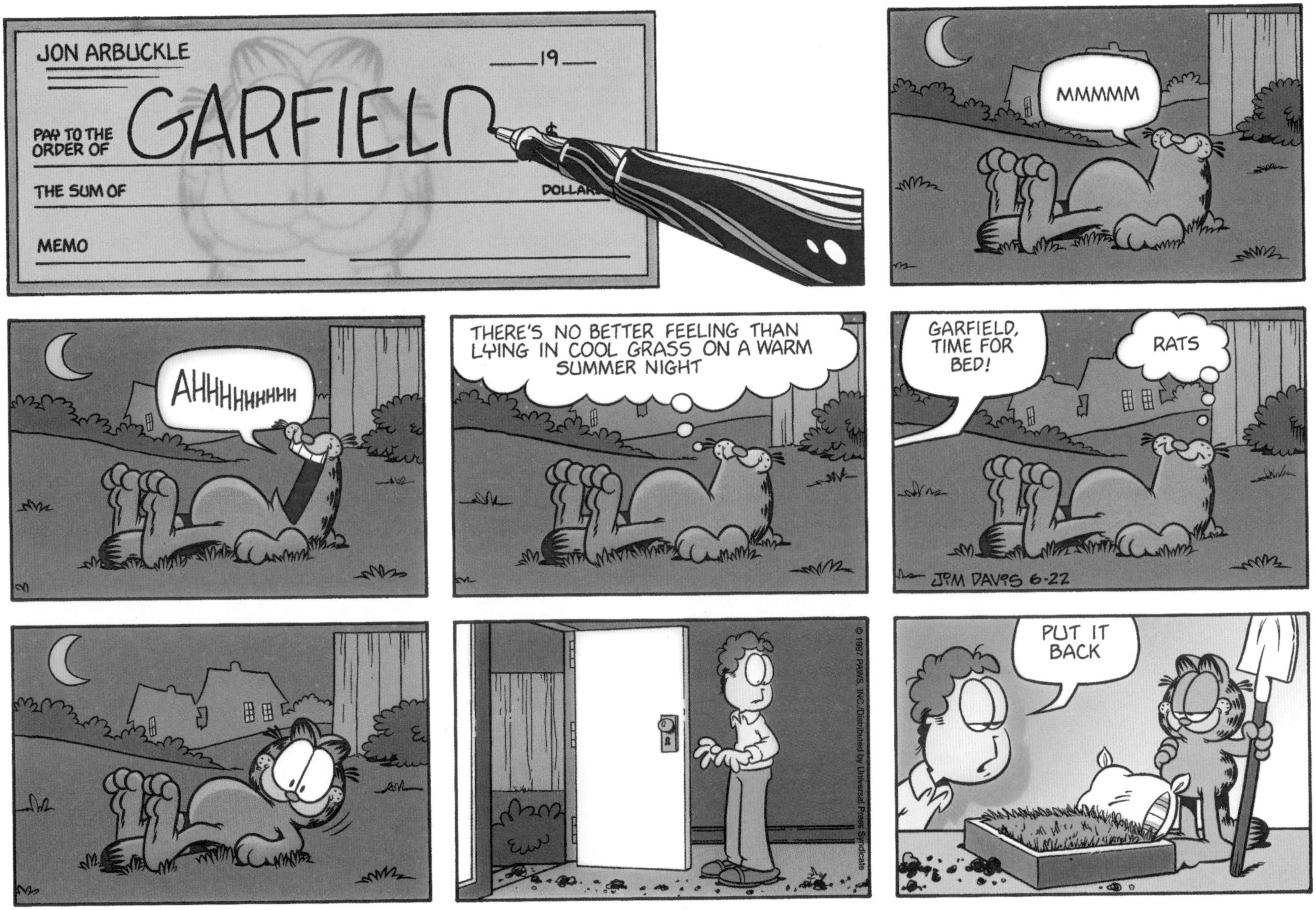
JON ARBUCKLE
19
PAY TO THE ORDER OF
GARFIELD
$
THE SUM OF
DOLLARS
MEMO
MMMMM
AHHHHHHHHH
THERE'S NO BETTER FEELING THAN LYING IN COOL GRASS ON A WARM SUMMER NIGHT
GARFIELD, TIME FOR BED!
RATS
JIM DAVIS 6-22
© 1997 PAWS, INC./Distributed by Universal Press Syndicate
PUT IT BACK

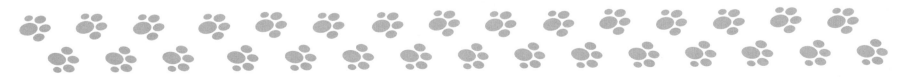

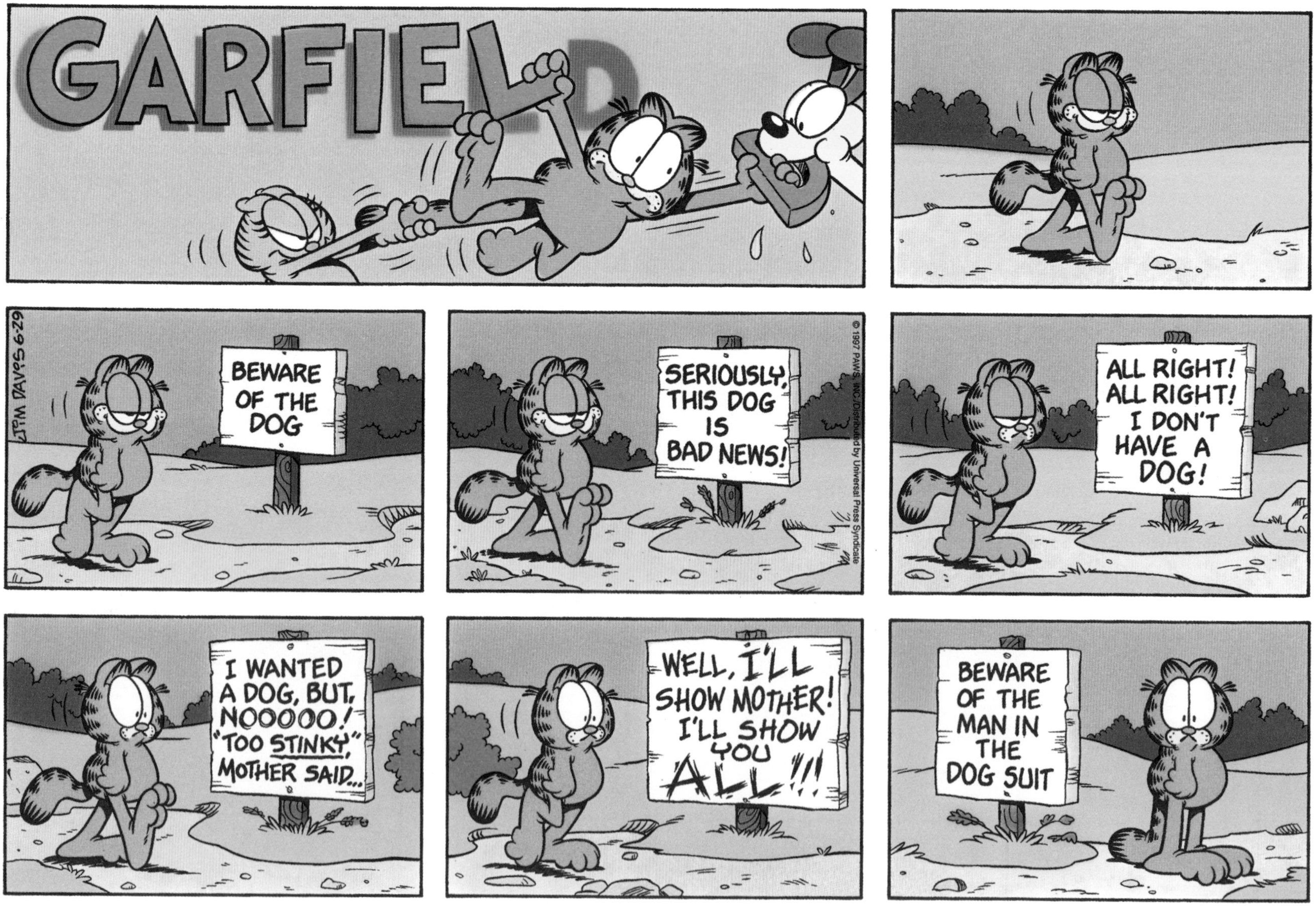
GARFIELD
JIM DAVIS 6-29
BEWARE OF THE DOG
SERIOUSLY, THIS DOG IS BAD NEWS!
© 1997 PAWS, INC./Distributed by Universal Press Syndicate
ALL RIGHT! ALL RIGHT! I DON'T HAVE A DOG!
I WANTED A DOG, BUT, NOOOOO! "TOO STINKY," MOTHER SAID...
WELL, I'LL SHOW MOTHER! I'LL SHOW YOU ALL!!!
BEWARE OF THE MAN IN THE DOG SUIT

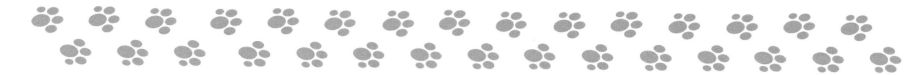

GARFIELD®
AHHHH
AHHHH
JIM DAVIS 7-6
AHHHHHHHHHHHHH
© 1997 PAWS, INC./Distributed by Universal Press Syndicate

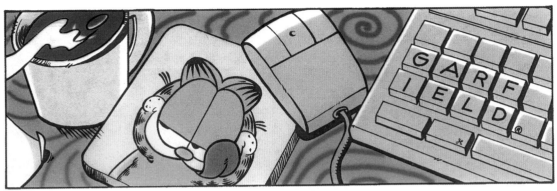

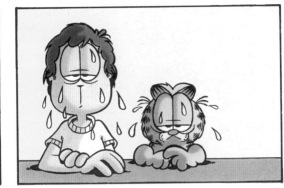

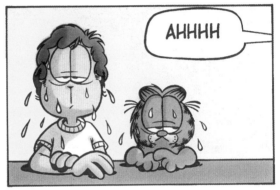

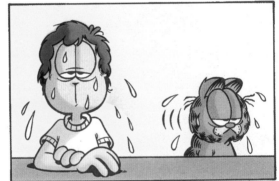

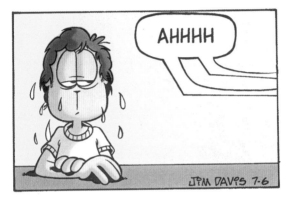

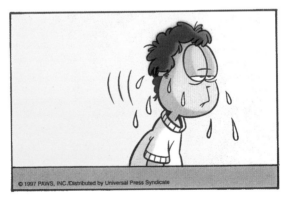

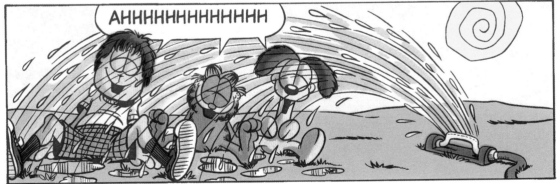

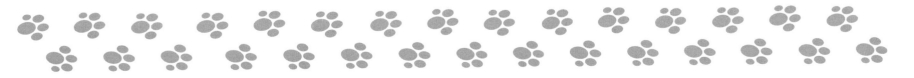

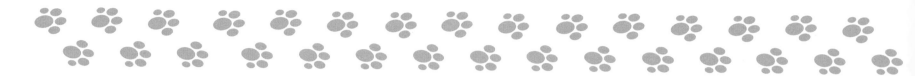

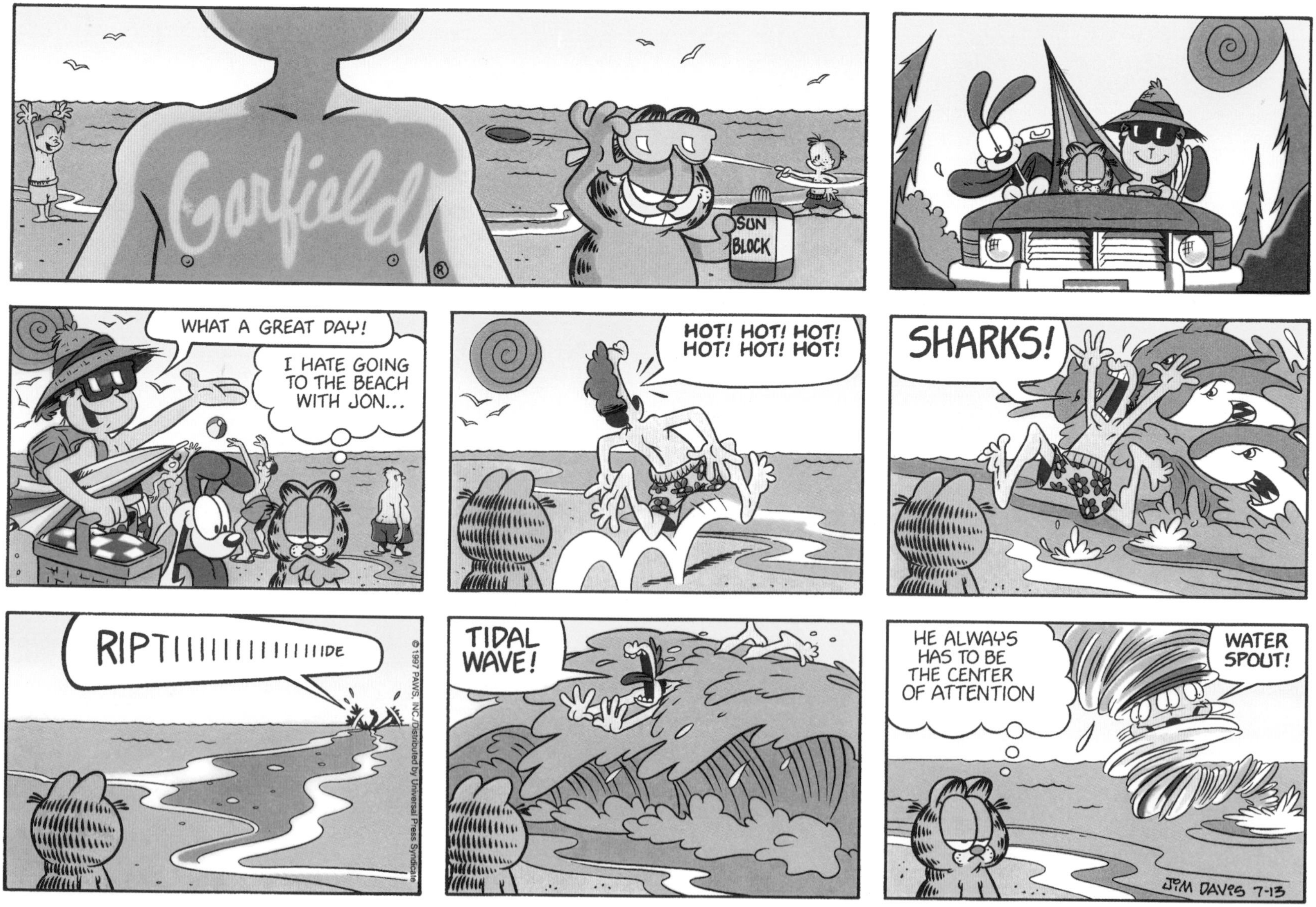
Garfield ®
SUN BLOCK
WHAT A GREAT DAY!
I HATE GOING TO THE BEACH WITH JON...
HOT! HOT! HOT! HOT! HOT! HOT!
SHARKS!
RIPTIIIIIIIIIIIIIIIIIDE
© 1997 PAWS, INC./Distributed by Universal Press Syndicate
TIDAL WAVE!
HE ALWAYS HAS TO BE THE CENTER OF ATTENTION
WATER SPOUT!
JIM DAVIS 7-13

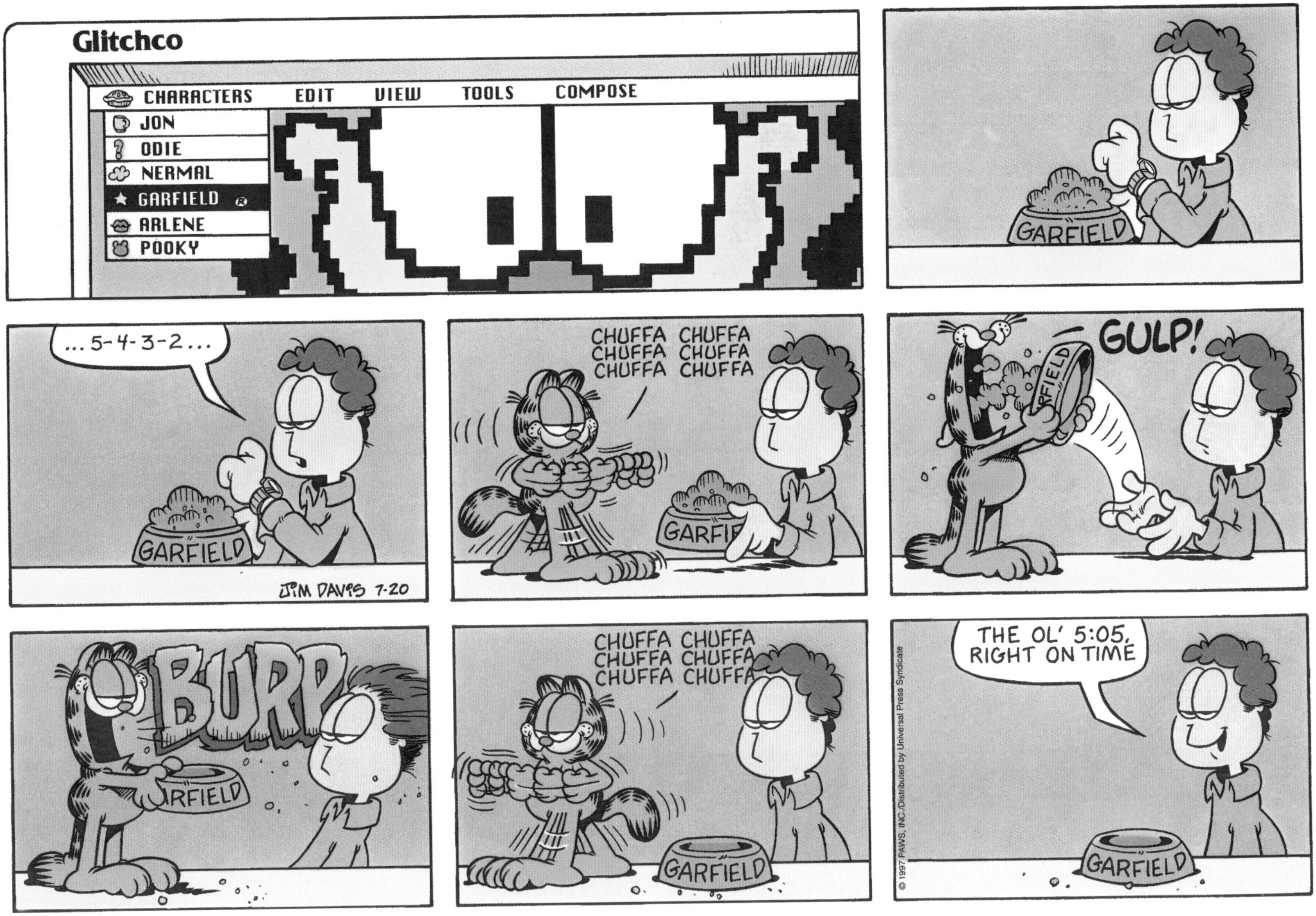
Glitchco
CHARACTERS
EDIT
VIEW
TOOLS
COMPOSE
JON
ODIE
NERMAL
GARFIELD ®
ARLENE
POOKY
GARFIELD
...5-4-3-2...
GARFIELD
JIM DAVIS 7-20
CHUFFA CHUFFA
CHUFFA CHUFFA
CHUFFA CHUFFA
GARFIE
GULP!
RFIELD
BURP
RFIELD
CHUFFA CHUFFA
CHUFFA CHUFFA
CHUFFA CHUFFA
GARFIELD
THE OL' 5:05, RIGHT ON TIME
GARFIELD
© 1997 PAWS, INC./Distributed by Universal Press Syndicate

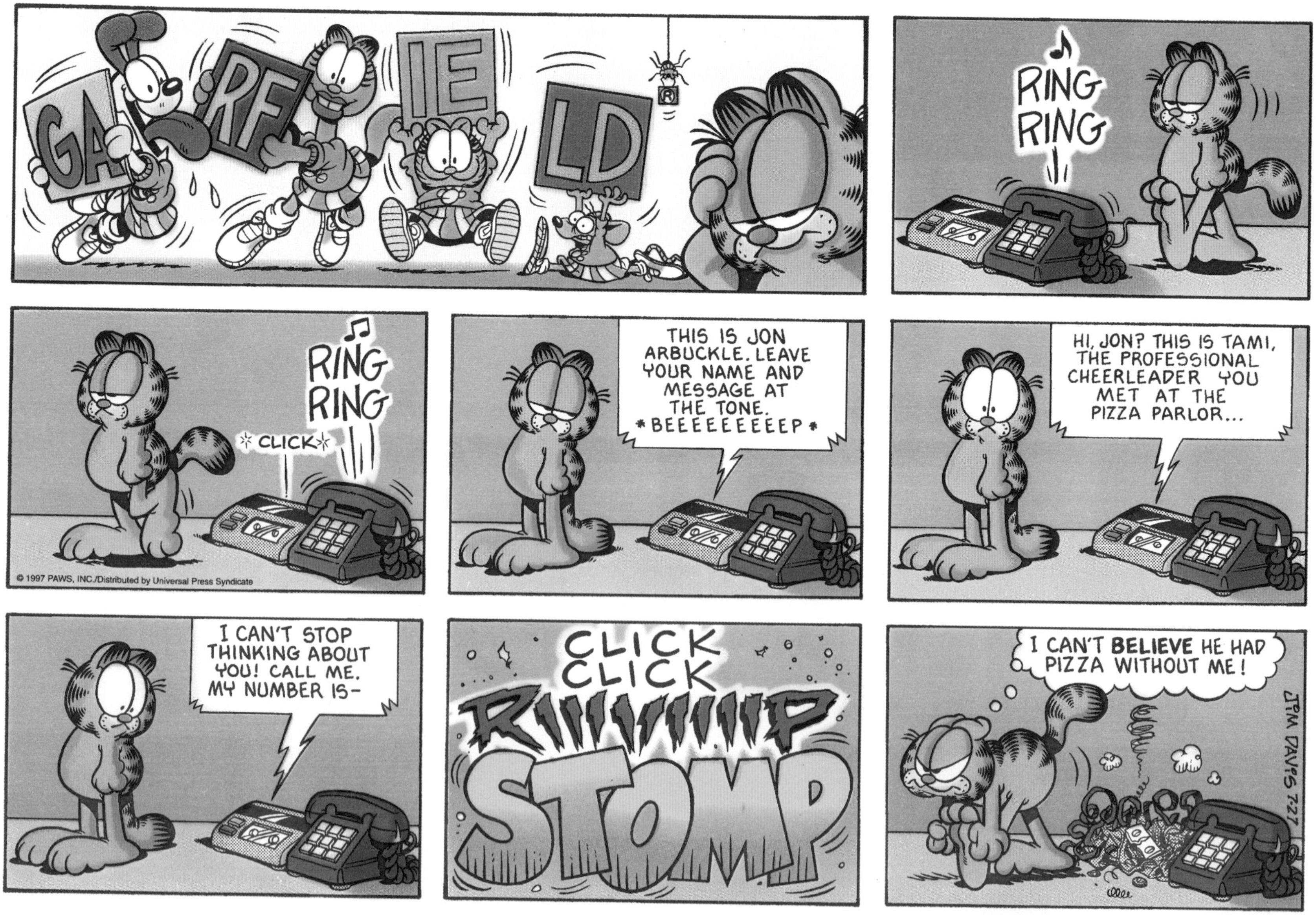
GARFIELD
®
RING RING
RING RING
CLICK
THIS IS JON ARBUCKLE. LEAVE YOUR NAME AND MESSAGE AT THE TONE. *BEEEEEEEEEP*
HI, JON? THIS IS TAMI, THE PROFESSIONAL CHEERLEADER YOU MET AT THE PIZZA PARLOR...
I CAN'T STOP THINKING ABOUT YOU! CALL ME. MY NUMBER IS-
CLICK CLICK
RIIIIIIIP
STOMP
I CAN'T **BELIEVE** HE HAD PIZZA WITHOUT ME!
JIM DAVIS 7-27
© 1997 PAWS, INC./Distributed by Universal Press Syndicate

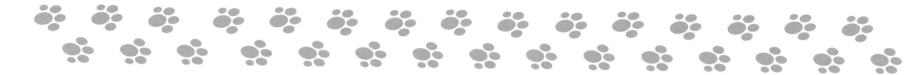

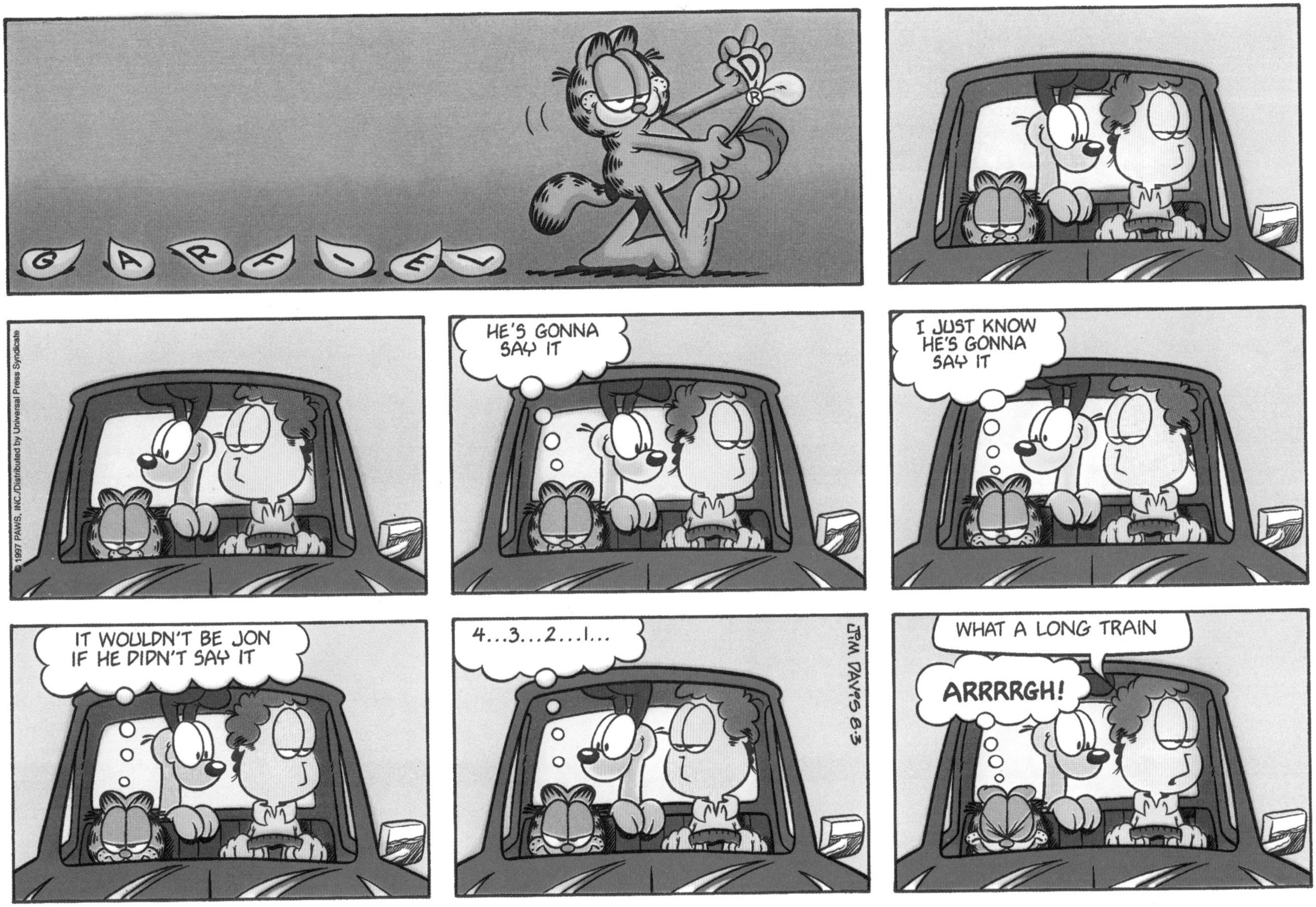
GARFIELD
© 1997 PAWS, INC./Distributed by Universal Press Syndicate
HE'S GONNA SAY IT
I JUST KNOW HE'S GONNA SAY IT
IT WOULDN'T BE JON IF HE DIDN'T SAY IT
4...3...2...1...
JIM DAVIS 8-3
WHAT A LONG TRAIN
ARRRRGH!

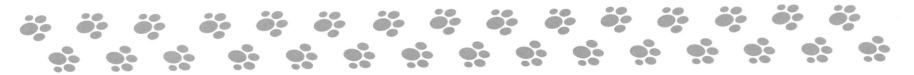

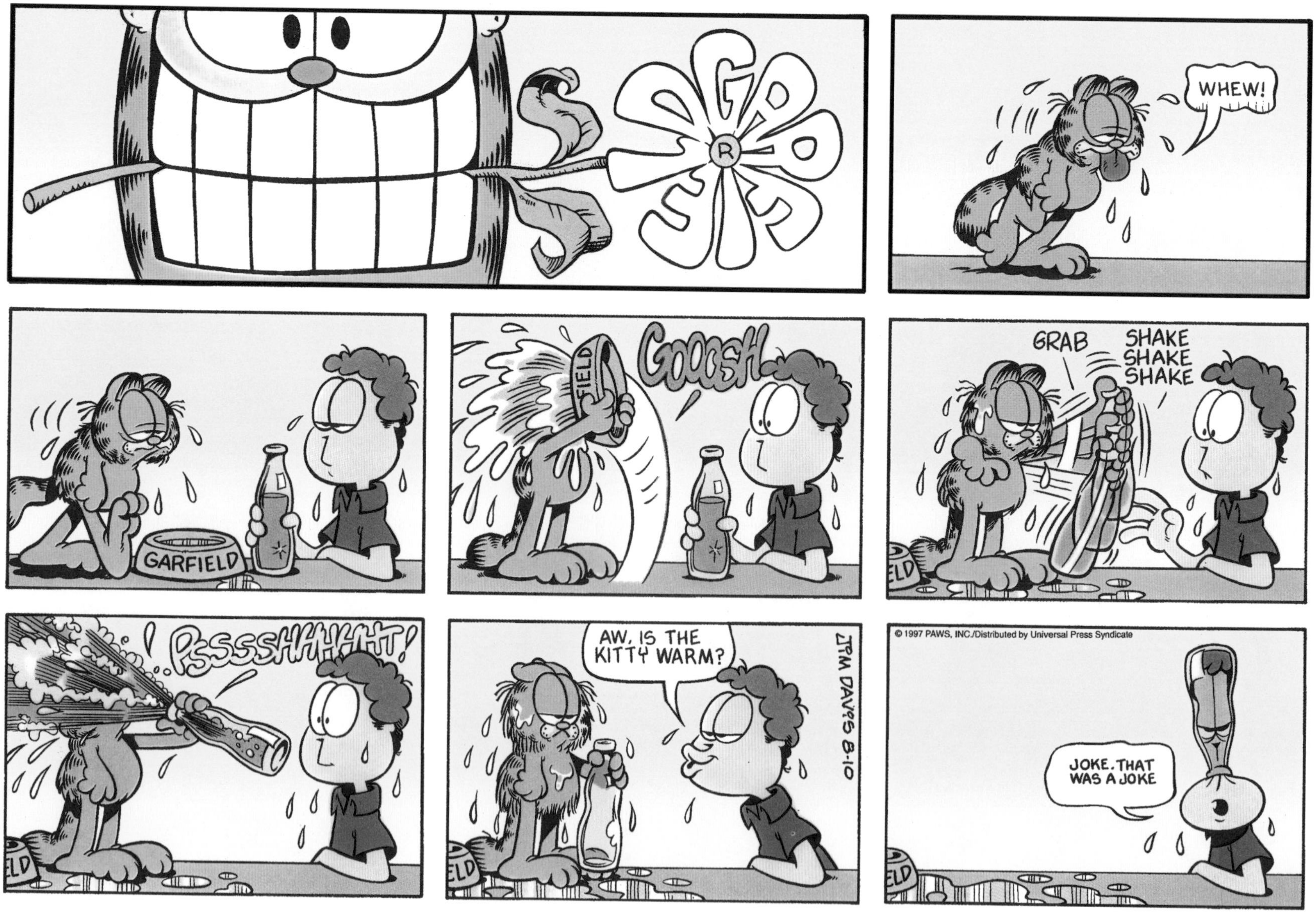
WHEW!
GARFIELD
FIELD
GOOOSH
GRAB
SHAKE
SHAKE
SHAKE
PSSSSHHHHHHT!
AW, IS THE KITTY WARM?
JIM DAVIS 8-10
© 1997 PAWS, INC./Distributed by Universal Press Syndicate
JOKE. THAT WAS A JOKE

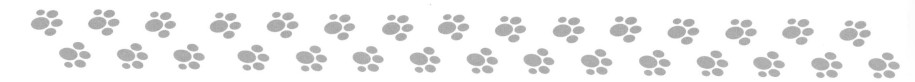

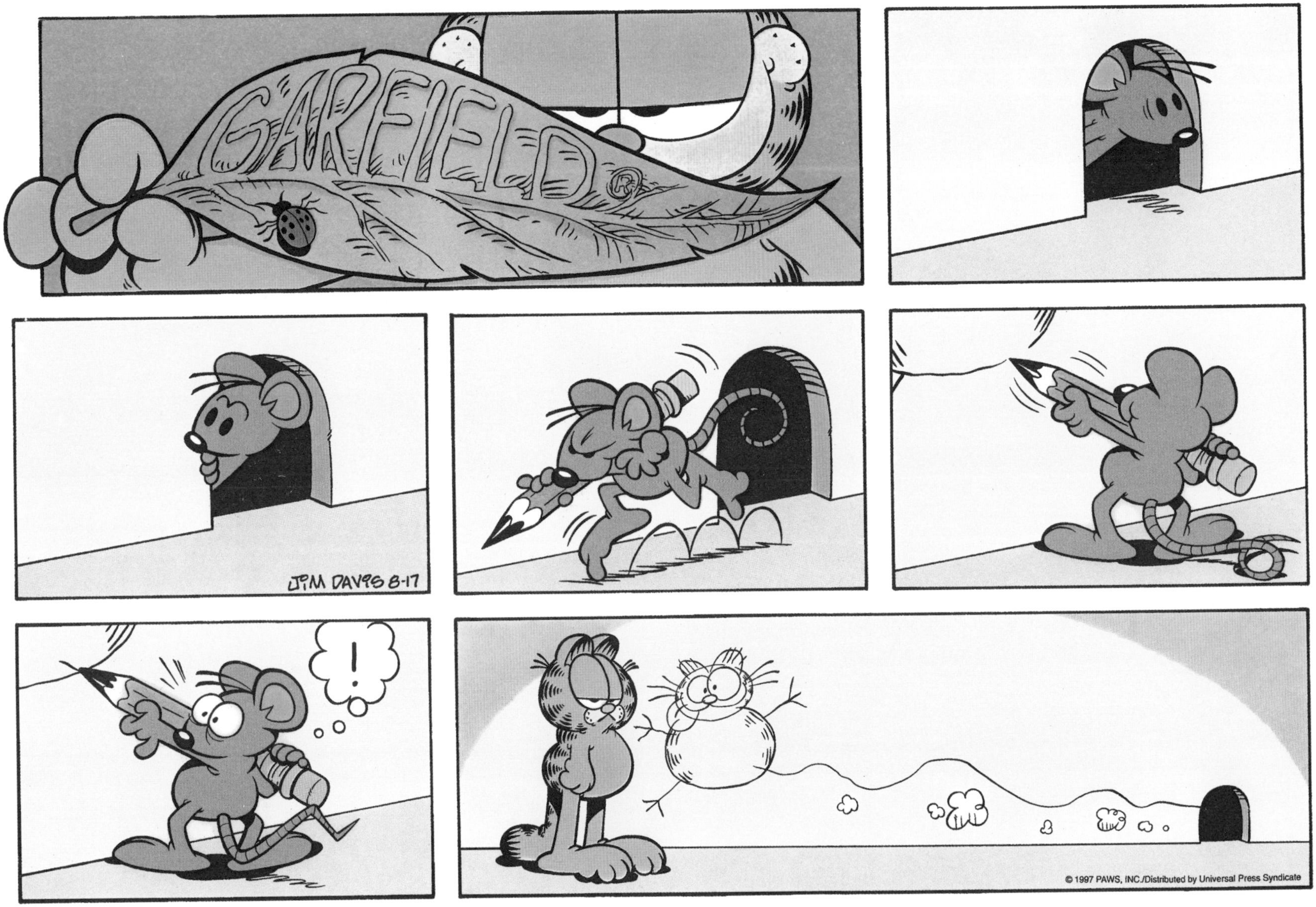
GARFIELD
JIM DAVIS 8-17
!
© 1997 PAWS, INC./Distributed by Universal Press Syndicate

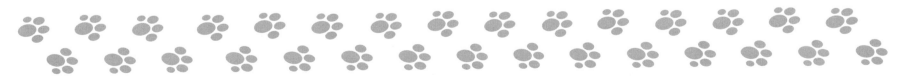

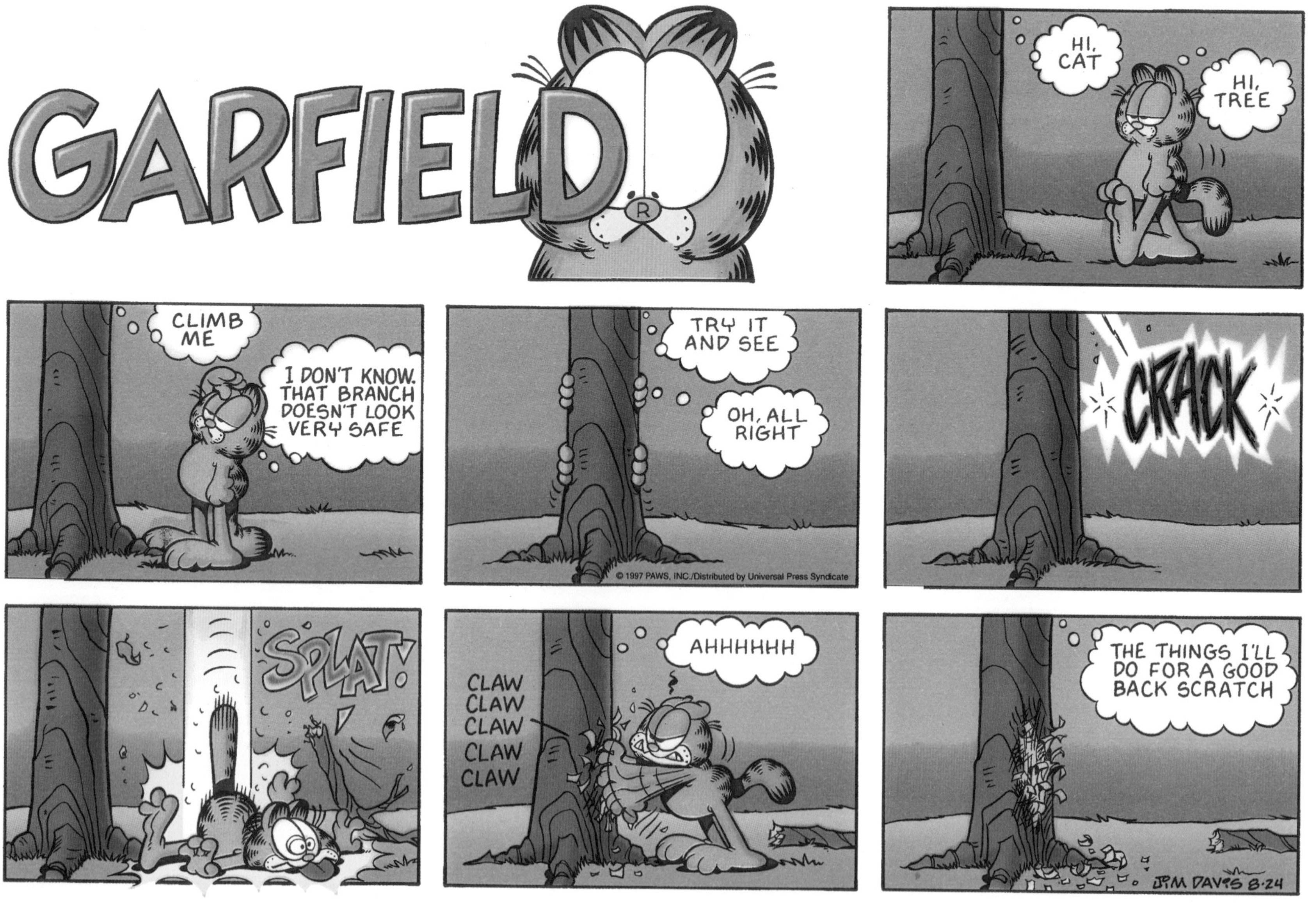
GARFIELD
HI, CAT
HI, TREE
CLIMB ME
I DON'T KNOW. THAT BRANCH DOESN'T LOOK VERY SAFE
TRY IT AND SEE
OH, ALL RIGHT
© 1997 PAWS, INC./Distributed by Universal Press Syndicate
CRACK
SPLAT
CLAW CLAW CLAW CLAW CLAW
AHHHHHH
THE THINGS I'LL DO FOR A GOOD BACK SCRATCH
JIM DAVIS 8-24

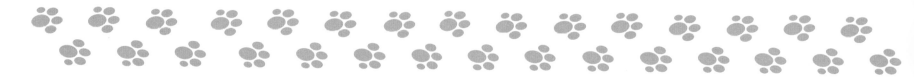

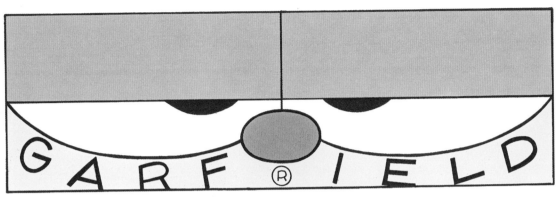

MOM FIXED ME UP WITH A BLIND DATE TONIGHT

SHE SAYS SHE'S GOT A GREAT SENSE OF HUMOR

EXCUSE ME

BWAH-HA HAHA! HA! HA! HA! HA! HAR HAR HAR

© 1997 PAWS, INC./Distributed by Universal Press Syndicate

GAH-HA! HA! GASP! SNORT! WAH HA! HA! HA! *WHEEEZE* COUGH... COUGH

JIM DAVIS 8-31

DO CONTINUE

SHE WON FIRST PLACE AT THE COUNTY FAIR IN THE PORK RIND EATING CONTEST

EXCUSE ME AGAIN

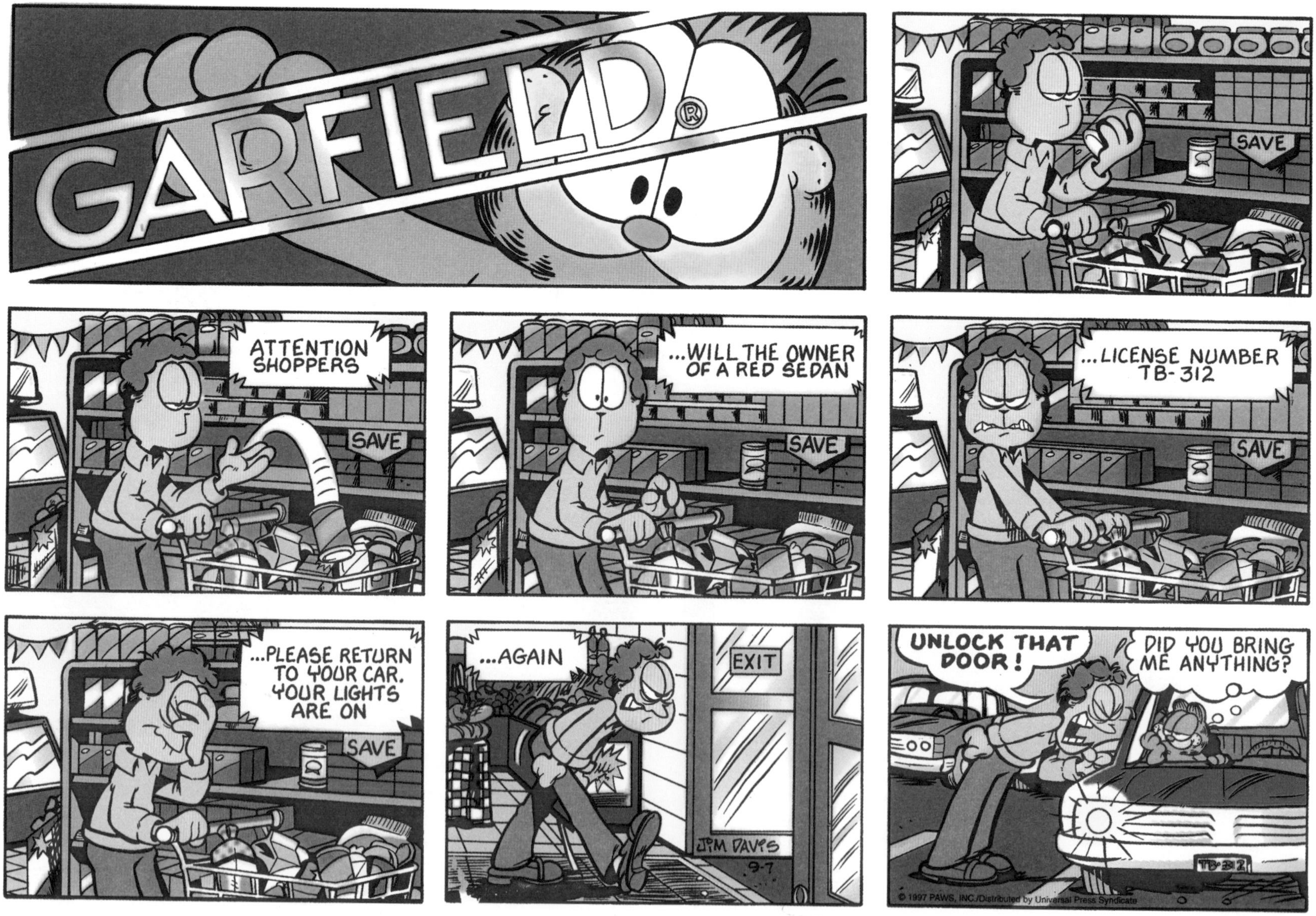
GARFIELD®
SAVE
ATTENTION SHOPPERS
SAVE
...WILL THE OWNER OF A RED SEDAN
SAVE
...LICENSE NUMBER TB-312
SAVE
...PLEASE RETURN TO YOUR CAR. YOUR LIGHTS ARE ON
SAVE
...AGAIN
EXIT
JIM DAVIS
9-7
UNLOCK THAT DOOR!
DID YOU BRING ME ANYTHING?
TB-312
© 1997 PAWS, INC./Distributed by Universal Press Syndicate

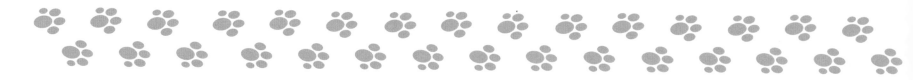

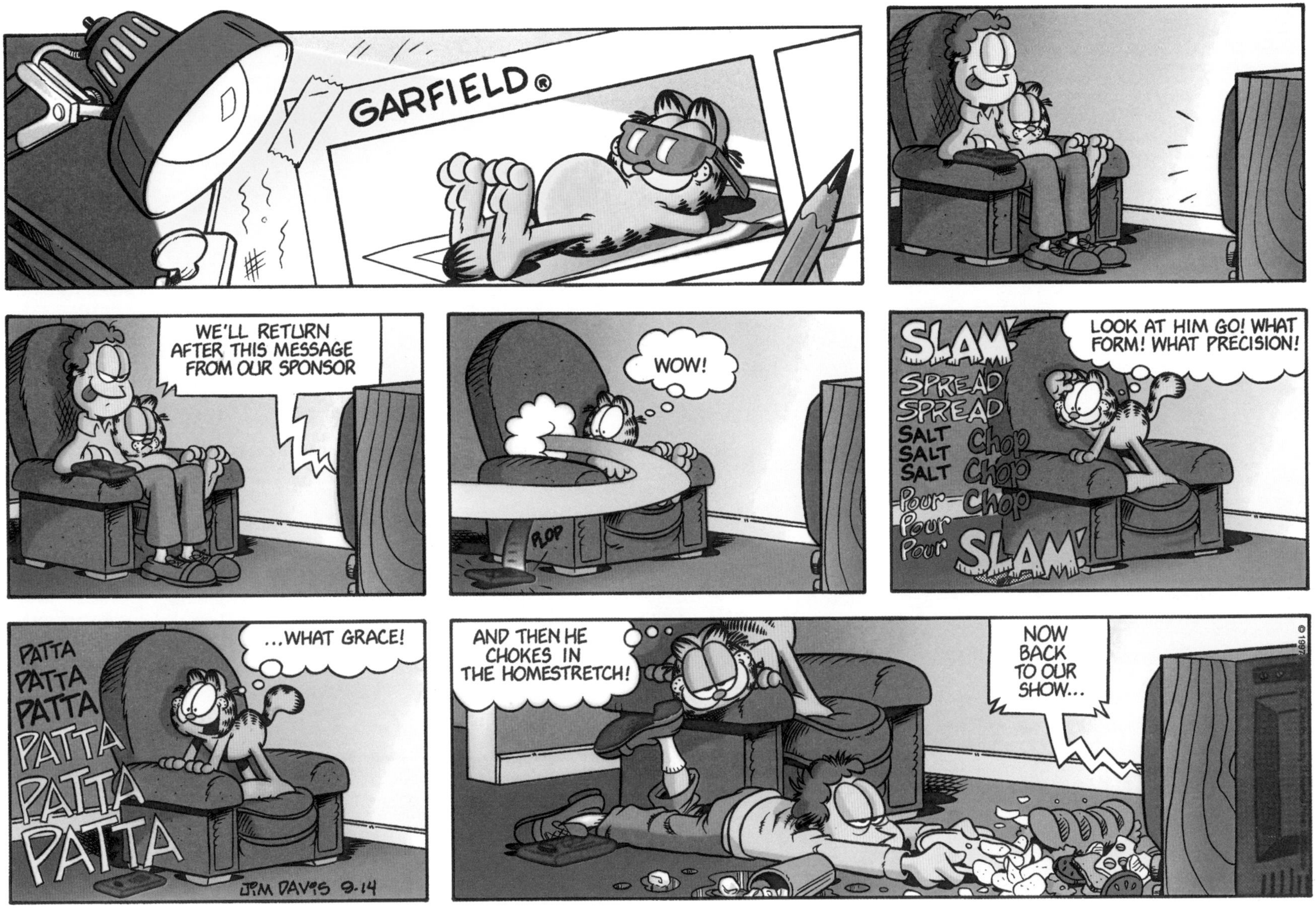
GARFIELD®
WE'LL RETURN AFTER THIS MESSAGE FROM OUR SPONSOR
WOW!
PLOP
SLAM!
SPREAD SPREAD
SALT SALT SALT
Chop Chop Chop
Pour Pour Pour
SLAM!
LOOK AT HIM GO! WHAT FORM! WHAT PRECISION!
PATTA PATTA PATTA PATTA PATTA PATTA
...WHAT GRACE!
JIM DAVIS 9-14
AND THEN HE CHOKES IN THE HOMESTRETCH!
NOW BACK TO OUR SHOW...
© 1997

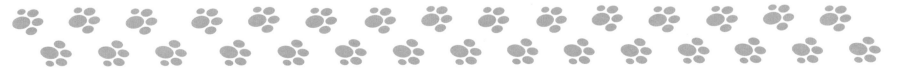

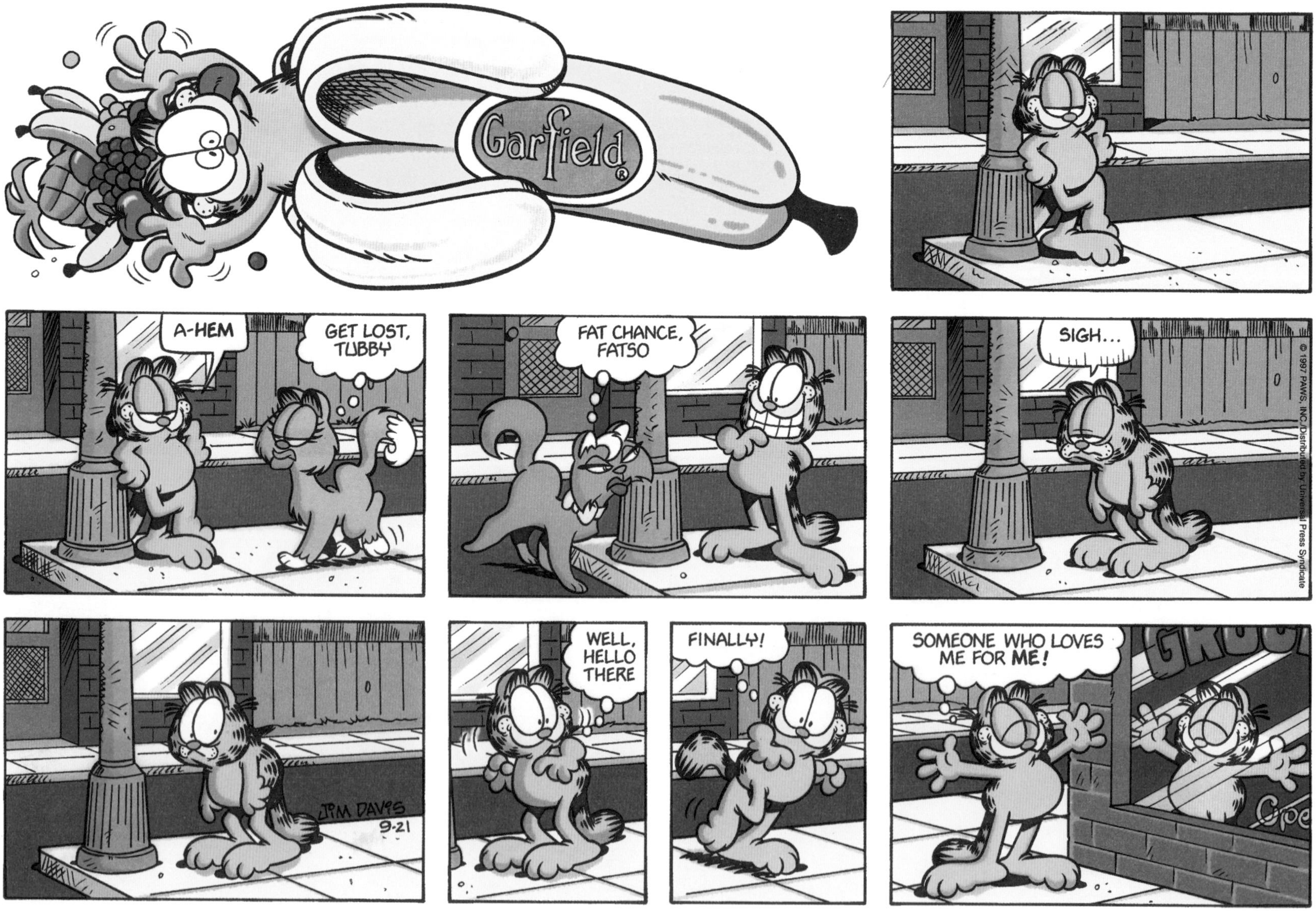
Garfield®
A-HEM
GET LOST, TUBBY
FAT CHANCE, FATSO
SIGH...
© 1997 PAWS, INC./Distributed by Universal Press Syndicate
JIM DAVIS 9-21
WELL, HELLO THERE
FINALLY!
SOMEONE WHO LOVES ME FOR ME!

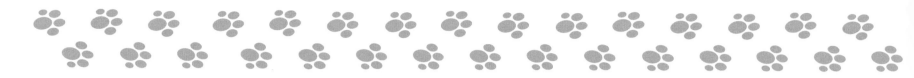

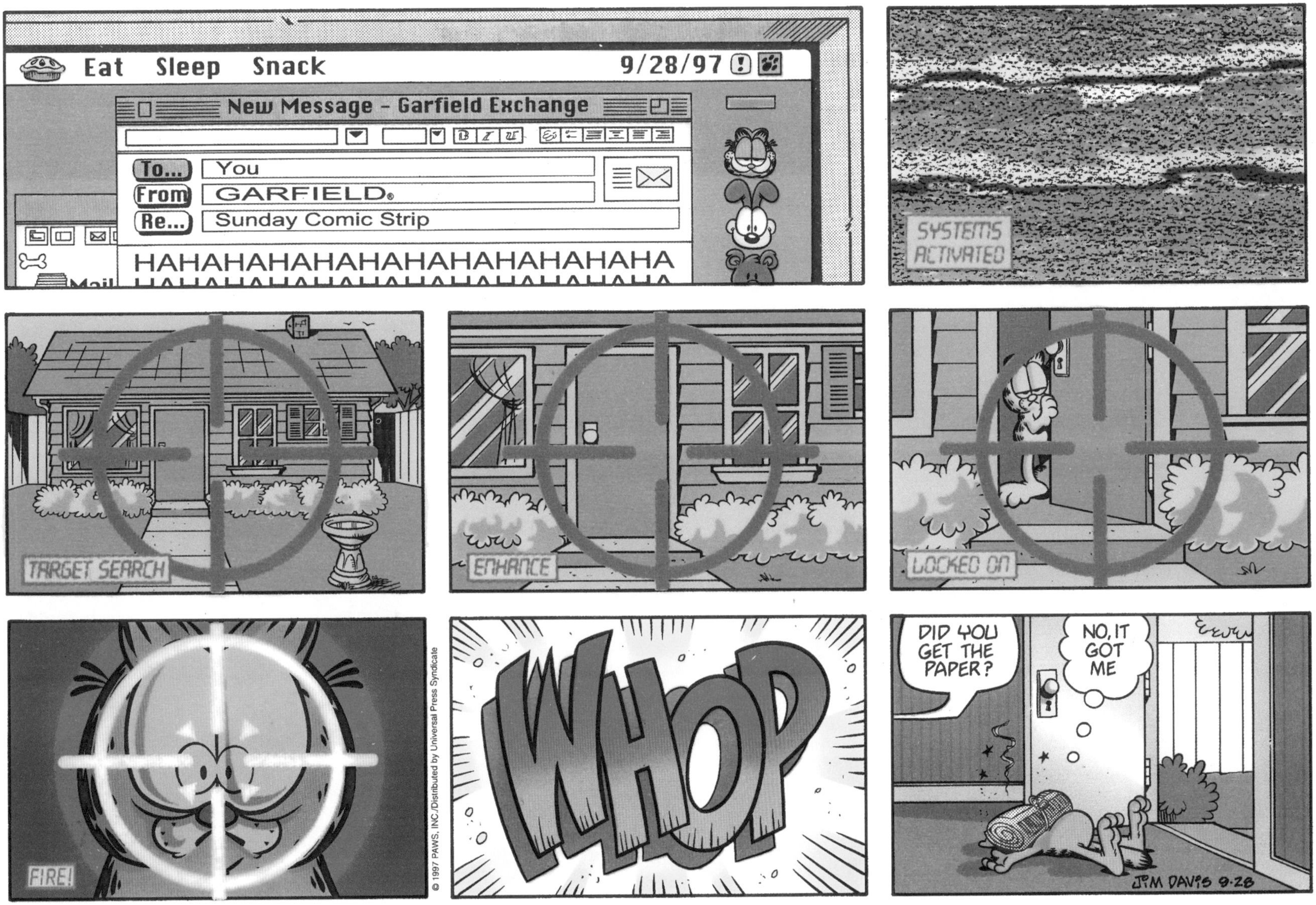
Eat Sleep Snack
9/28/97
New Message - Garfield Exchange
To... You
From GARFIELD®
Re... Sunday Comic Strip
HAHAHAHAHAHAHAHAHAHAHAHAHAHA
SYSTEMS ACTIVATED
TARGET SEARCH
ENHANCE
LOCKED ON
FIRE!
WHOP
DID YOU GET THE PAPER?
NO, IT GOT ME
JIM DAVIS 9-28

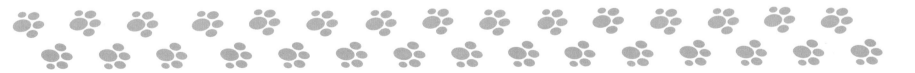

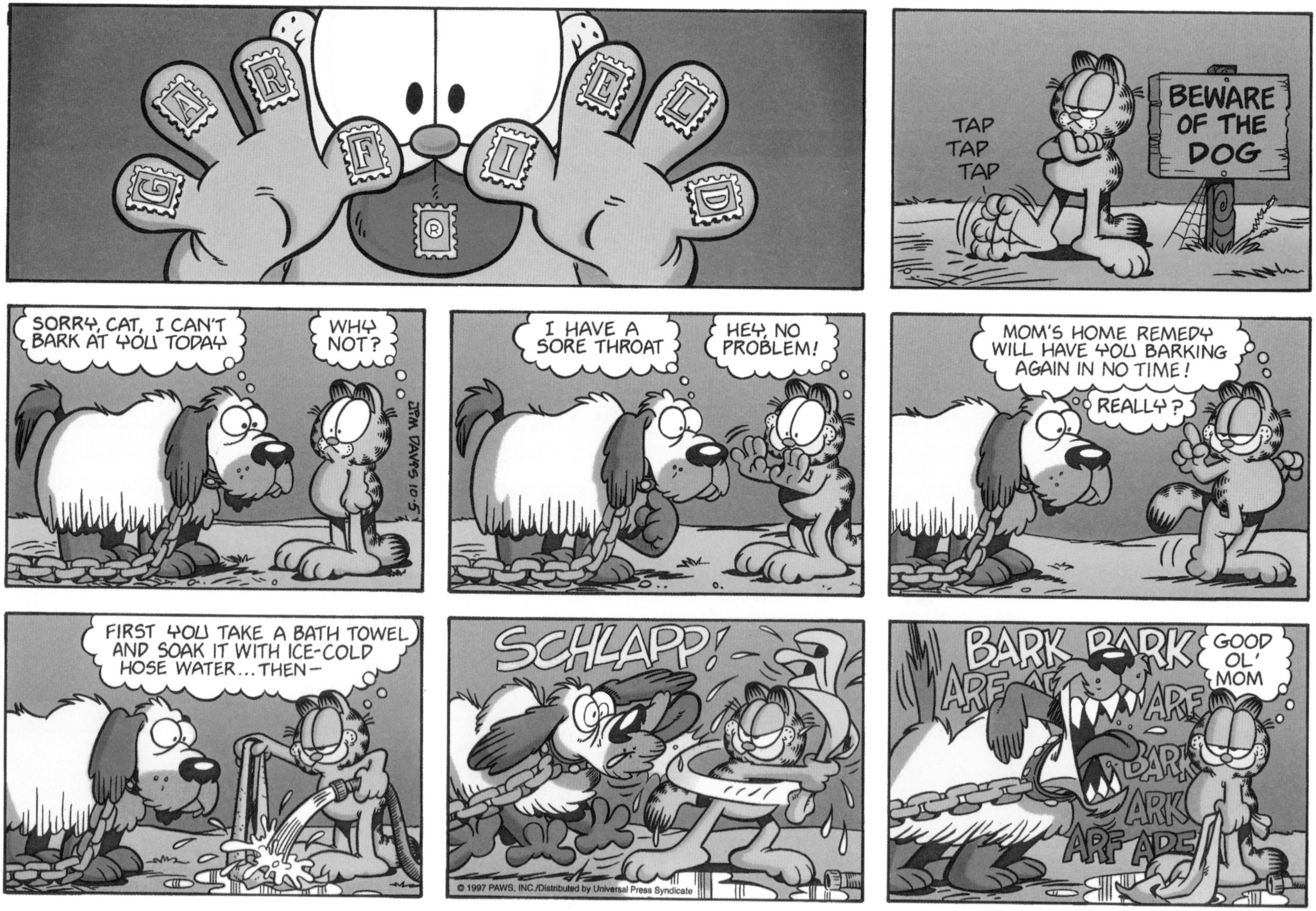
GARFIELD®
TAP
TAP
TAP
BEWARE OF THE DOG
SORRY, CAT, I CAN'T BARK AT YOU TODAY
WHY NOT?
JPM DAVIS 10-5
I HAVE A SORE THROAT
HEY, NO PROBLEM!
MOM'S HOME REMEDY WILL HAVE YOU BARKING AGAIN IN NO TIME!
REALLY?
FIRST YOU TAKE A BATH TOWEL AND SOAK IT WITH ICE-COLD HOSE WATER... THEN—
SCHLAPP!
© 1997 PAWS, INC./Distributed by Universal Press Syndicate
BARK BARK
ARF
ARF
BARK
ARK
ARF ARF
GOOD OL' MOM

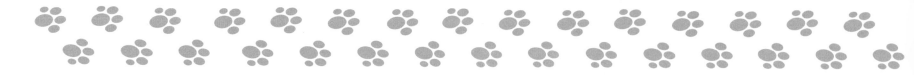

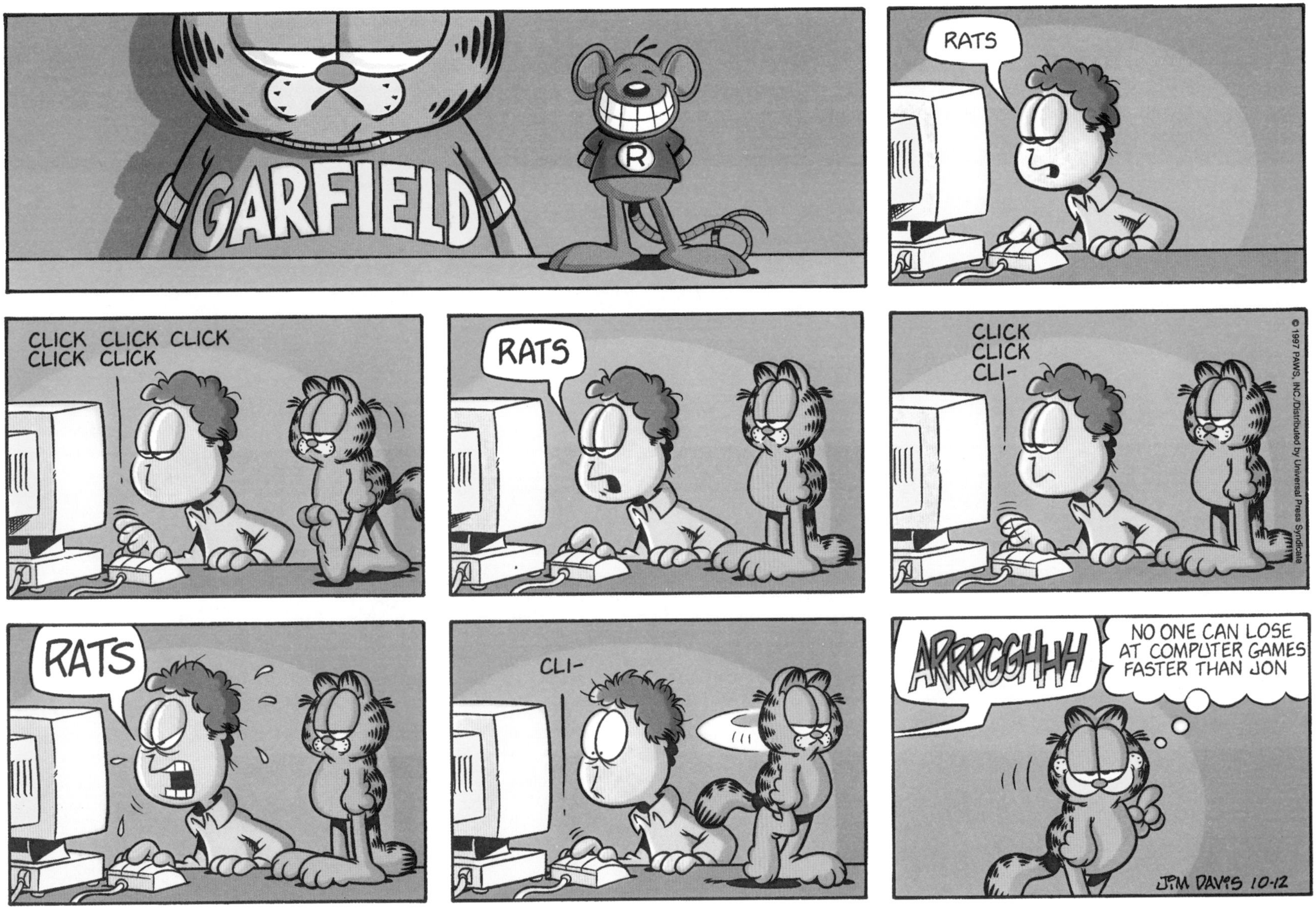
GARFIELD
RATS
CLICK CLICK CLICK CLICK CLICK
RATS
CLICK CLICK CLI-
© 1997 PAWS, INC./Distributed by Universal Press Syndicate
RATS
CLI-
ARRRGGHHH
NO ONE CAN LOSE AT COMPUTER GAMES FASTER THAN JON
JIM DAVIS 10-12

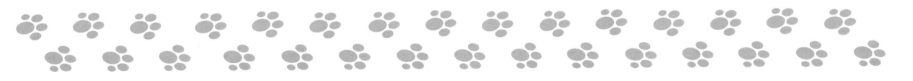

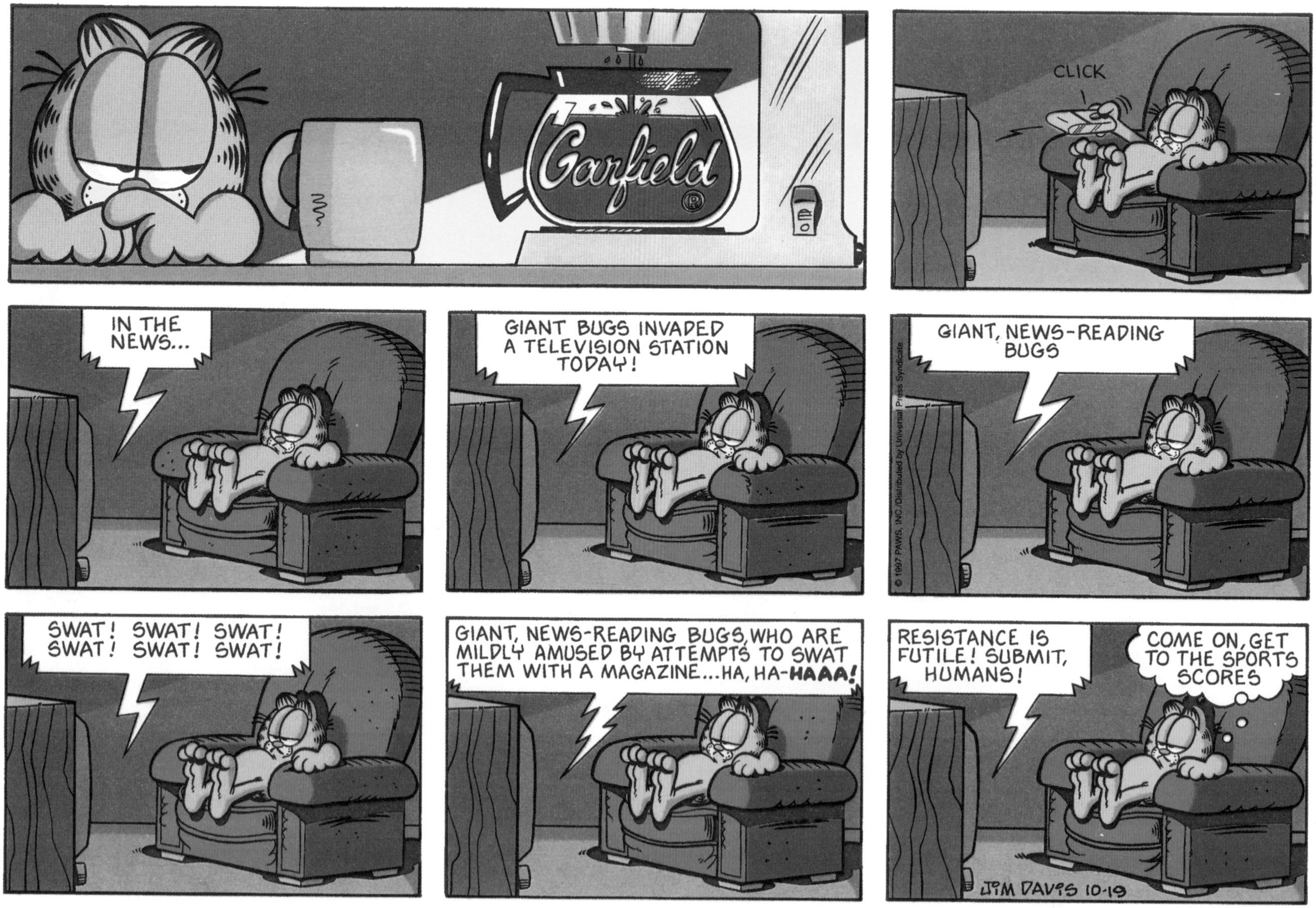
Garfield®
CLICK
IN THE NEWS...
GIANT BUGS INVADED A TELEVISION STATION TODAY!
GIANT, NEWS-READING BUGS
© 1997 PAWS, INC./Distributed by Universal Press Syndicate
SWAT! SWAT! SWAT! SWAT! SWAT! SWAT!
GIANT, NEWS-READING BUGS, WHO ARE MILDLY AMUSED BY ATTEMPTS TO SWAT THEM WITH A MAGAZINE...HA, HA-HAAA!
RESISTANCE IS FUTILE! SUBMIT, HUMANS!
COME ON, GET TO THE SPORTS SCORES
JIM DAVIS 10-19

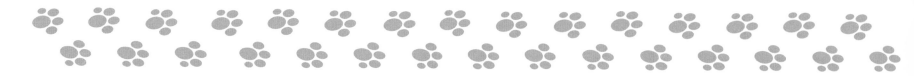

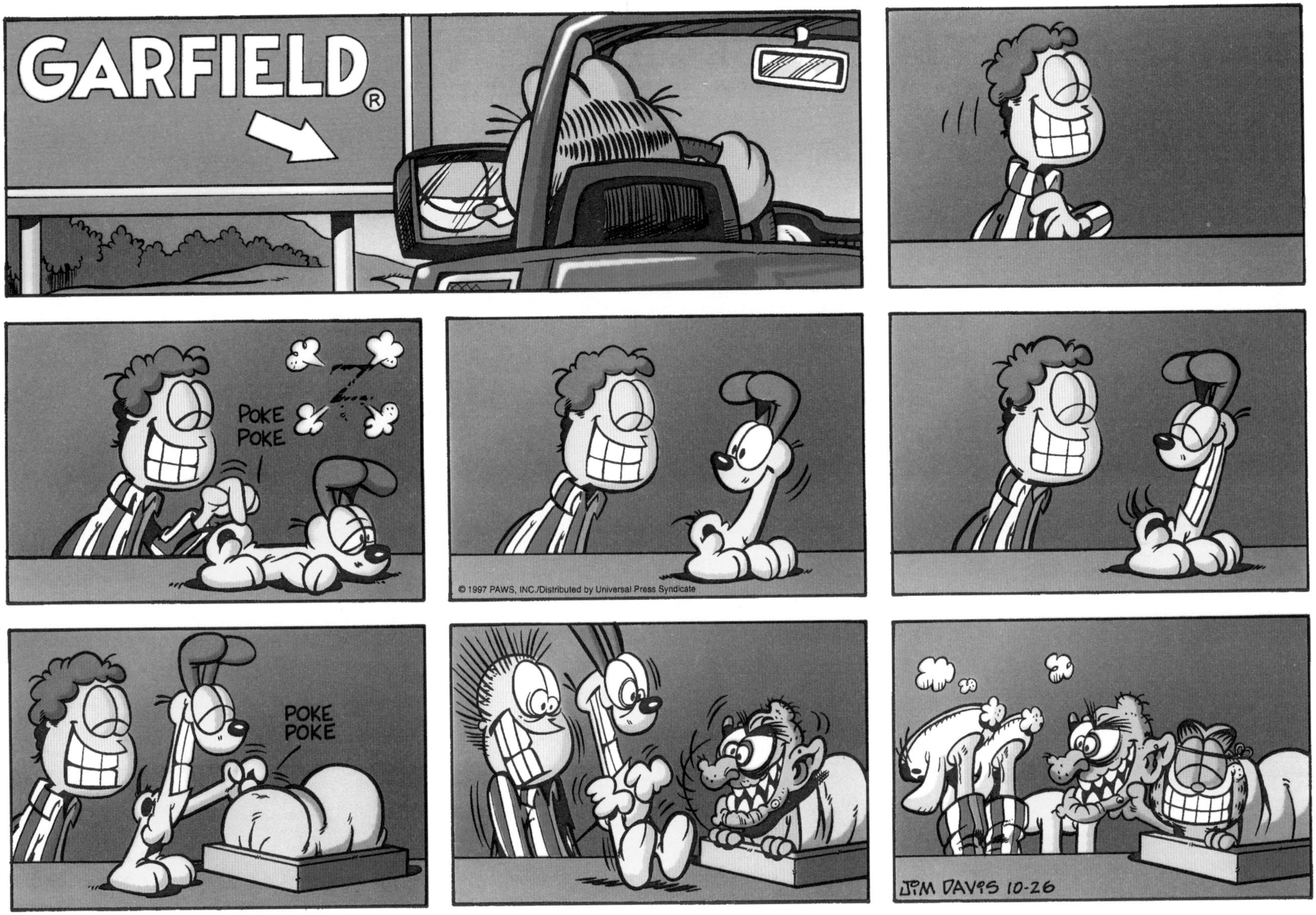
GARFIELD®
POKE POKE
© 1997 PAWS, INC./Distributed by Universal Press Syndicate
POKE POKE
JIM DAVIS 10-26

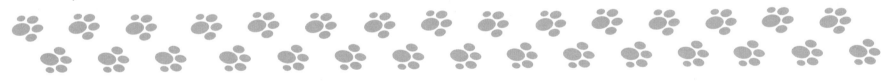

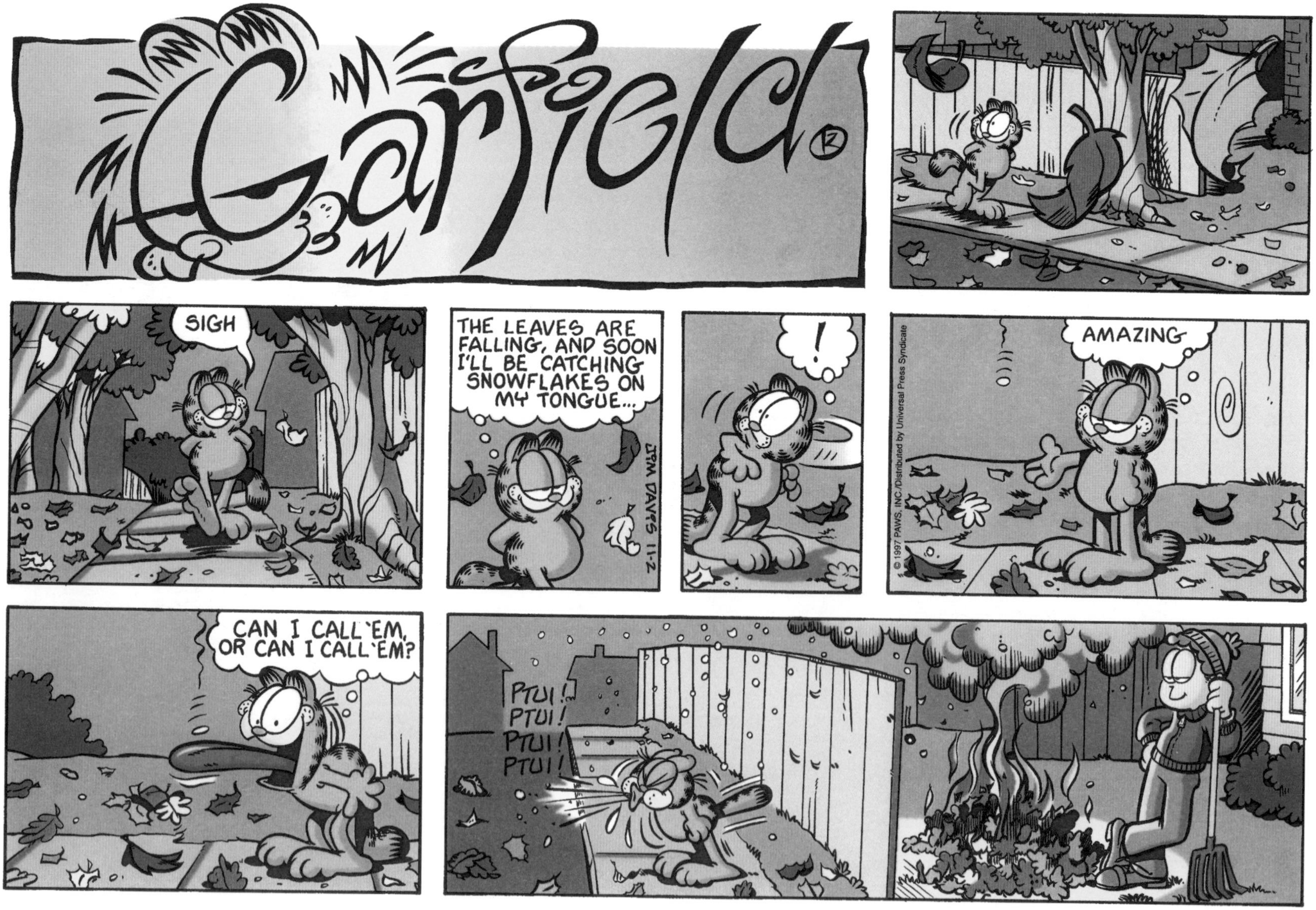
Garfield
SIGH
THE LEAVES ARE FALLING, AND SOON I'LL BE CATCHING SNOWFLAKES ON MY TONGUE...
JIM DAVIS 11-2
!
AMAZING
© 1997 PAWS, INC./Distributed by Universal Press Syndicate
CAN I CALL 'EM, OR CAN I CALL 'EM?
PTUI!
PTUI!
PTUI!
PTUI!

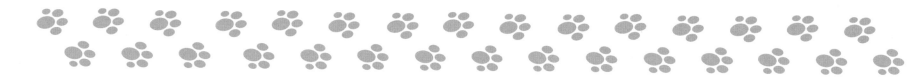

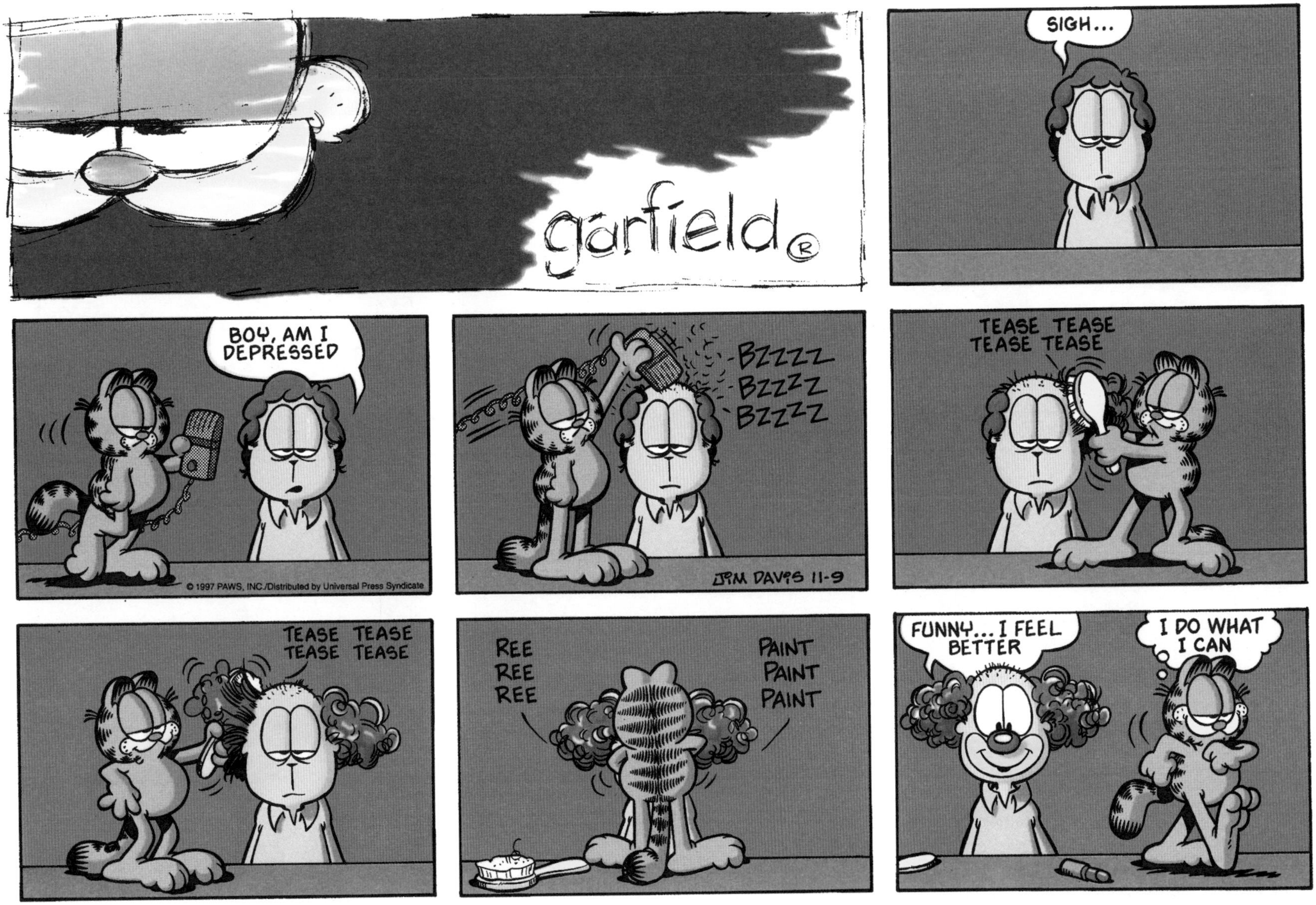
garfield ®
SIGH...
BOY, AM I DEPRESSED
© 1997 PAWS, INC./Distributed by Universal Press Syndicate
BZZZZ
BZZZZ
BZZZZ
JIM DAVIS 11-9
TEASE TEASE
TEASE TEASE
TEASE TEASE
TEASE TEASE
REE
REE
REE
PAINT
PAINT
PAINT
FUNNY... I FEEL BETTER
I DO WHAT I CAN

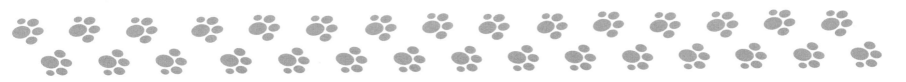

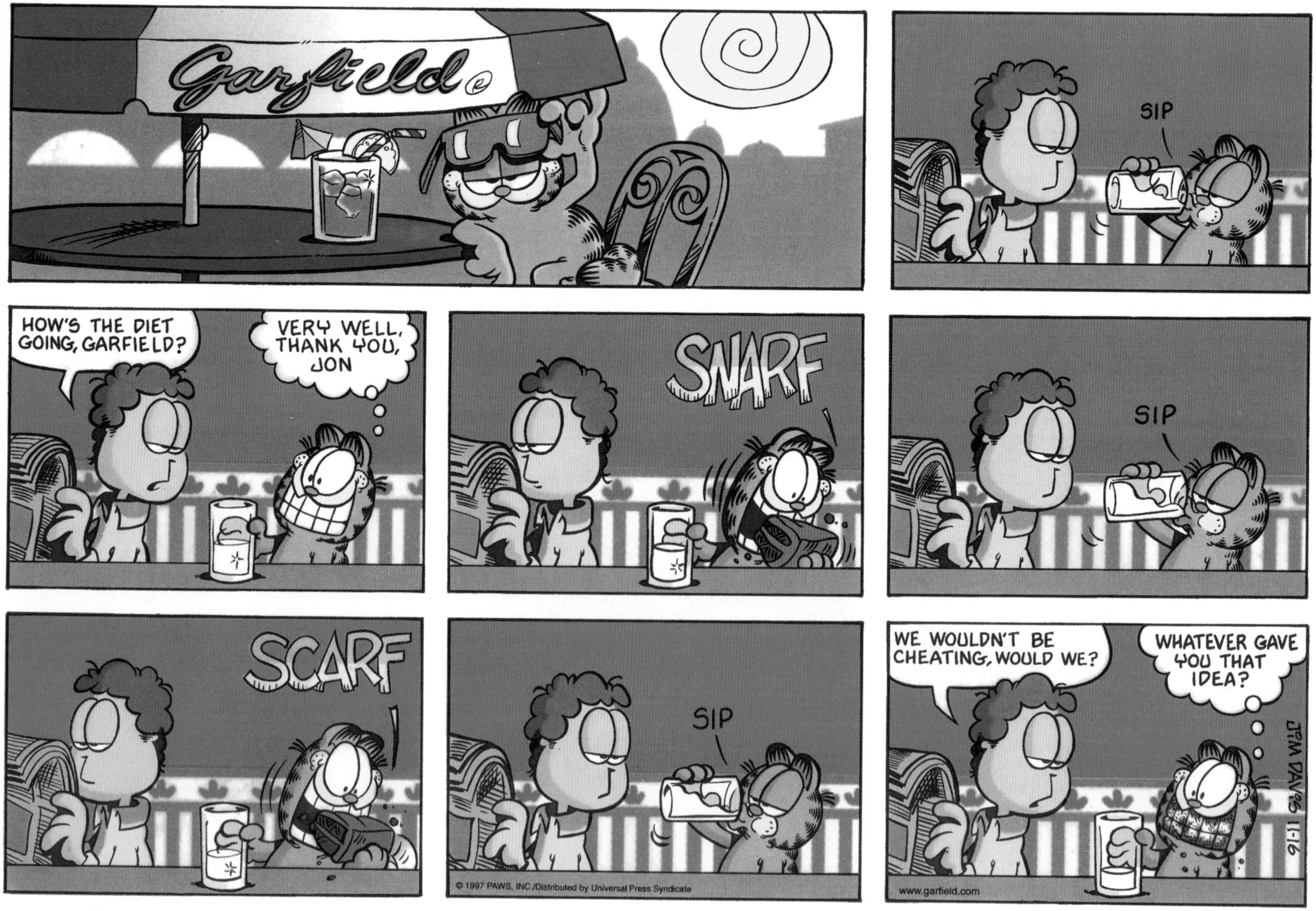

Garfield
SIP
HOW'S THE DIET GOING, GARFIELD?
VERY WELL, THANK YOU, JON
SNARF
SIP
SCARF
SIP
WE WOULDN'T BE CHEATING, WOULD WE?
WHATEVER GAVE YOU THAT IDEA?
JPM DAVIS 11-16
© 1997 PAWS, INC./Distributed by Universal Press Syndicate
www.garfield.com

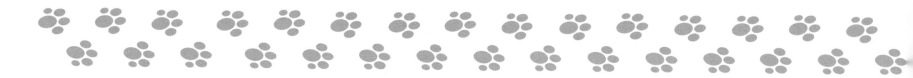

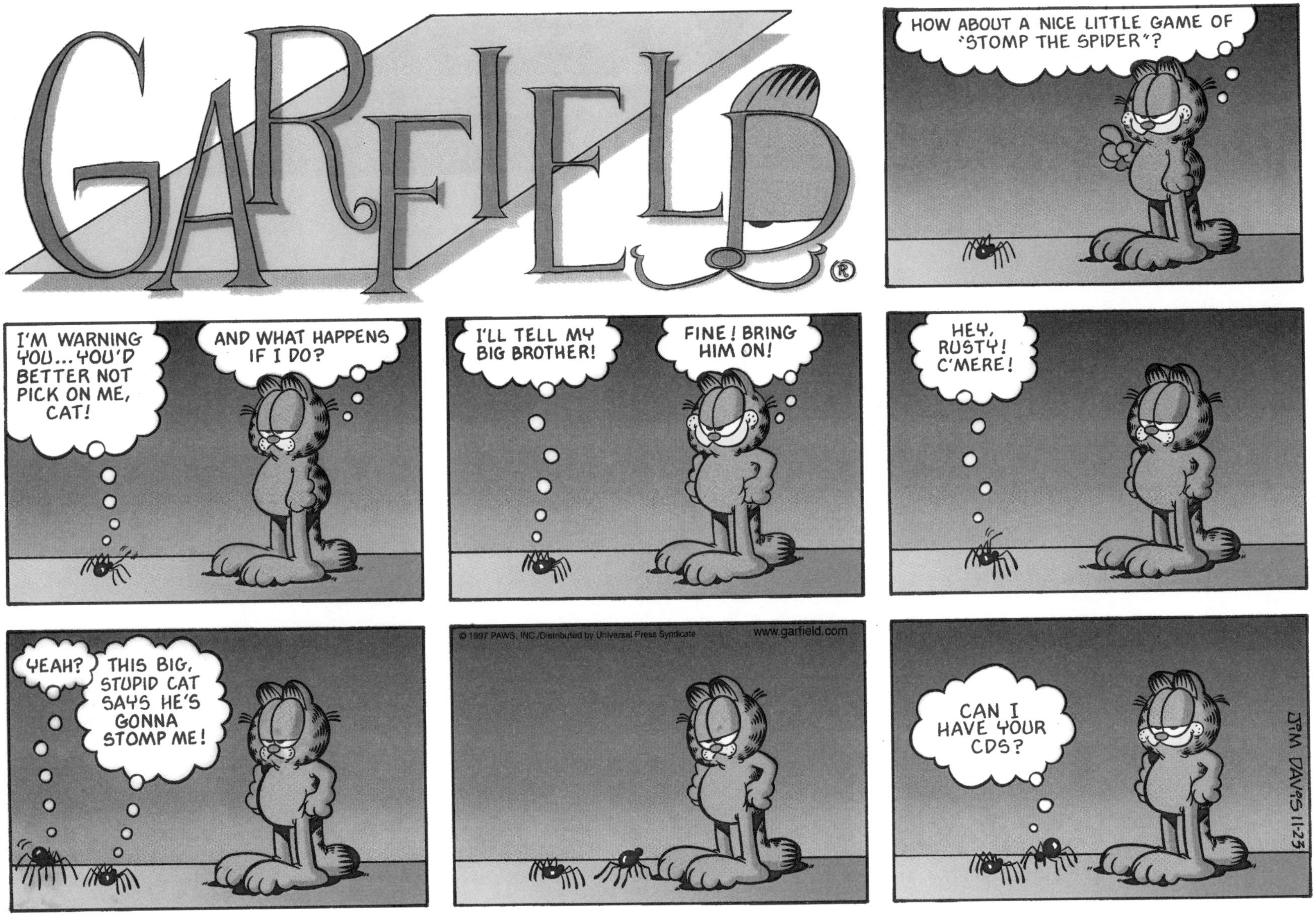
GARFIELD
HOW ABOUT A NICE LITTLE GAME OF "STOMP THE SPIDER"?
I'M WARNING YOU...YOU'D BETTER NOT PICK ON ME, CAT!
AND WHAT HAPPENS IF I DO?
I'LL TELL MY BIG BROTHER!
FINE! BRING HIM ON!
HEY, RUSTY! C'MERE!
YEAH?
THIS BIG, STUPID CAT SAYS HE'S GONNA STOMP ME!
© 1997 PAWS, INC./Distributed by Universal Press Syndicate
www.garfield.com
CAN I HAVE YOUR CDS?
JIM DAVIS 11-23

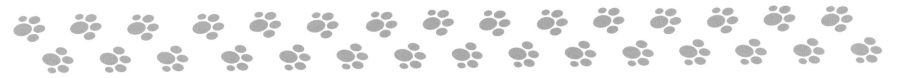

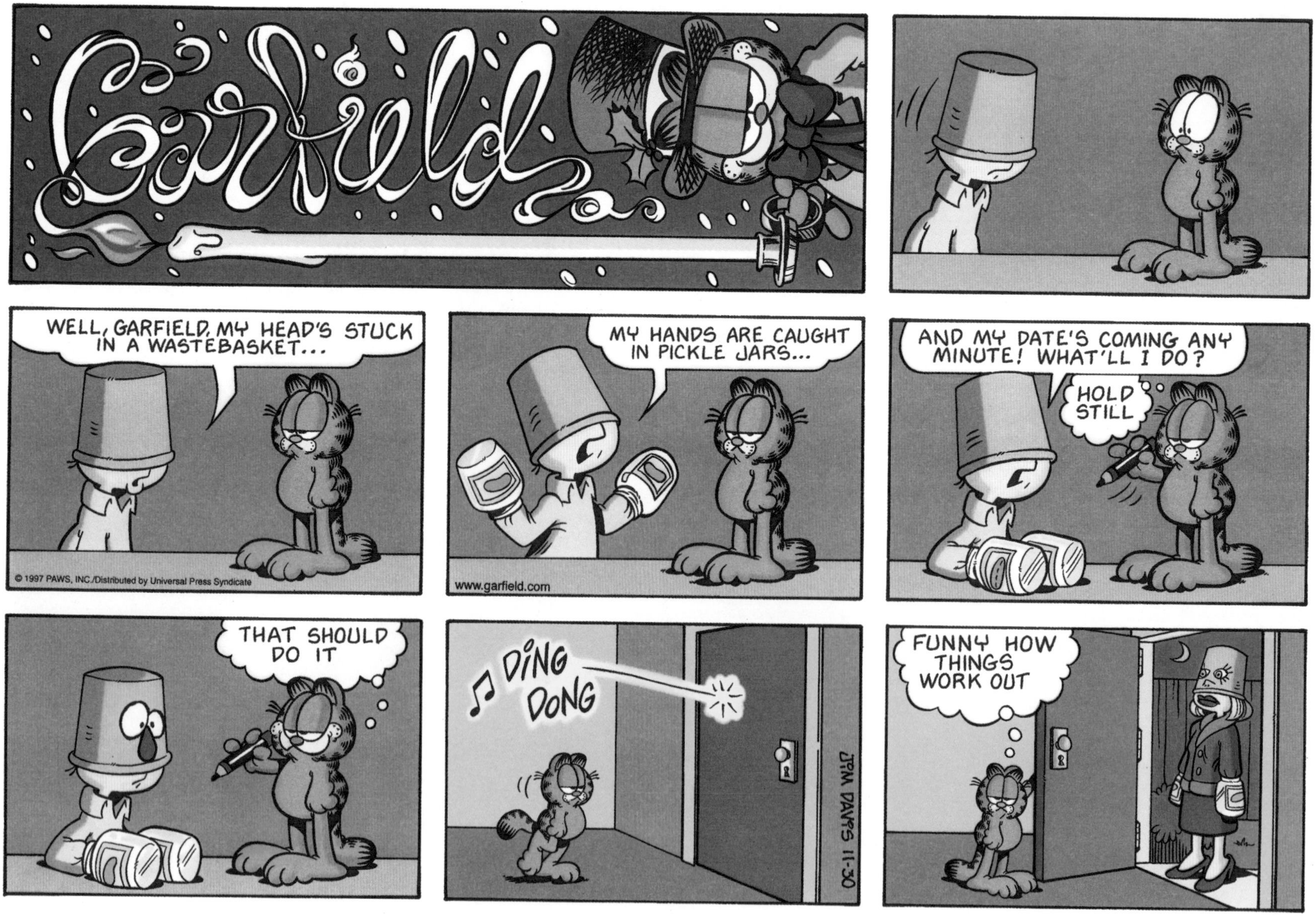
Garfield
WELL, GARFIELD, MY HEAD'S STUCK IN A WASTEBASKET...
© 1997 PAWS, INC./Distributed by Universal Press Syndicate
MY HANDS ARE CAUGHT IN PICKLE JARS...
www.garfield.com
AND MY DATE'S COMING ANY MINUTE! WHAT'LL I DO?
HOLD STILL
THAT SHOULD DO IT
DING DONG
JIM DAVIS 11-30
FUNNY HOW THINGS WORK OUT

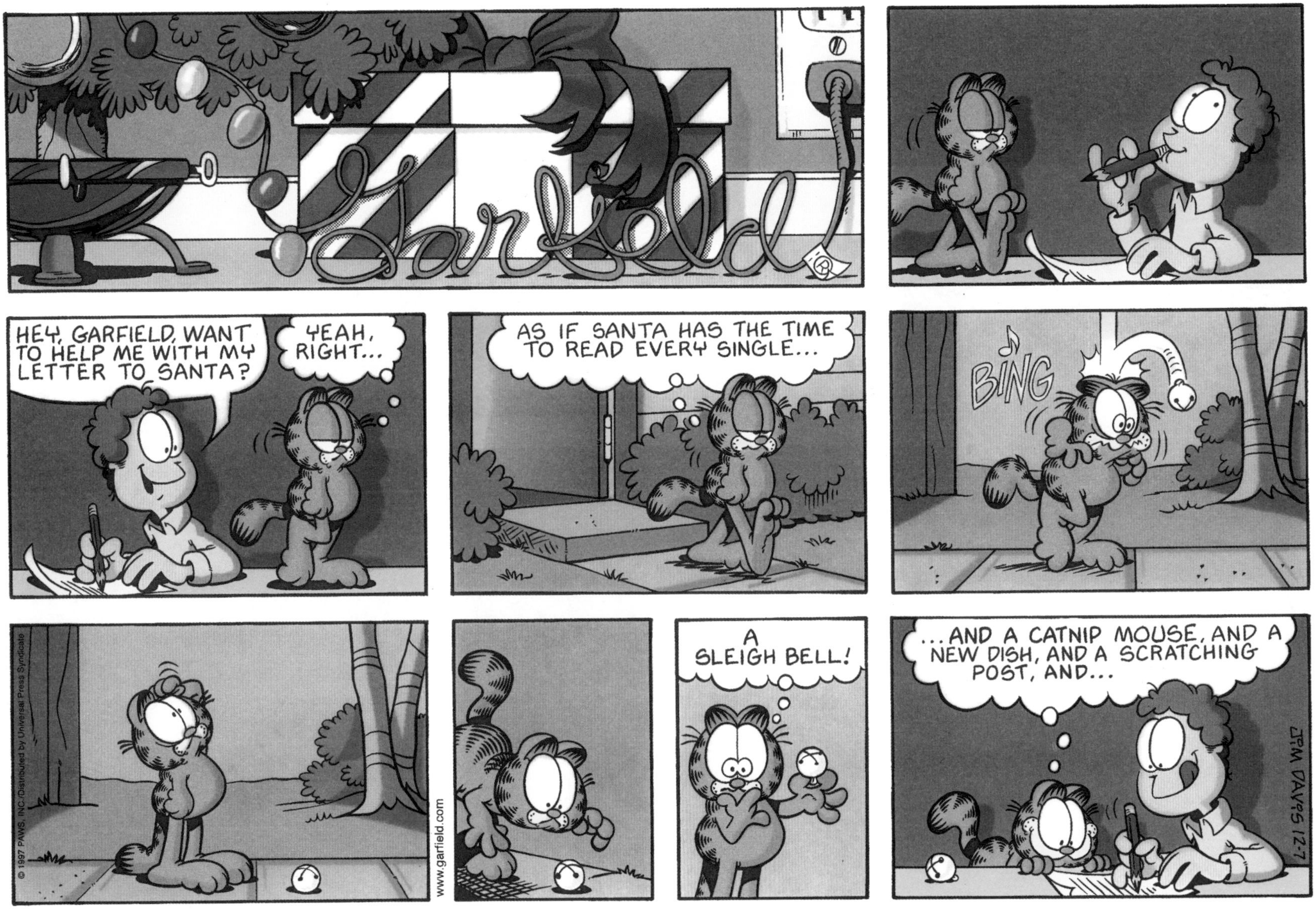
Garfield
HEY, GARFIELD, WANT TO HELP ME WITH MY LETTER TO SANTA?
YEAH, RIGHT...
AS IF SANTA HAS THE TIME TO READ EVERY SINGLE...
BING
© 1997 PAWS, INC./Distributed by Universal Press Syndicate
www.garfield.com
A SLEIGH BELL!
...AND A CATNIP MOUSE, AND A NEW DISH, AND A SCRATCHING POST, AND...
JPM DAVIS 12-7

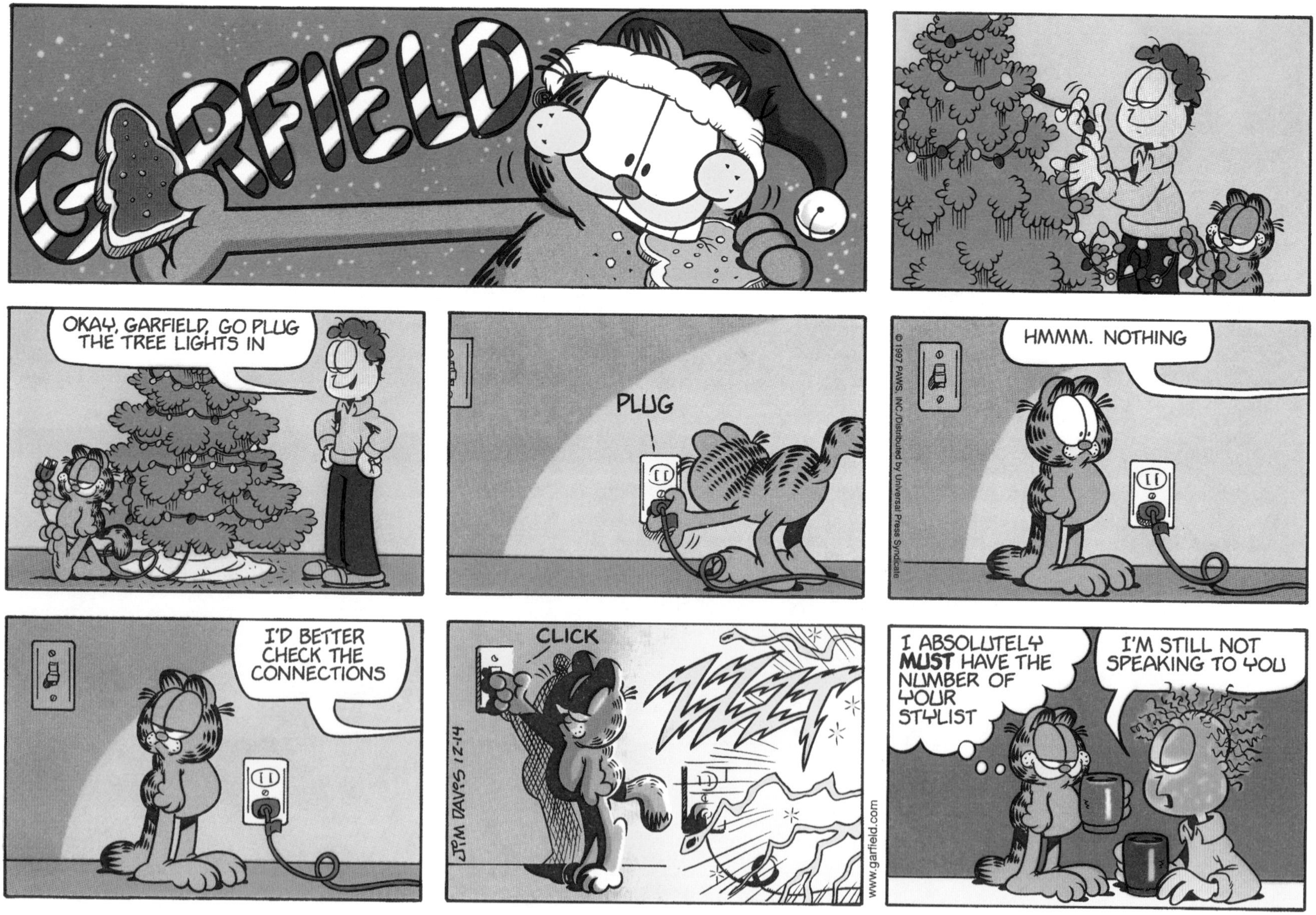
GARFIELD
OKAY, GARFIELD, GO PLUG THE TREE LIGHTS IN
PLUG
HMMM. NOTHING
© 1997 PAWS, INC./Distributed by Universal Press Syndicate
I'D BETTER CHECK THE CONNECTIONS
CLICK
JIM DAVIS 12-14
www.garfield.com
I ABSOLUTELY **MUST** HAVE THE NUMBER OF YOUR STYLIST
I'M STILL NOT SPEAKING TO YOU

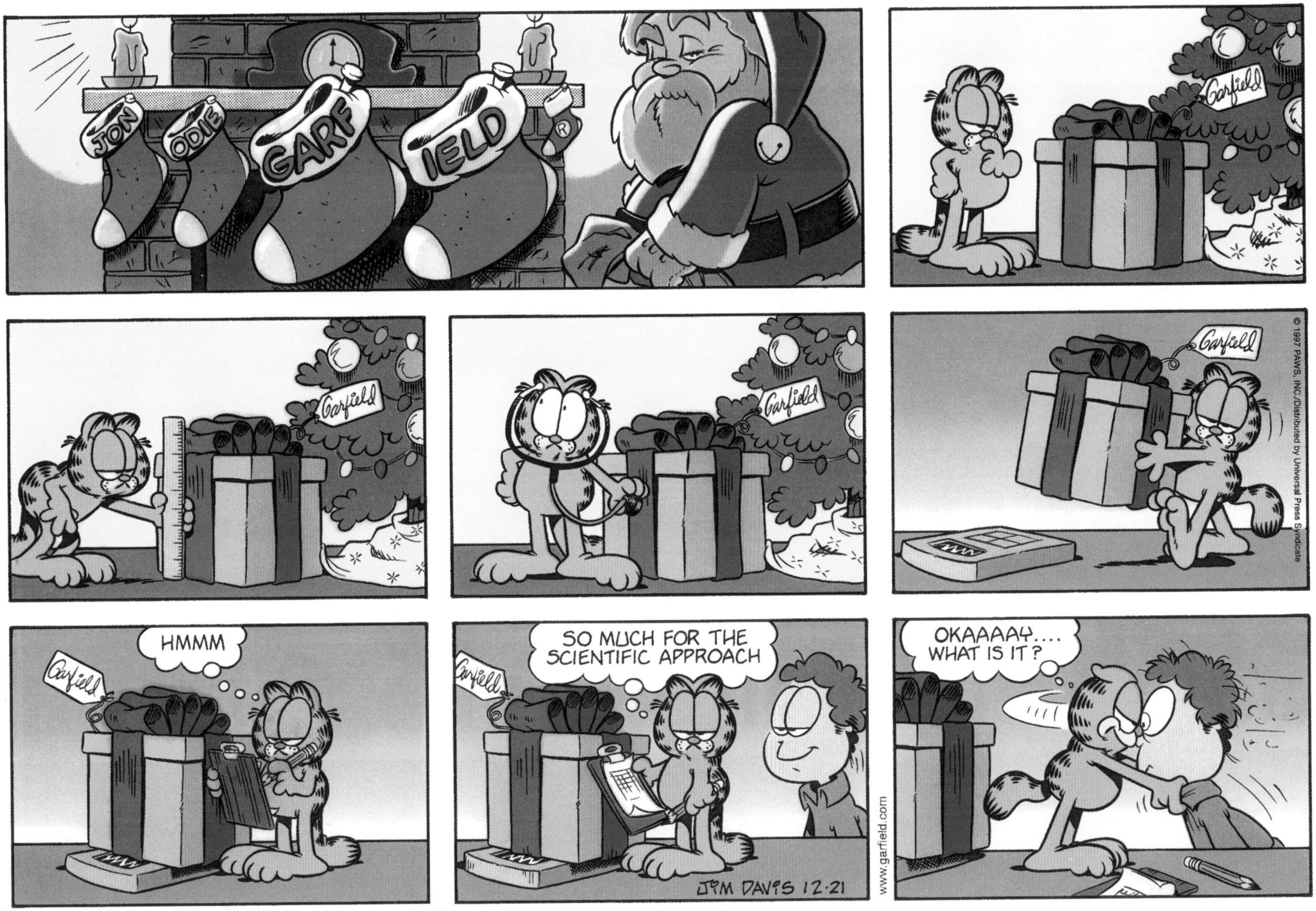
JON
ODIE
GARF
IELD
Garfield
Garfield
Garfield
© 1997 PAWS, INC./Distributed by Universal Press Syndicate
Garfield
HMMM
Garfield
SO MUCH FOR THE SCIENTIFIC APPROACH
JIM DAVIS 12·21
www.garfield.com
OKAAAAY.... WHAT IS IT?

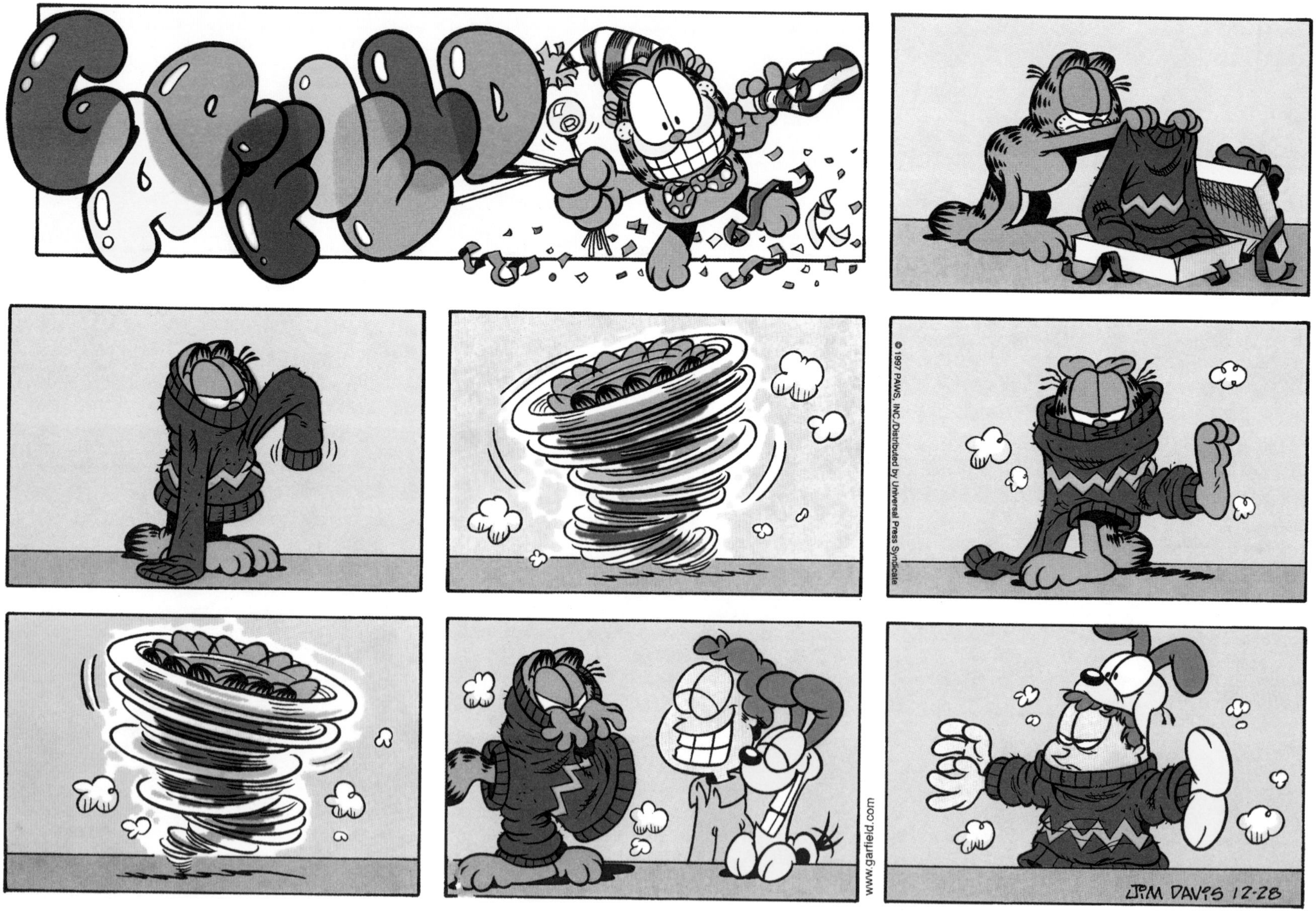
GARFIELD
© 1997 PAWS, INC./Distributed by Universal Press Syndicate
www.garfield.com
JIM DAVIS 12-28

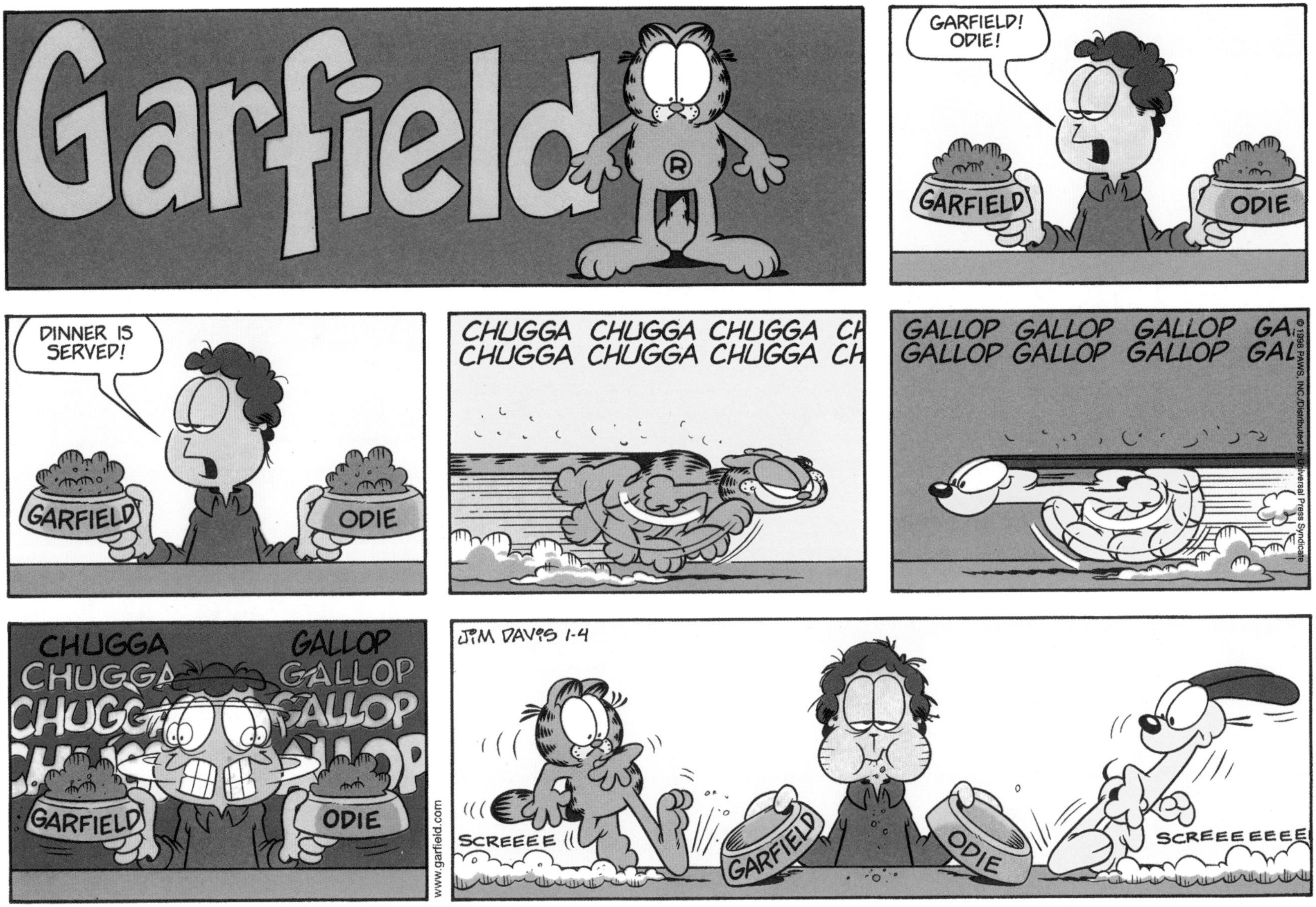

Garfield
GARFIELD! ODIE!
GARFIELD
ODIE
DINNER IS SERVED!
GARFIELD
ODIE
CHUGGA CHUGGA CHUGGA CH
CHUGGA CHUGGA CHUGGA CH
GALLOP GALLOP GALLOP GA
GALLOP GALLOP GALLOP GAL
© 1998 PAWS, INC./Distributed by Universal Press Syndicate
CHUGGA
GALLOP
CHUGGA
GALLOP
GARFIELD
ODIE
www.garfield.com
JIM DAVIS 1-4
SCREEEE
GARFIELD
ODIE
SCREEEEEEE

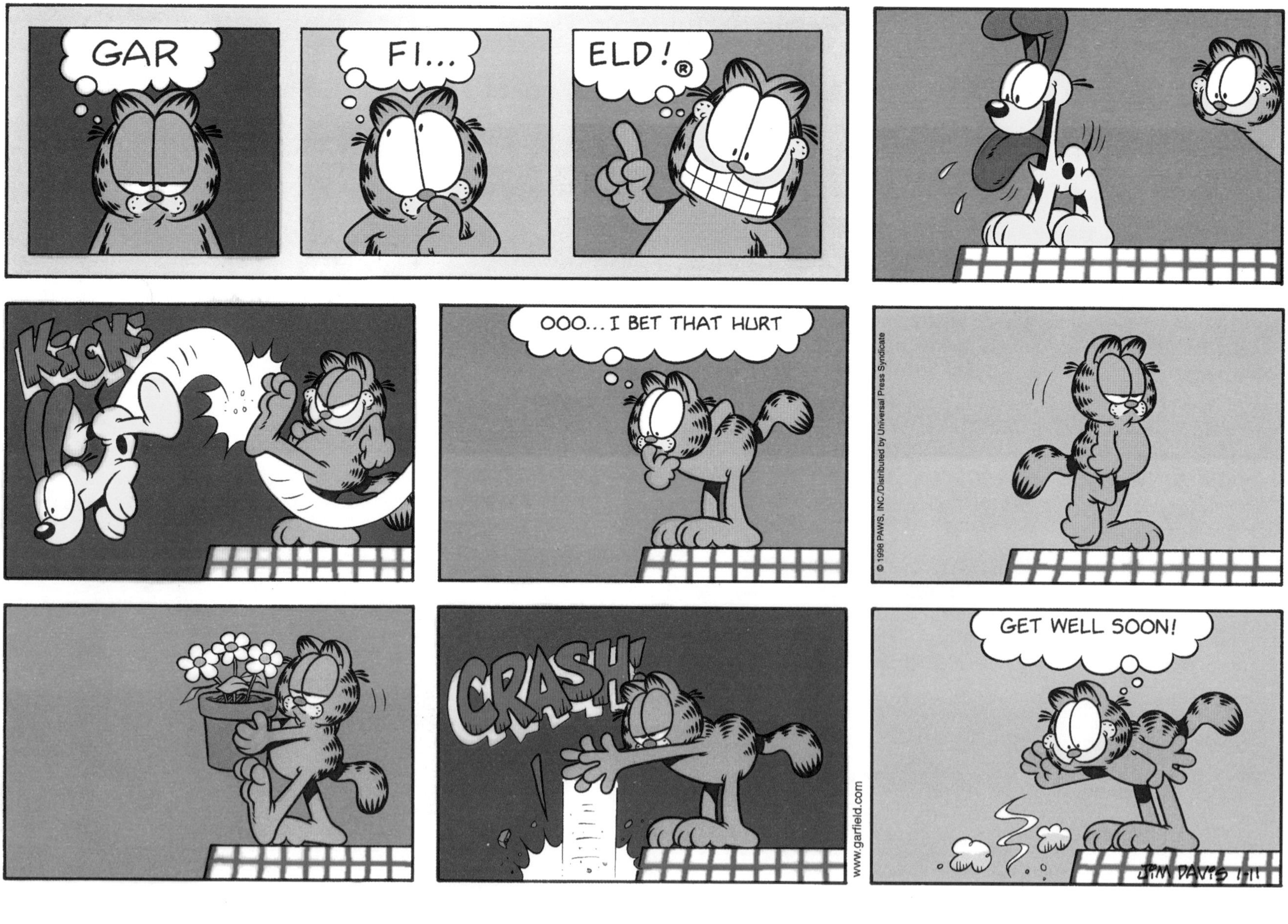
GAR
FI...
ELD!®
KICK!
OOO... I BET THAT HURT
CRASH!
GET WELL SOON!
© 1998 PAWS, INC./Distributed by Universal Press Syndicate
www.garfield.com
JIM DAVIS 1-11

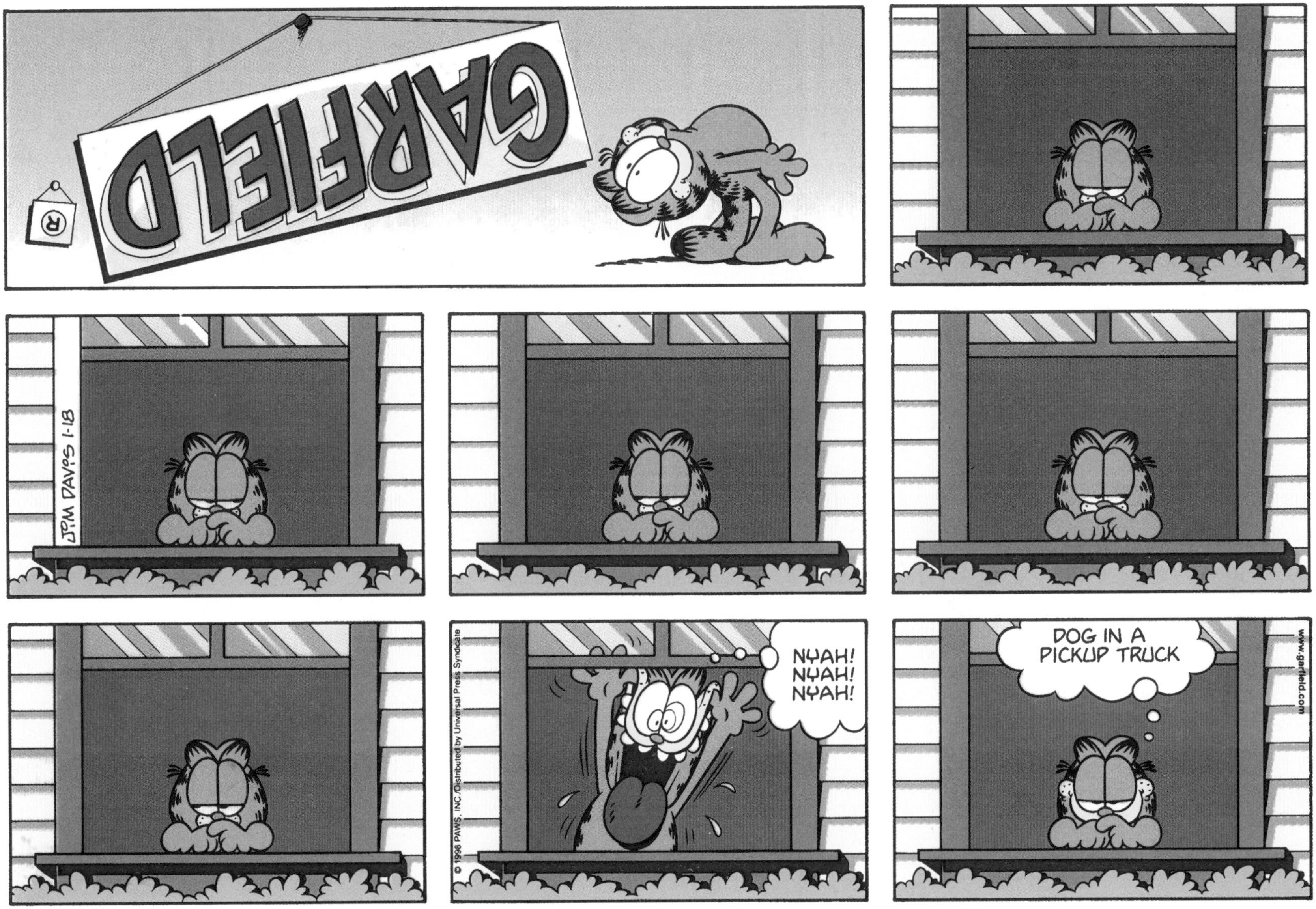
GARFIELD
JPM DAVPS 1-18
© 1998 PAWS, INC./Distributed by Universal Press Syndicate
NYAH! NYAH! NYAH!
DOG IN A PICKUP TRUCK
www.garfield.com

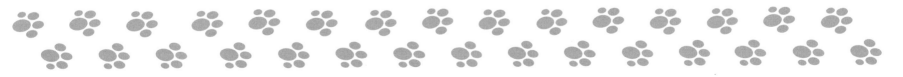

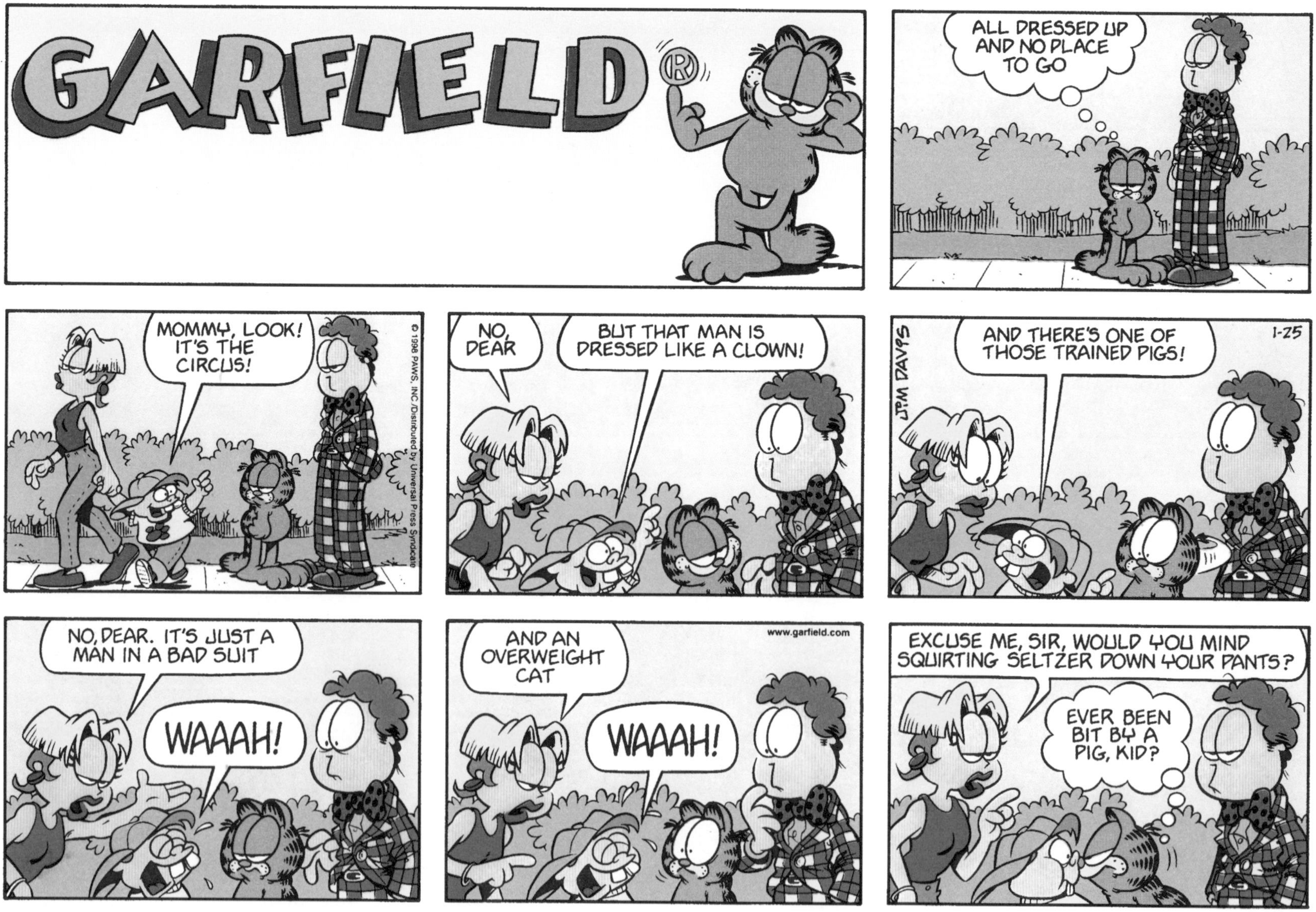
GARFIELD ®
ALL DRESSED UP AND NO PLACE TO GO
MOMMY, LOOK! IT'S THE CIRCUS!
© 1998 PAWS, INC./Distributed by Universal Press Syndicate
NO, DEAR
BUT THAT MAN IS DRESSED LIKE A CLOWN!
JPM DAV95
1-25
AND THERE'S ONE OF THOSE TRAINED PIGS!
NO, DEAR. IT'S JUST A MAN IN A BAD SUIT
WAAAH!
www.garfield.com
AND AN OVERWEIGHT CAT
WAAAH!
EXCUSE ME, SIR, WOULD YOU MIND SQUIRTING SELTZER DOWN YOUR PANTS?
EVER BEEN BIT BY A PIG, KID?

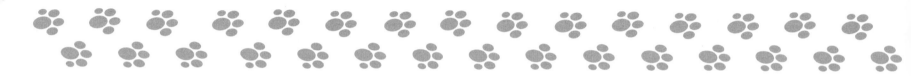

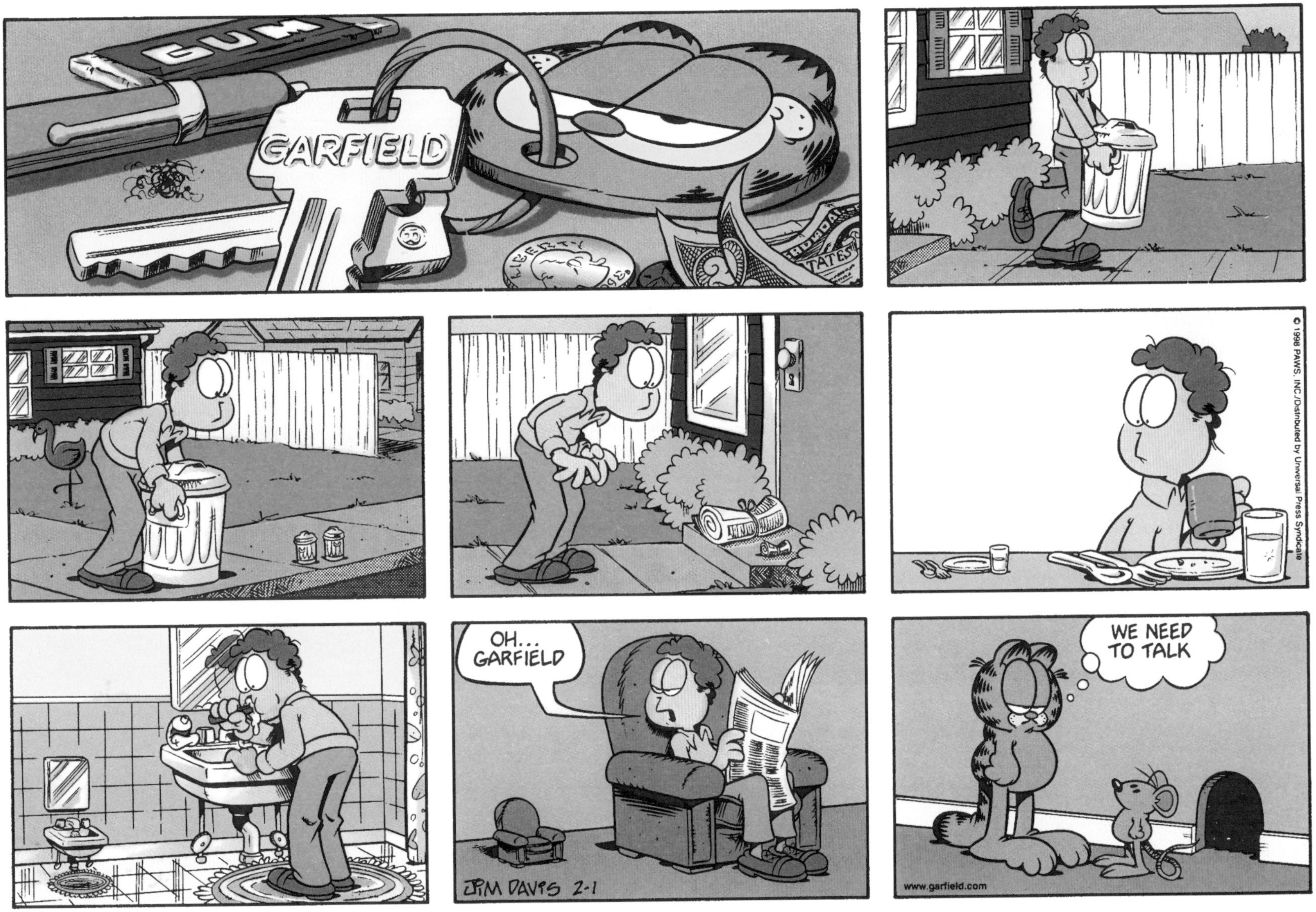
GUM
GARFIELD
© 1998 PAWS, INC./Distributed by Universal Press Syndicate
OH... GARFIELD
JIM DAVIS 2-1
WE NEED TO TALK
www.garfield.com

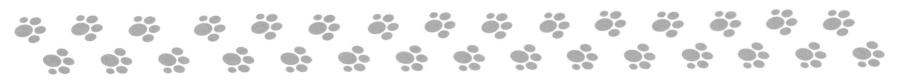

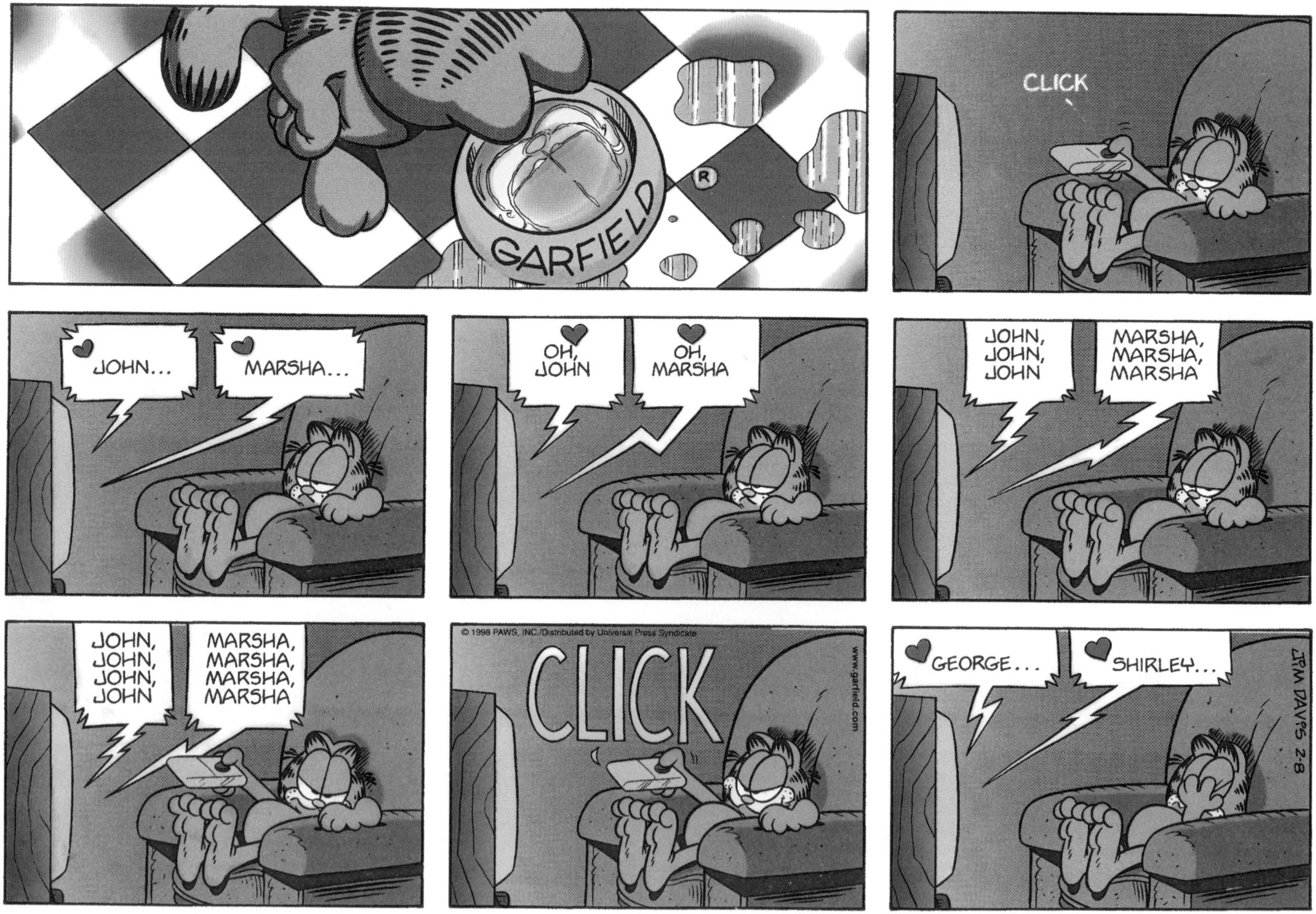
GARFIELD
CLICK
JOHN...
MARSHA...
OH, JOHN
OH, MARSHA
JOHN, JOHN, JOHN
MARSHA, MARSHA, MARSHA
JOHN, JOHN, JOHN, JOHN
MARSHA, MARSHA, MARSHA, MARSHA
© 1998 PAWS, INC./Distributed by Universal Press Syndicate
www.garfield.com
CLICK
GEORGE...
SHIRLEY...
JIM DAVIS 2-8

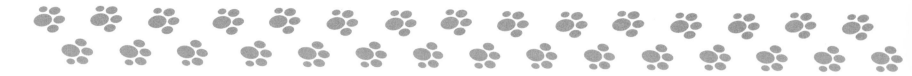

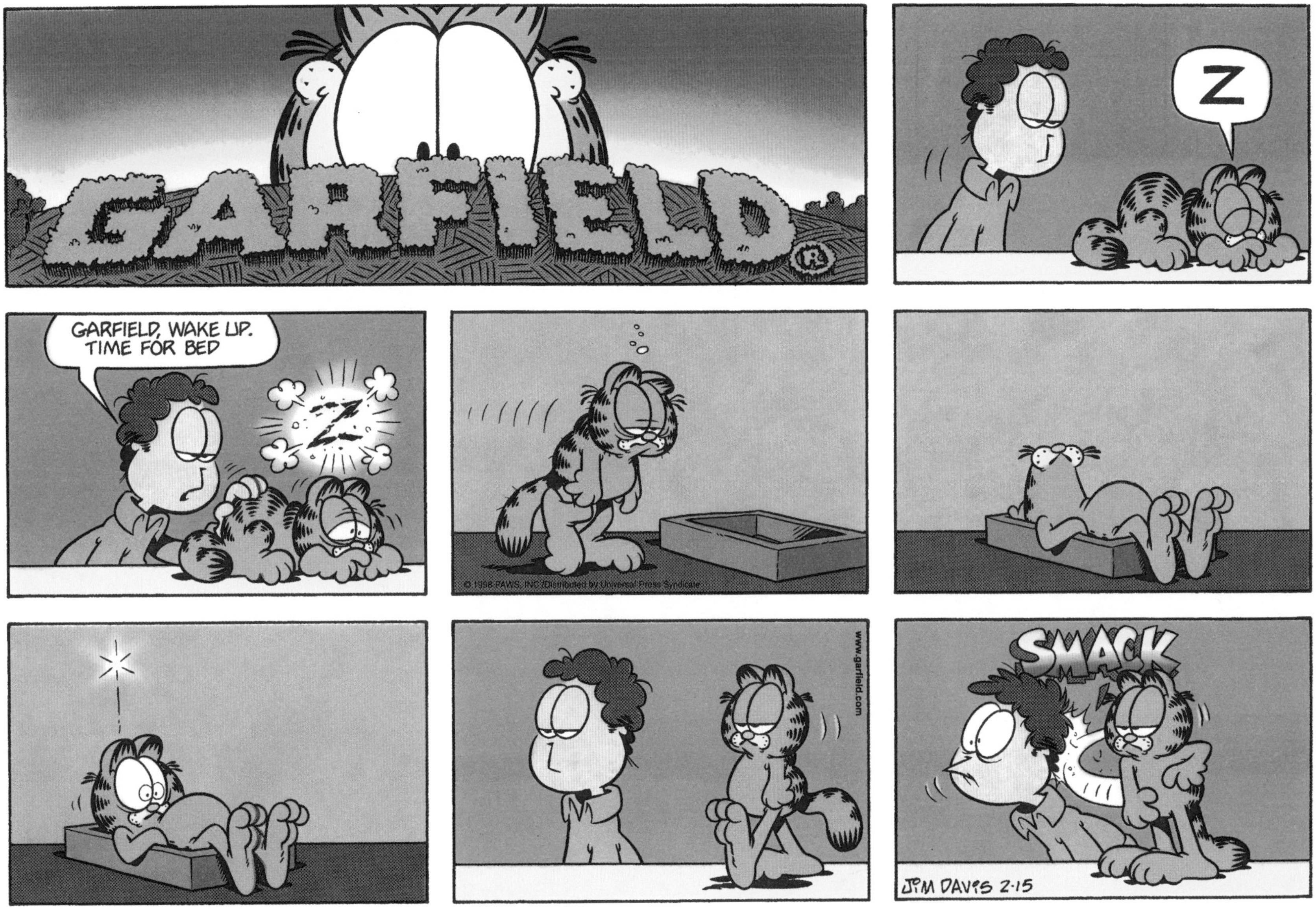
GARFIELD
Z
GARFIELD, WAKE UP. TIME FOR BED
Z
© 1998 PAWS, INC./Distributed by Universal Press Syndicate
www.garfield.com
SMACK
JIM DAVIS 2-15

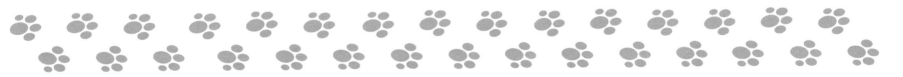

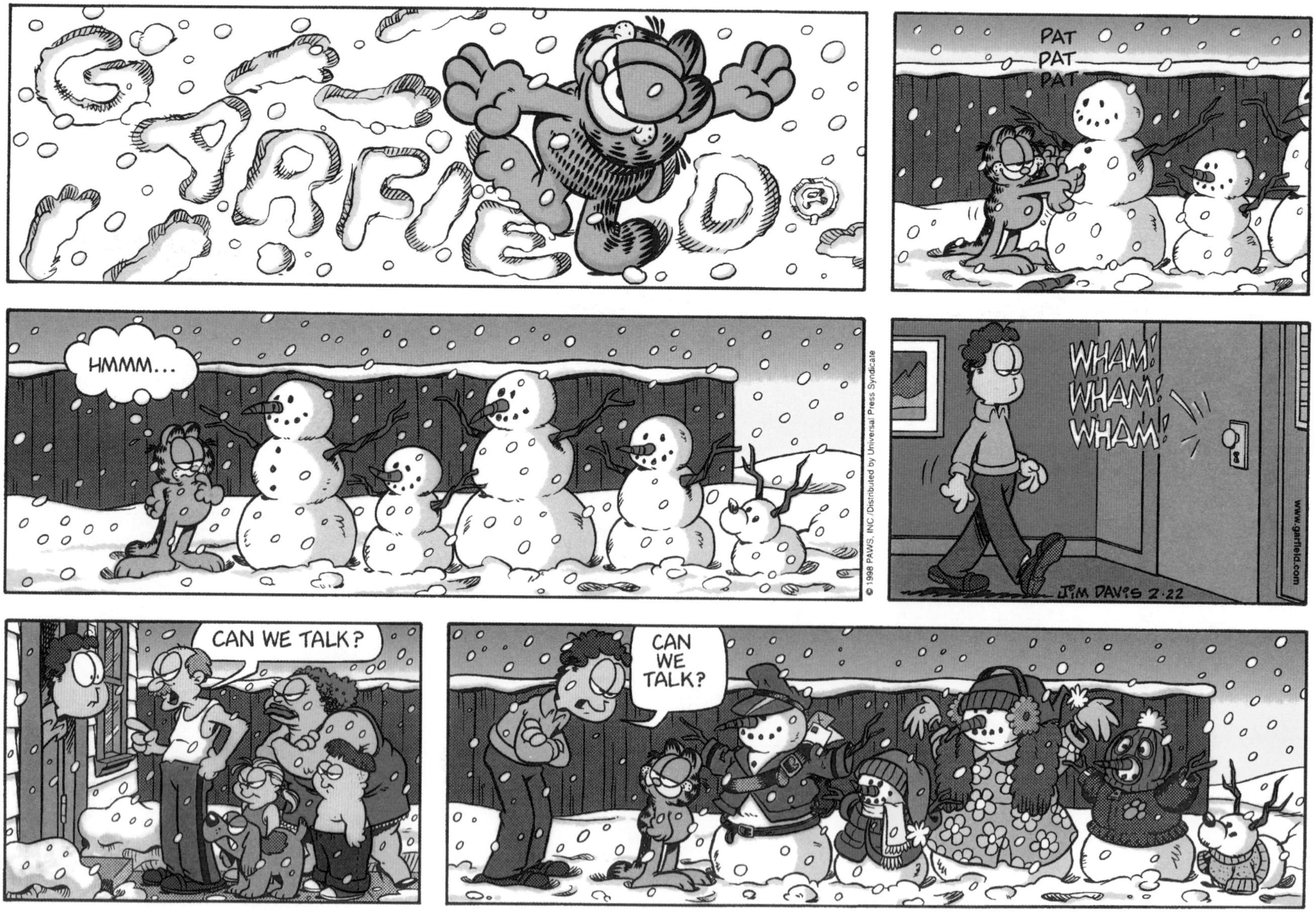
GARFIELD®
PAT
PAT
PAT
HMMM...
© 1998 PAWS, INC./Distributed by Universal Press Syndicate
WHAM!
WHAM!
WHAM!
JIM DAVIS 2-22
www.garfield.com
CAN WE TALK?
CAN WE TALK?

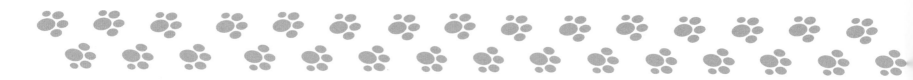

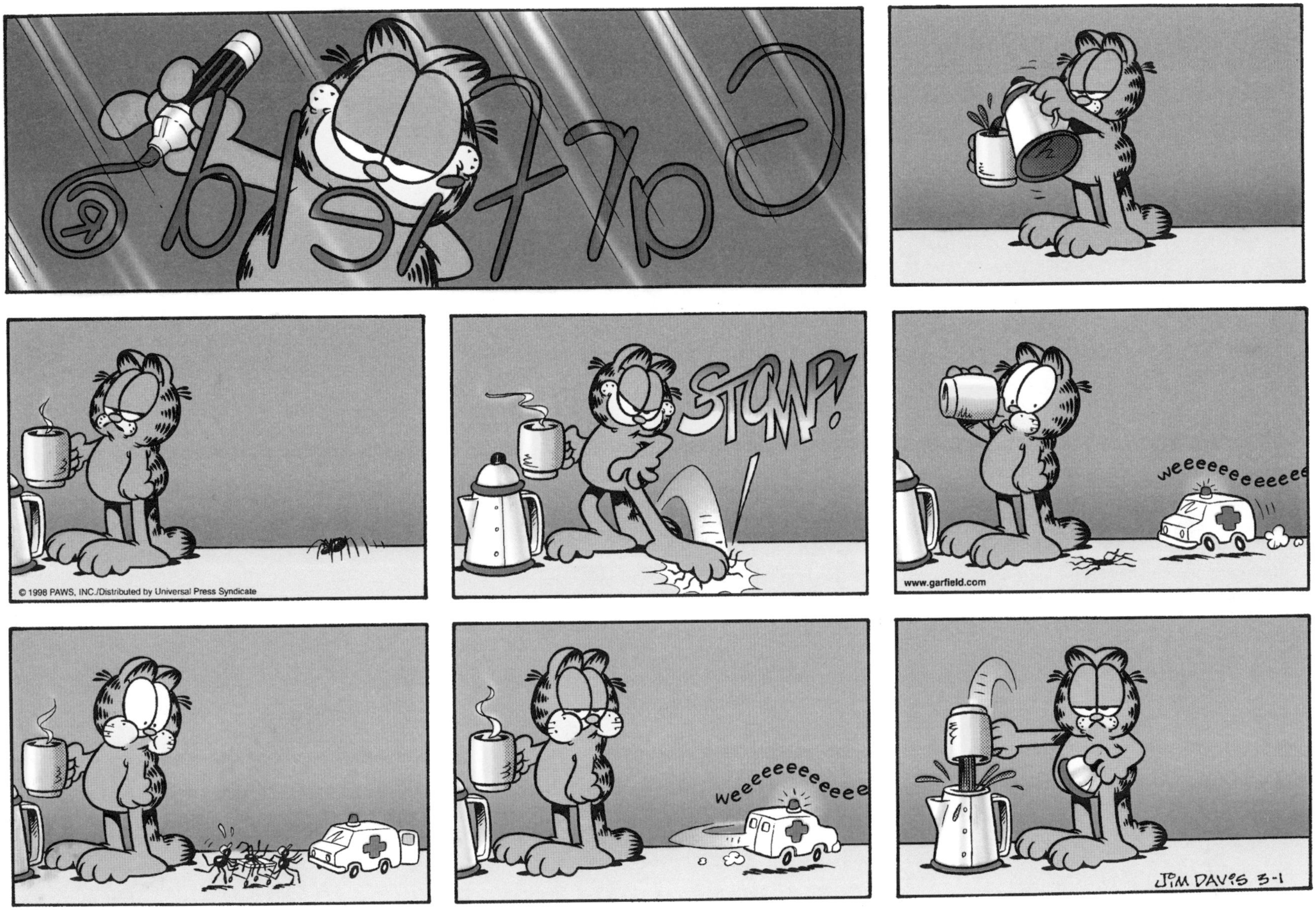
Garfield®
© 1998 PAWS, INC./Distributed by Universal Press Syndicate
STOMP!
weeeeeeeeeeee
www.garfield.com
weeeeeeeeeeee
JIM DAVIS 3-1

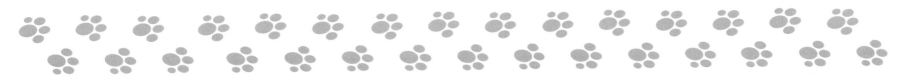

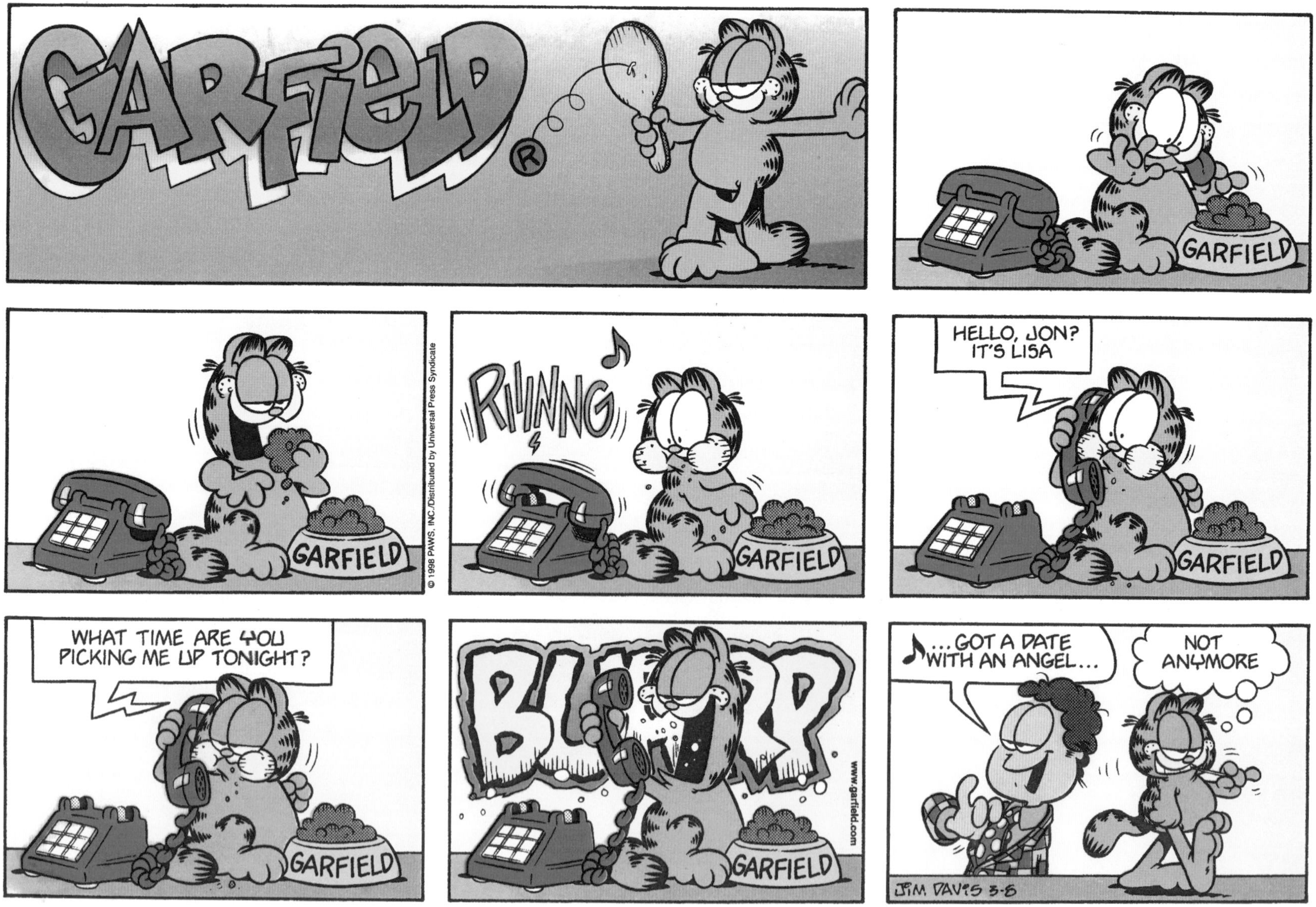

GARFIELD®
GARFIELD
© 1998 PAWS, INC./Distributed by Universal Press Syndicate
RIIINNG
HELLO, JON? IT'S LISA
WHAT TIME ARE YOU PICKING ME UP TONIGHT?
www.garfield.com
♪ ...GOT A DATE WITH AN ANGEL...
NOT ANYMORE
JIM DAVIS 3-8

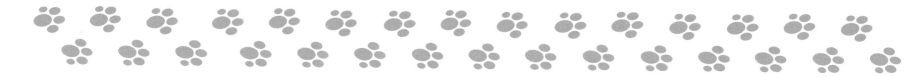

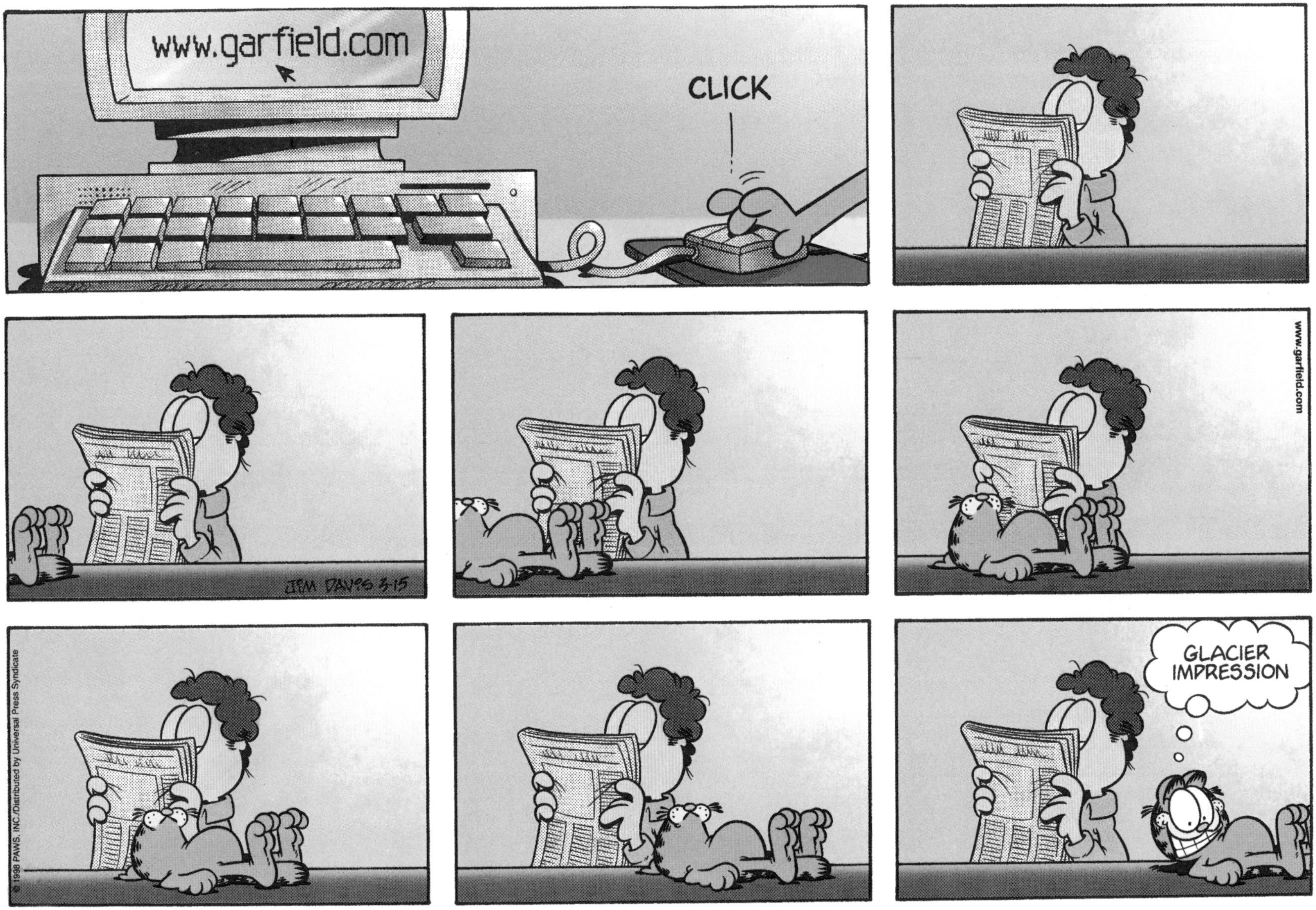
www.garfield.com
CLICK
JIM DAVIS 3-15
www.garfield.com
© 1998 PAWS, INC./Distributed by Universal Press Syndicate
GLACIER IMPRESSION

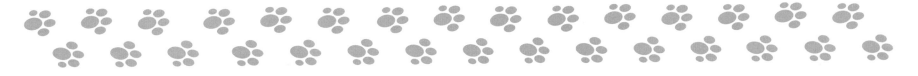

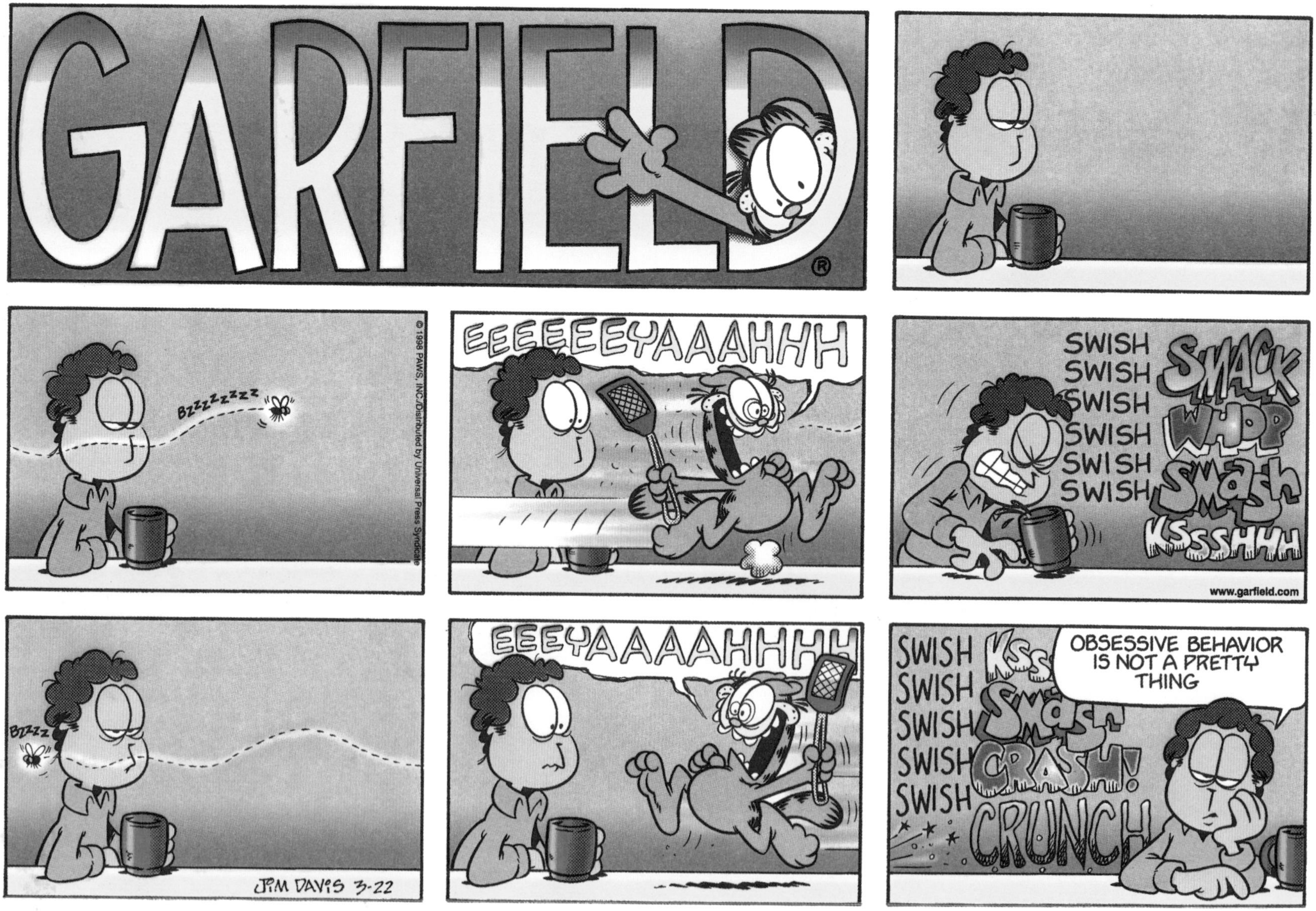

GARFIELD®
© 1998 PAWS, INC./Distributed by Universal Press Syndicate
BZZZZZZZZ
EEEEEEEYAAAHHH
SWISH SWISH SWISH SWISH SWISH SWISH
SMACK WHOP SMASH KSSSHHH
www.garfield.com
BZZZZ
JIM DAVIS 3-22
EEEEYAAAAAHHHH
SWISH SWISH SWISH SWISH SWISH
KSS SMASH CRASH! CRUNCH
OBSESSIVE BEHAVIOR IS NOT A PRETTY THING

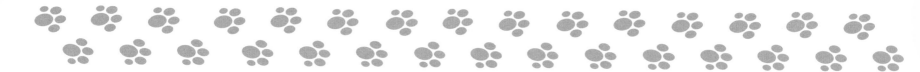

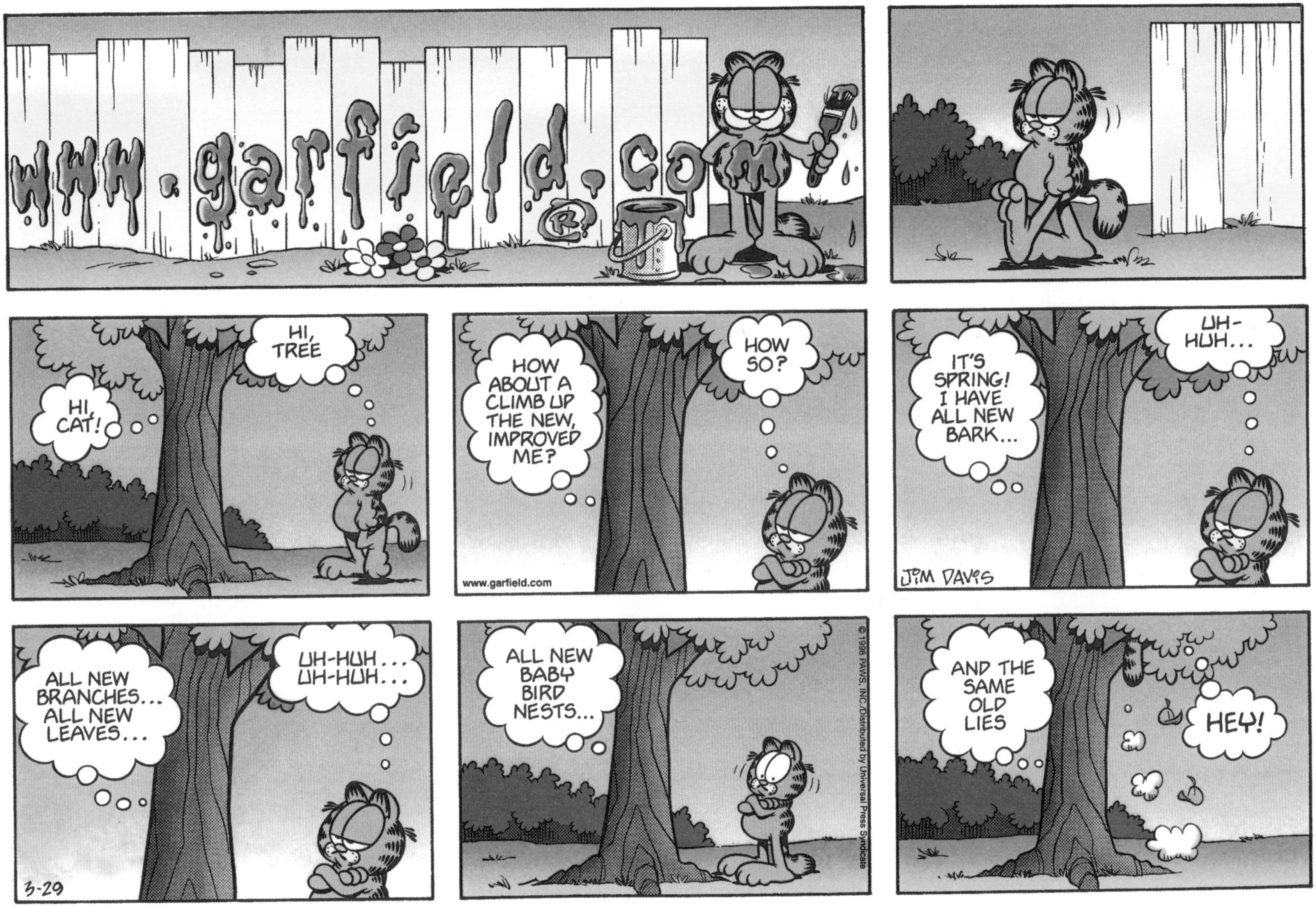
www.garfield.com
HI, TREE
HI, CAT!
HOW ABOUT A CLIMB UP THE NEW, IMPROVED ME?
HOW SO?
www.garfield.com
IT'S SPRING! I HAVE ALL NEW BARK...
UH-HUH...
JIM DAVIS
ALL NEW BRANCHES... ALL NEW LEAVES...
UH-HUH... UH-HUH...
3-29
ALL NEW BABY BIRD NESTS...
© 1998 PAWS, INC./Distributed by Universal Press Syndicate
AND THE SAME OLD LIES
HEY!

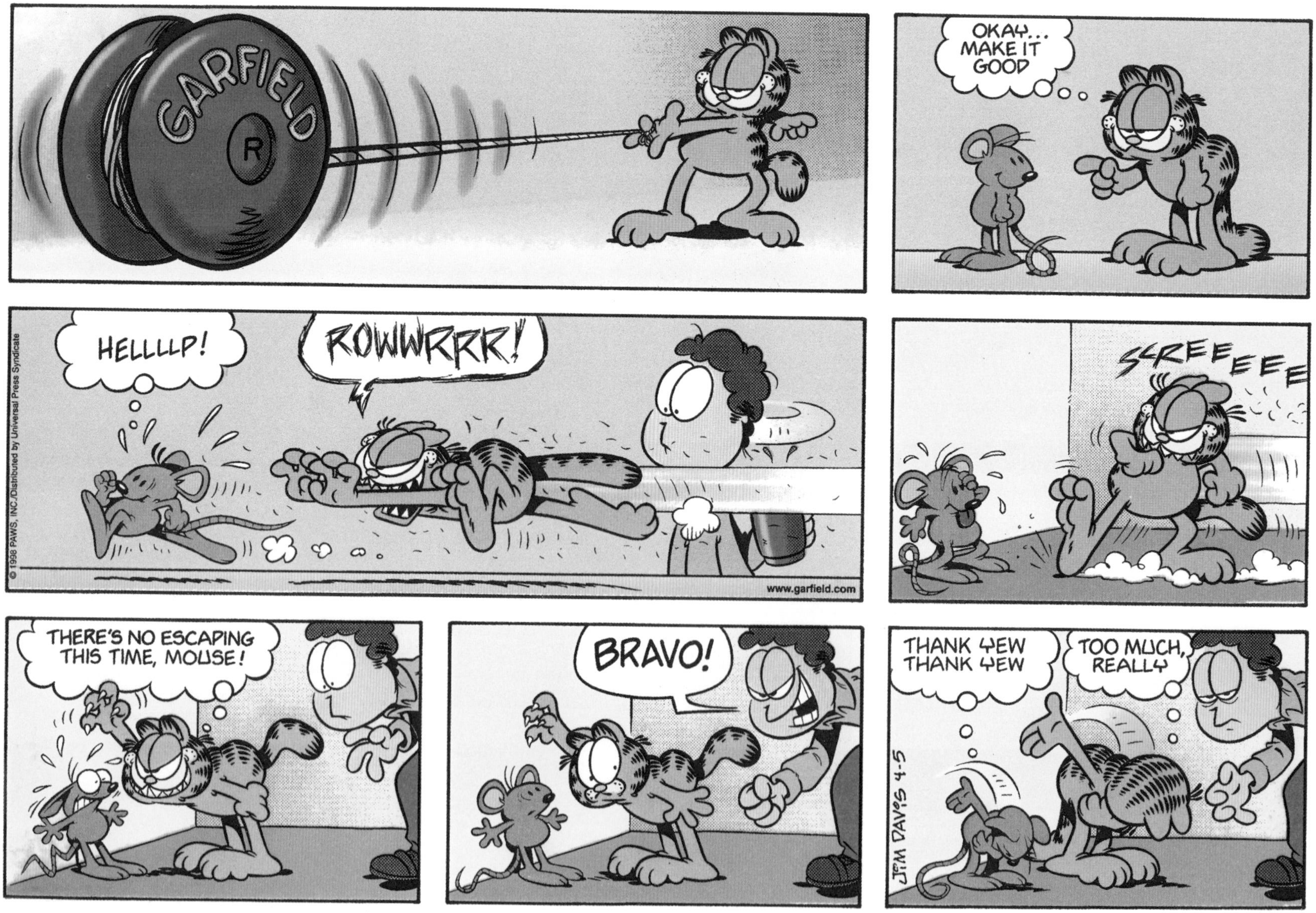
GARFIELD
R
OKAY... MAKE IT GOOD
HELLLLP!
ROWWRRR!
© 1998 PAWS, INC./Distributed by Universal Press Syndicate
www.garfield.com
SCREEEEEEE
THERE'S NO ESCAPING THIS TIME, MOUSE!
BRAVO!
JIM DAVIS 4-5
THANK YEW THANK YEW
TOO MUCH, REALLY

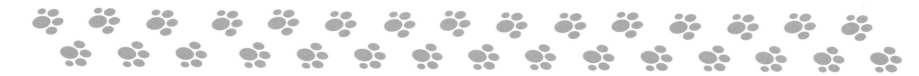

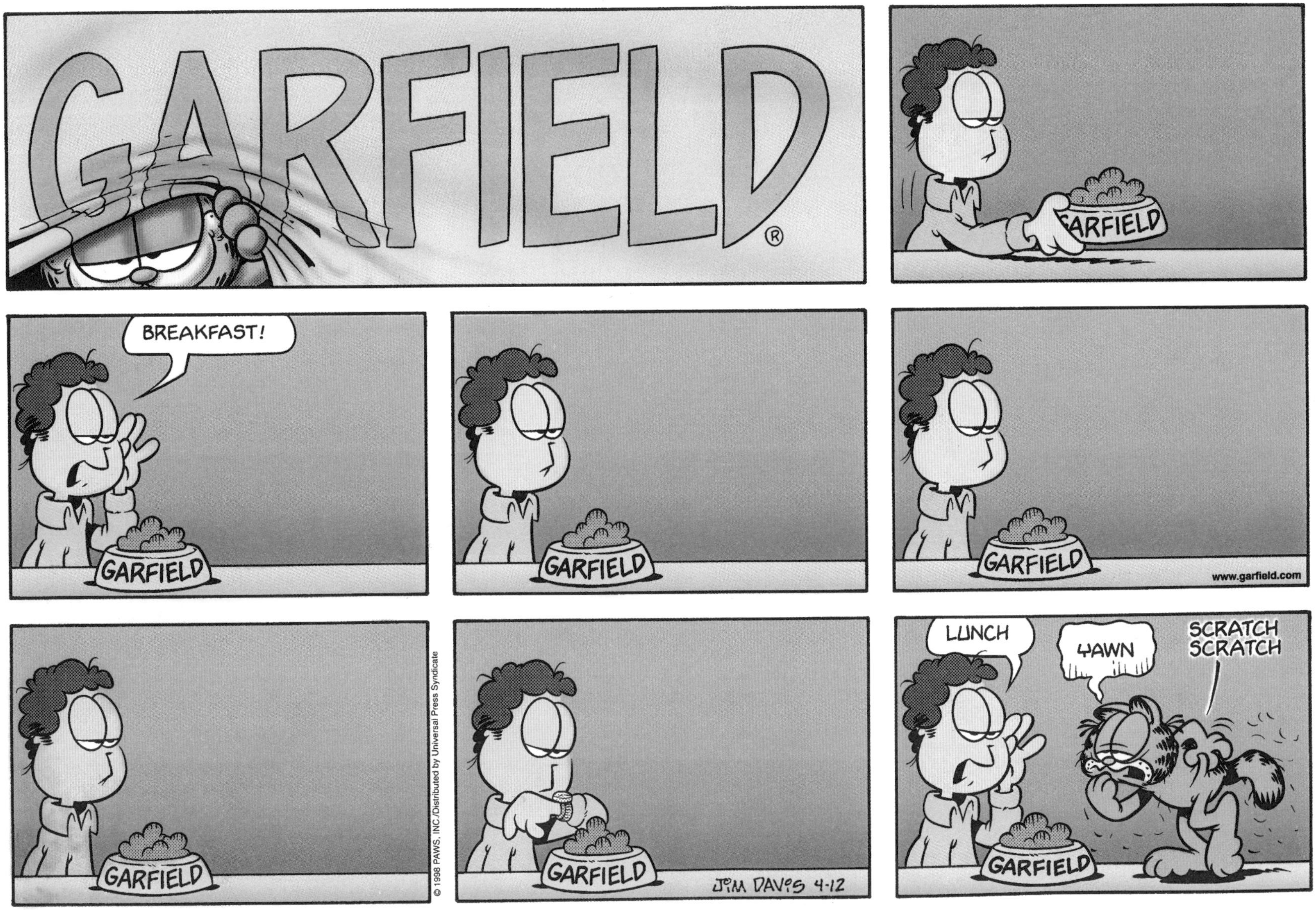
GARFIELD
BREAKFAST!
GARFIELD
www.garfield.com
JIM DAVIS 4-12
LUNCH
YAWN
SCRATCH SCRATCH

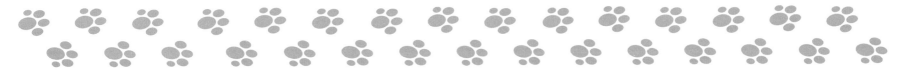

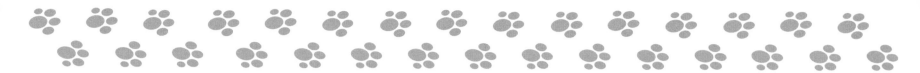

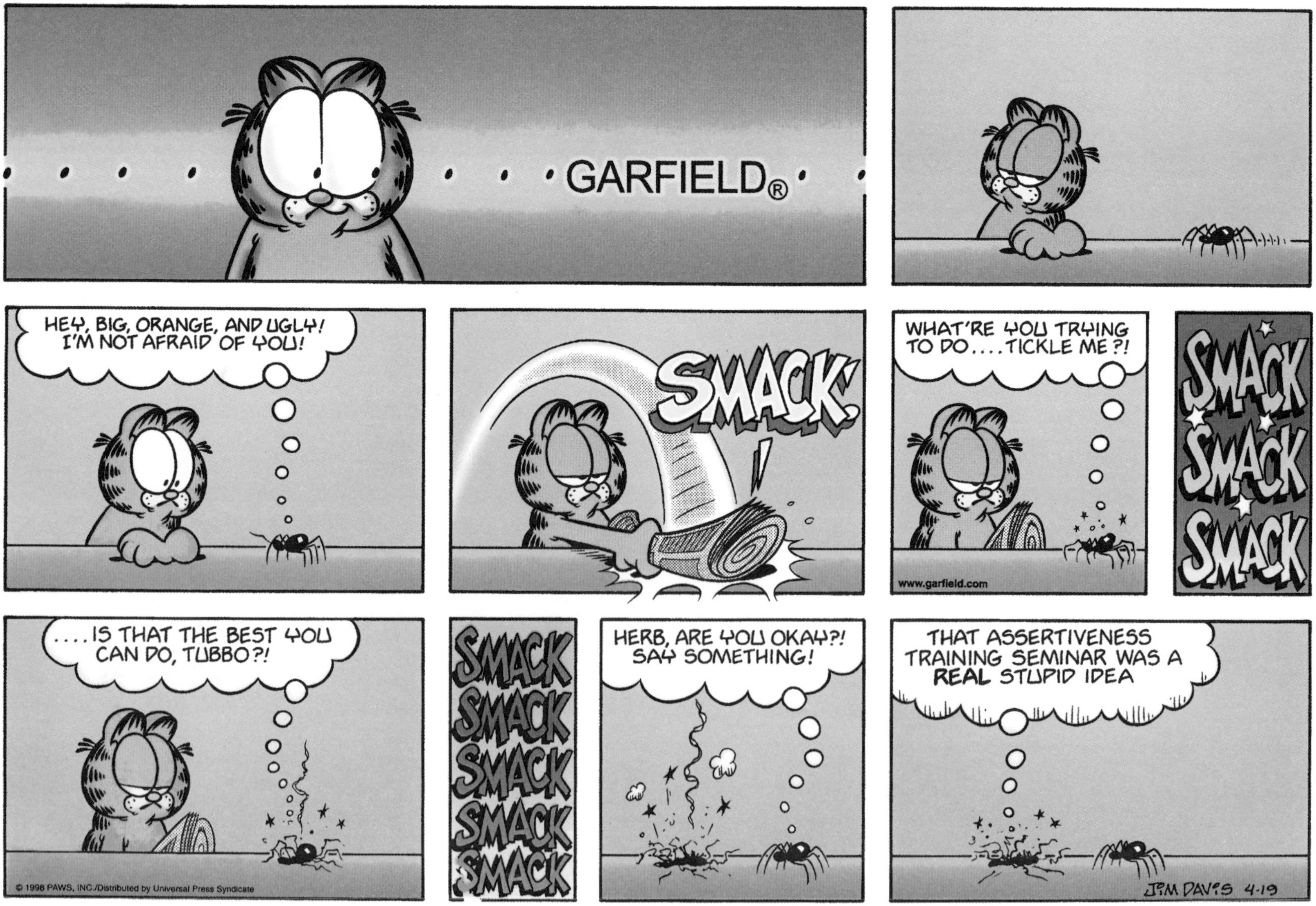
GARFIELD®
HEY, BIG, ORANGE, AND UGLY! I'M NOT AFRAID OF YOU!
SMACK!
WHAT'RE YOU TRYING TO DO.... TICKLE ME?!
www.garfield.com
SMACK SMACK SMACK
....IS THAT THE BEST YOU CAN DO, TUBBO?!
© 1998 PAWS, INC./Distributed by Universal Press Syndicate
SMACK SMACK SMACK SMACK SMACK
HERB, ARE YOU OKAY?! SAY SOMETHING!
THAT ASSERTIVENESS TRAINING SEMINAR WAS A **REAL** STUPID IDEA
JIM DAVIS 4-19

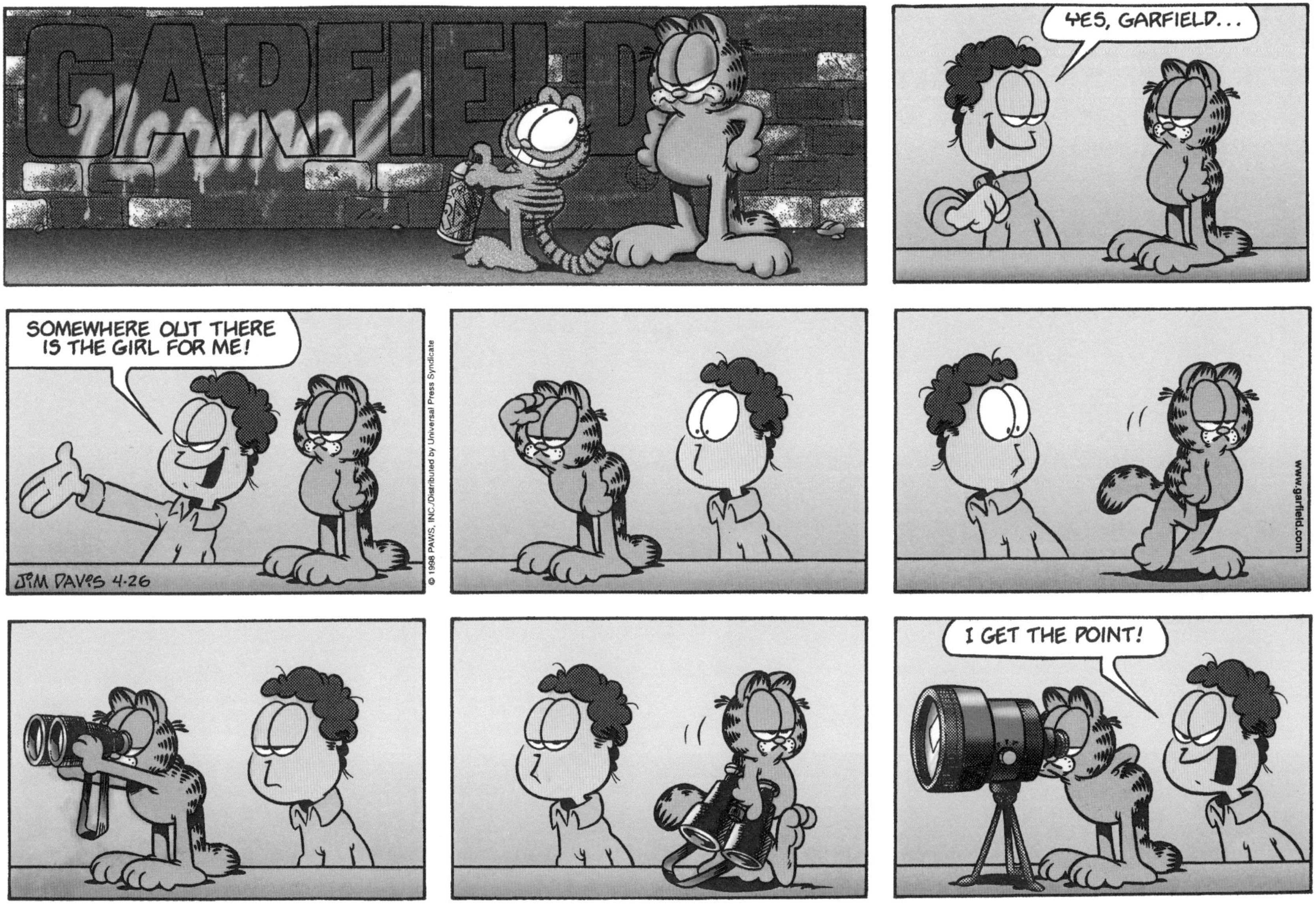
GARFIELD
YES, GARFIELD...
SOMEWHERE OUT THERE IS THE GIRL FOR ME!
JIM DAVIS 4-26
© 1998 PAWS, INC./Distributed by Universal Press Syndicate
www.garfield.com
I GET THE POINT!

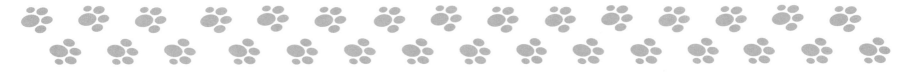

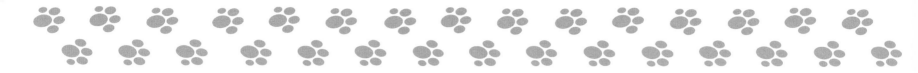

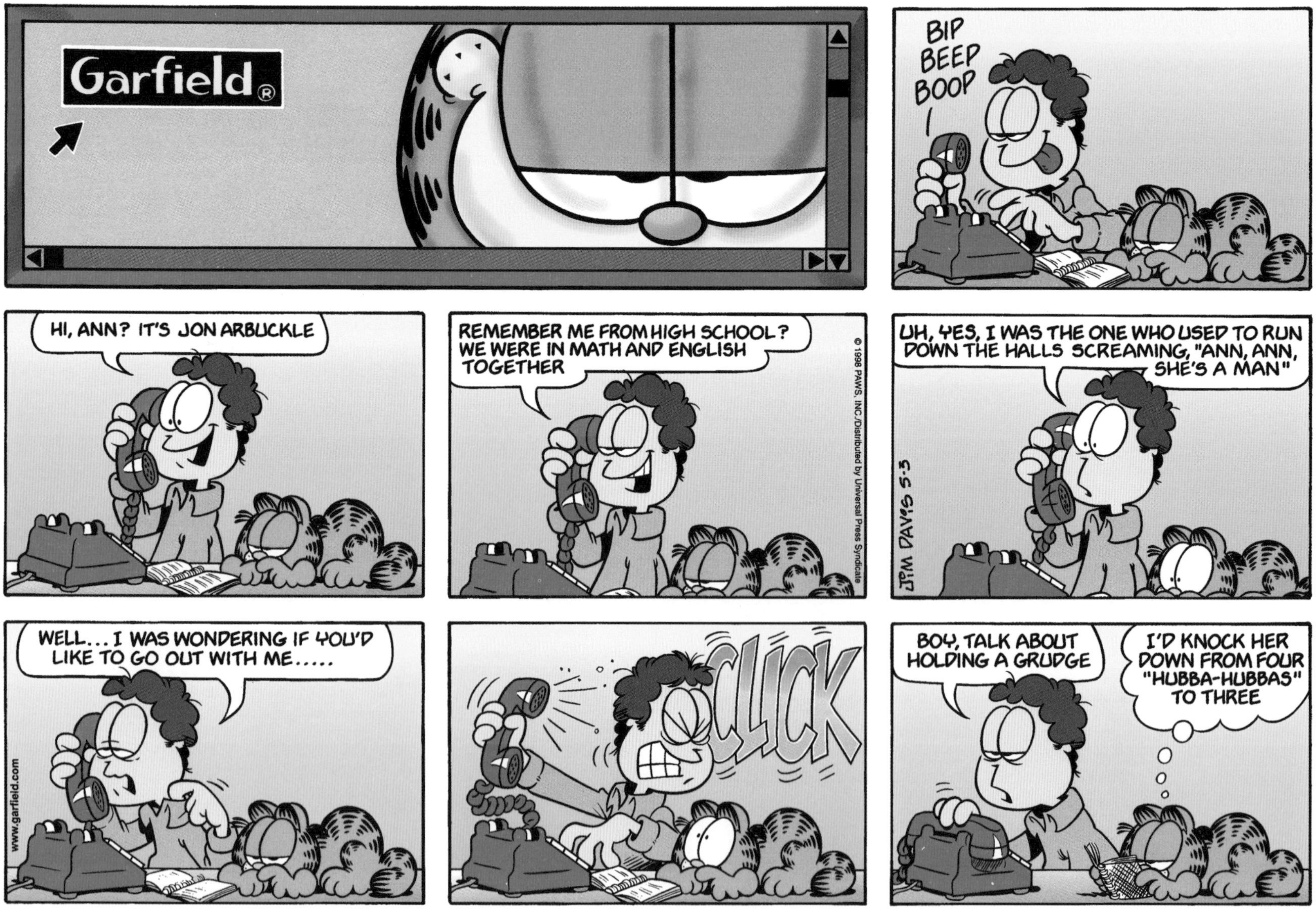
Garfield®
BIP BEEP BOOP
HI, ANN? IT'S JON ARBUCKLE
REMEMBER ME FROM HIGH SCHOOL? WE WERE IN MATH AND ENGLISH TOGETHER
© 1998 PAWS, INC./Distributed by Universal Press Syndicate
JIM DAVIS 5-3
UH, YES, I WAS THE ONE WHO USED TO RUN DOWN THE HALLS SCREAMING, "ANN, ANN, SHE'S A MAN"
WELL... I WAS WONDERING IF YOU'D LIKE TO GO OUT WITH ME.....
www.garfield.com
CLICK
BOY, TALK ABOUT HOLDING A GRUDGE
I'D KNOCK HER DOWN FROM FOUR "HUBBA-HUBBAS" TO THREE

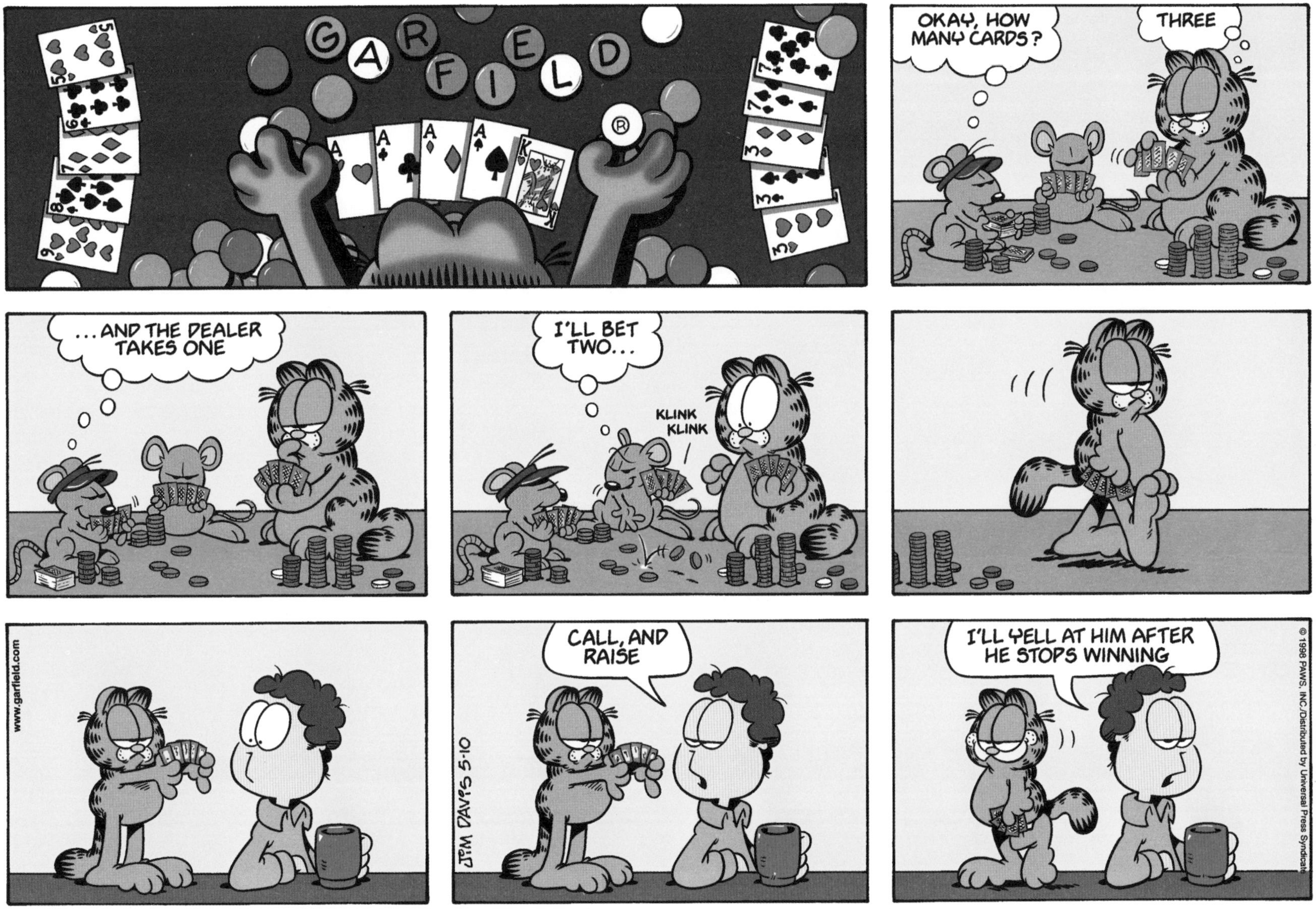
GARFIELD®
OKAY, HOW MANY CARDS?
THREE
...AND THE DEALER TAKES ONE
I'LL BET TWO...
KLINK KLINK
www.garfield.com
JIM DAVIS 5-10
CALL, AND RAISE
I'LL YELL AT HIM AFTER HE STOPS WINNING
© 1998 PAWS, INC./Distributed by Universal Press Syndicate

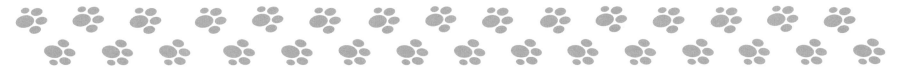

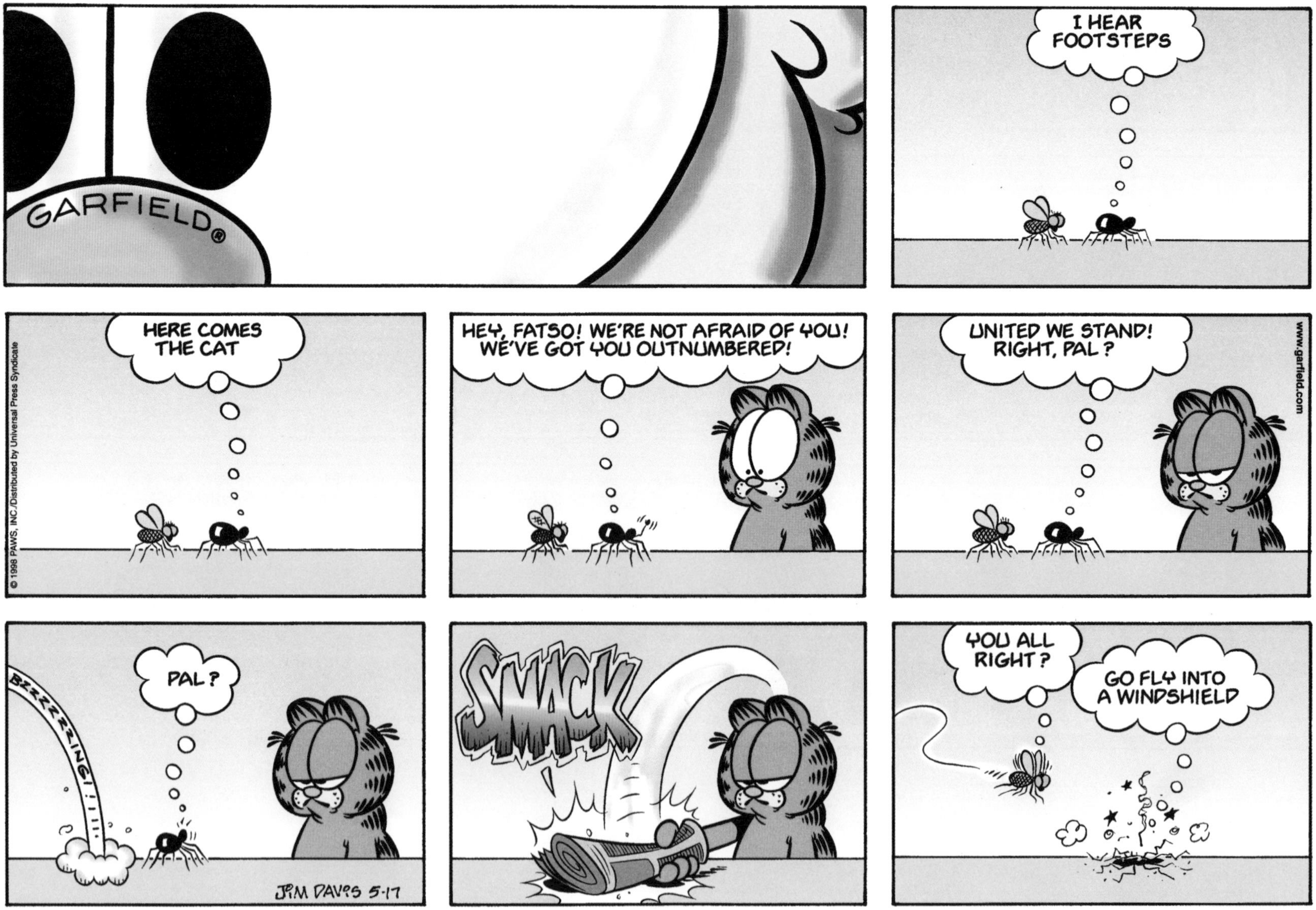
GARFIELD®
I HEAR FOOTSTEPS
HERE COMES THE CAT
HEY, FATSO! WE'RE NOT AFRAID OF YOU! WE'VE GOT YOU OUTNUMBERED!
UNITED WE STAND! RIGHT, PAL?
PAL?
BZZZZRING!
SMACK
YOU ALL RIGHT?
GO FLY INTO A WINDSHIELD
© 1998 PAWS, INC./Distributed by Universal Press Syndicate
www.garfield.com
JIM DAVIS 5-17

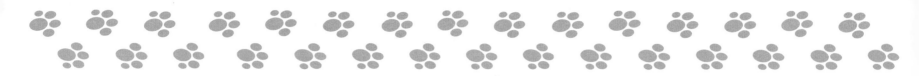

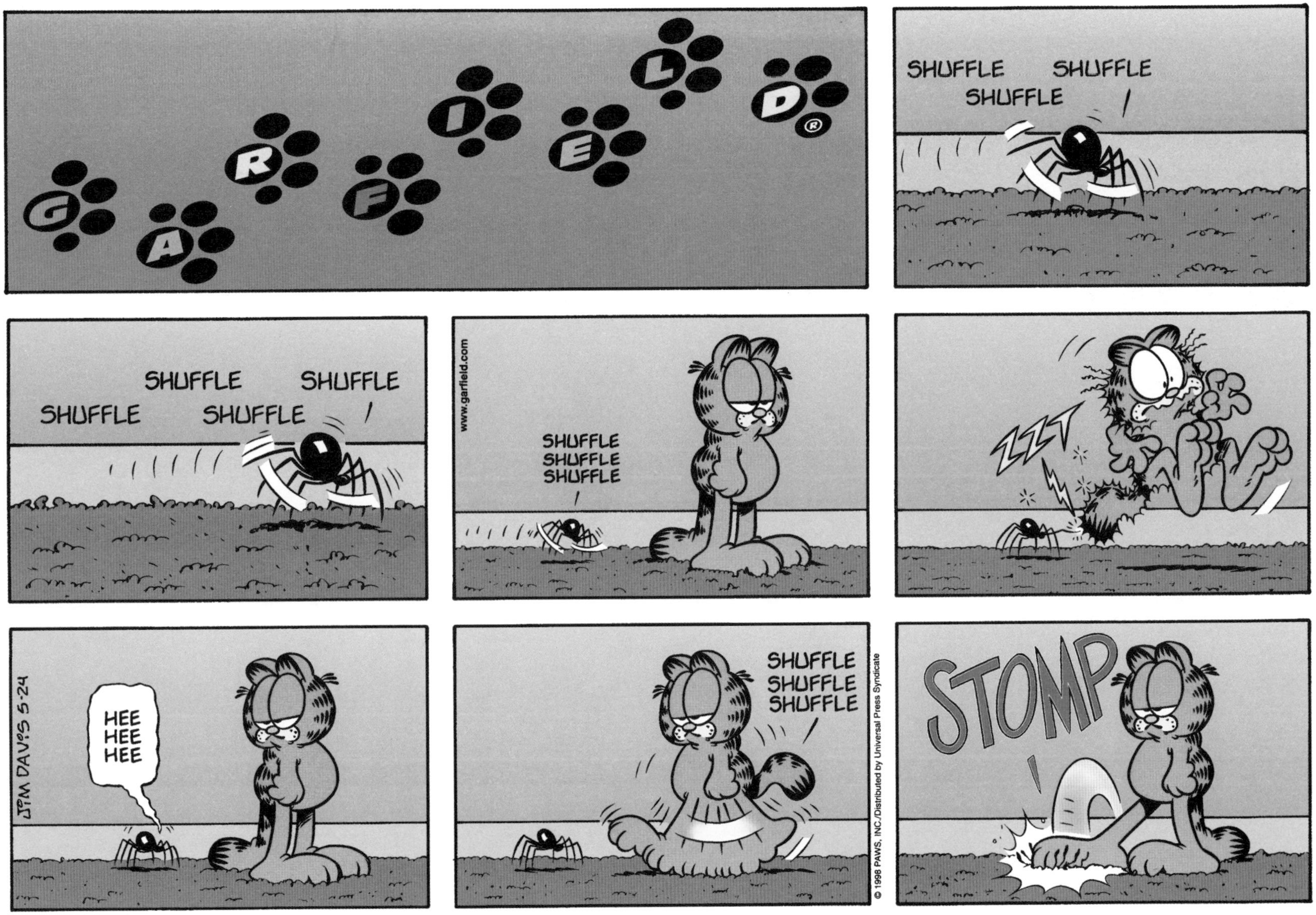
GARFIELD®
SHUFFLE
SHUFFLE
SHUFFLE
SHUFFLE
SHUFFLE
SHUFFLE
SHUFFLE
www.garfield.com
SHUFFLE
SHUFFLE
SHUFFLE
ZZZT
JIM DAVIS 5-24
HEE
HEE
HEE
SHUFFLE
SHUFFLE
SHUFFLE
© 1998 PAWS, INC./Distributed by Universal Press Syndicate
STOMP

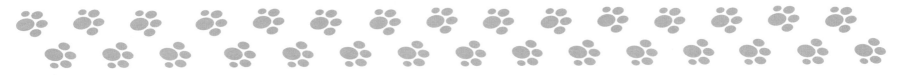

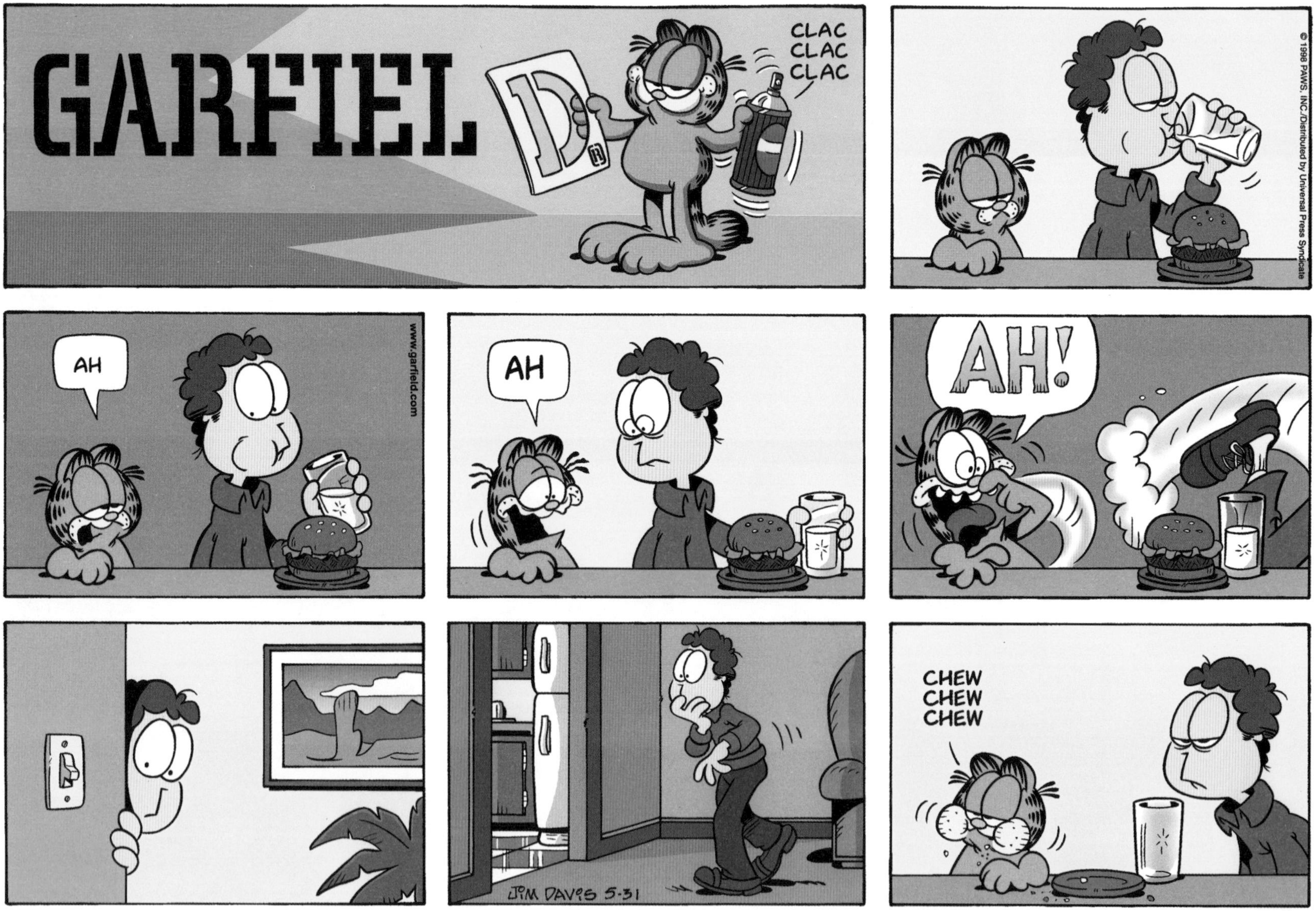

GARFIEL
D
CLAC
CLAC
CLAC
© 1998 PAWS, INC./Distributed by Universal Press Syndicate
www.garfield.com
AH
AH
AH!
JIM DAVIS 5-31
CHEW
CHEW
CHEW

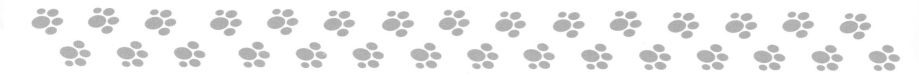

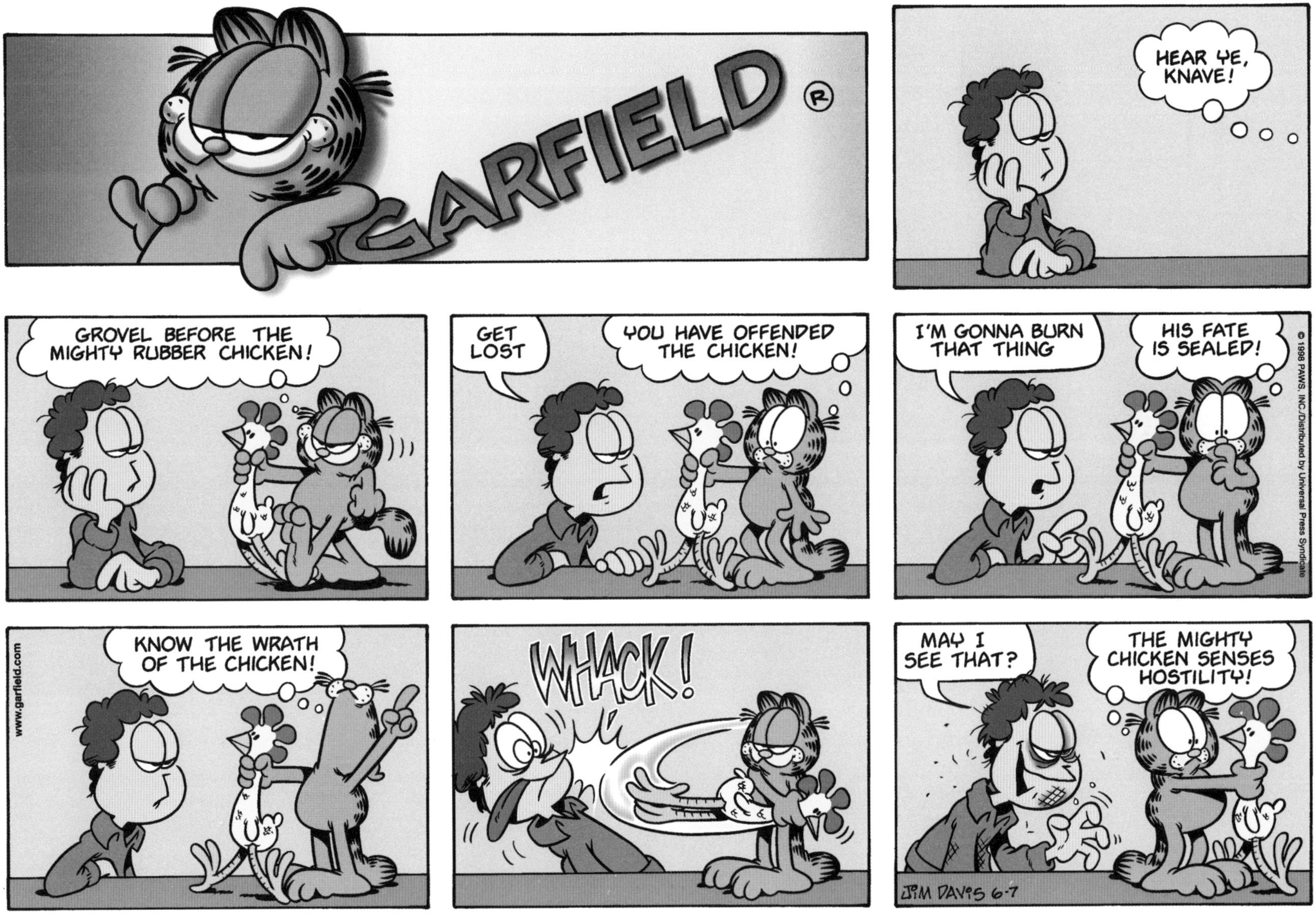
GARFIELD ®
HEAR YE, KNAVE!
GROVEL BEFORE THE MIGHTY RUBBER CHICKEN!
GET LOST
YOU HAVE OFFENDED THE CHICKEN!
I'M GONNA BURN THAT THING
HIS FATE IS SEALED!
© 1998 PAWS, INC./Distributed by Universal Press Syndicate
www.garfield.com
KNOW THE WRATH OF THE CHICKEN!
WHACK!
MAY I SEE THAT?
THE MIGHTY CHICKEN SENSES HOSTILITY!
JIM DAVIS 6-7

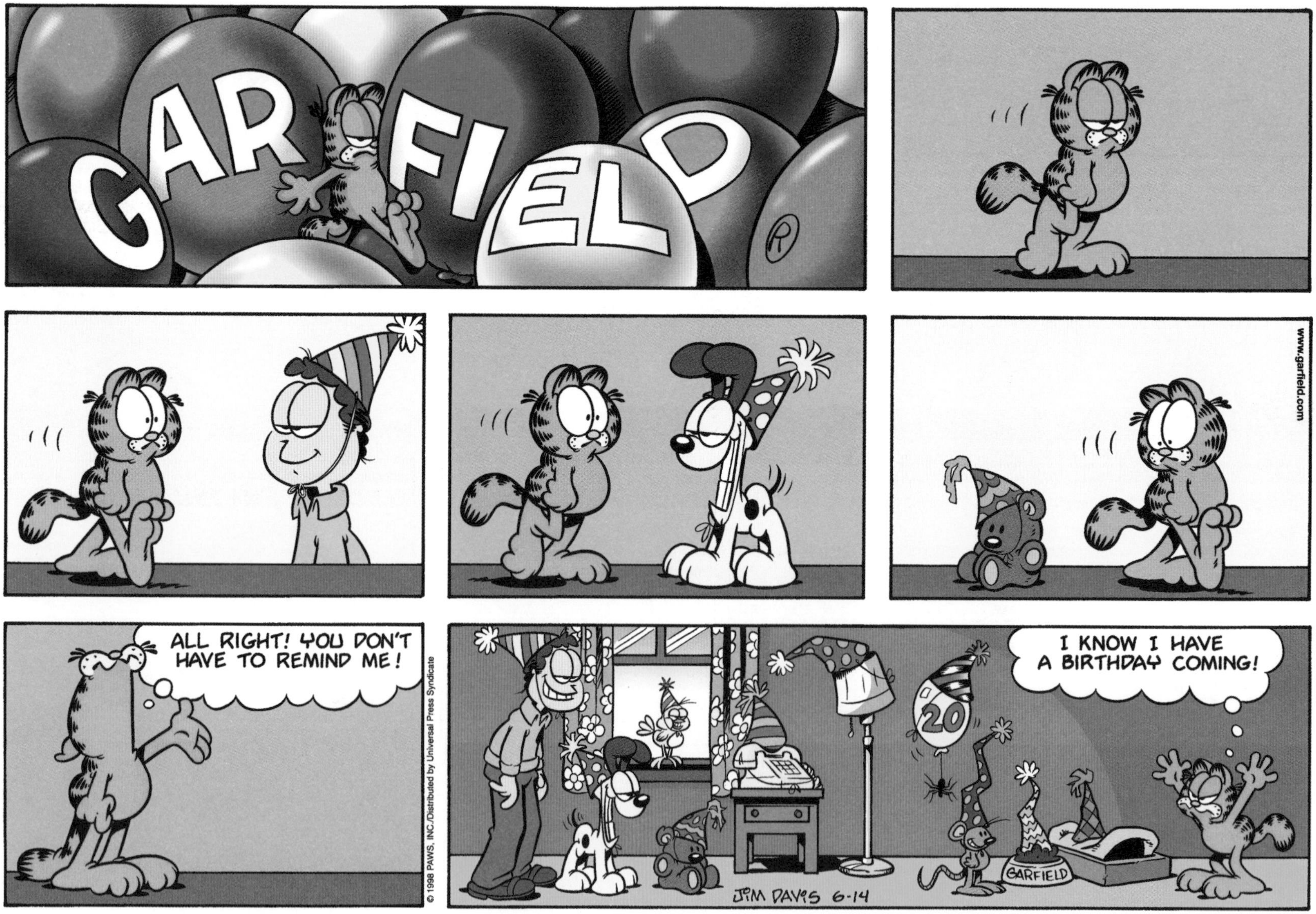
GARFIELD ®
ALL RIGHT! YOU DON'T HAVE TO REMIND ME!
I KNOW I HAVE A BIRTHDAY COMING!
20
GARFIELD
JIM DAVIS 6-14
www.garfield.com
© 1998 PAWS, INC./Distributed by Universal Press Syndicate

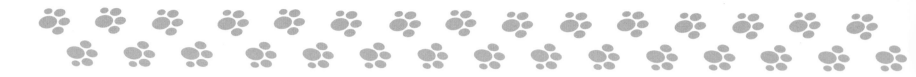

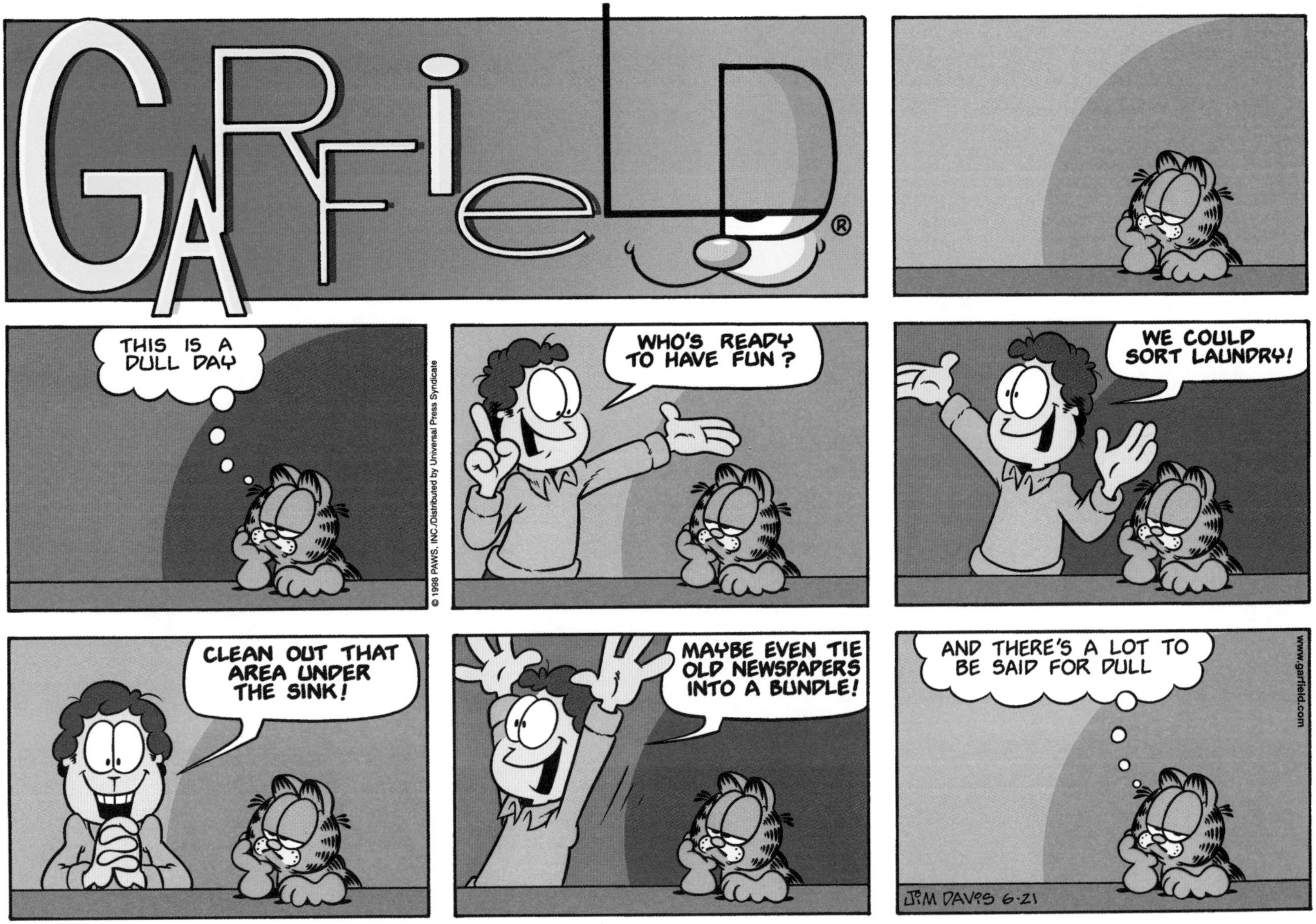
GARFIELD®
THIS IS A DULL DAY
WHO'S READY TO HAVE FUN ?
WE COULD SORT LAUNDRY!
CLEAN OUT THAT AREA UNDER THE SINK!
MAYBE EVEN TIE OLD NEWSPAPERS INTO A BUNDLE!
AND THERE'S A LOT TO BE SAID FOR DULL
© 1998 PAWS, INC./Distributed by Universal Press Syndicate
www.garfield.com
JIM DAVIS 6·21

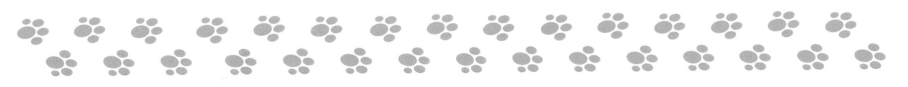

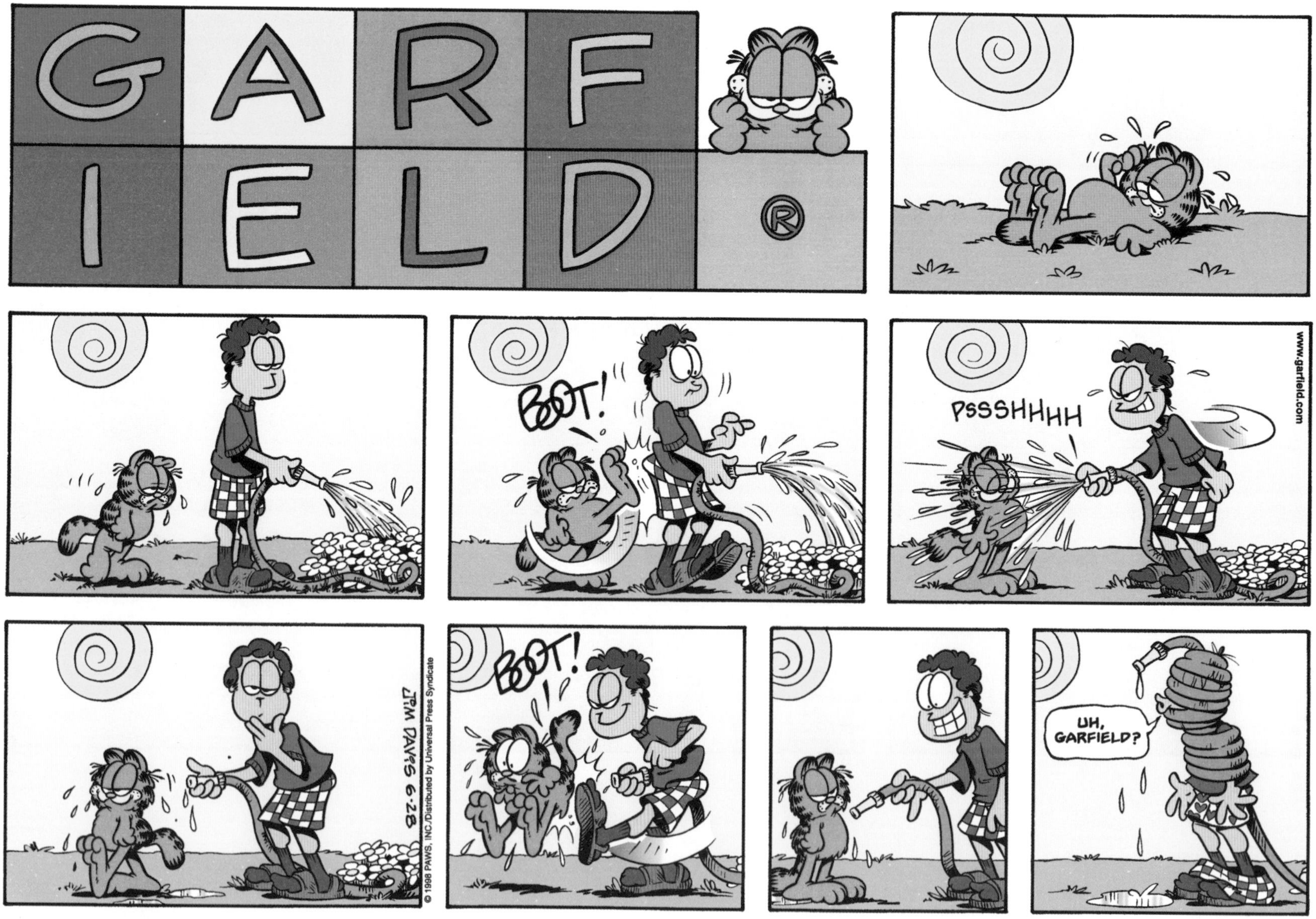
GARFIELD ®
BOOT!
www.garfield.com
PSSSHHHHH
JIM DAVIS 6-28
© 1998 PAWS, INC./Distributed by Universal Press Syndicate
BOOT!
UH, GARFIELD?

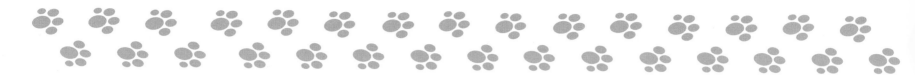

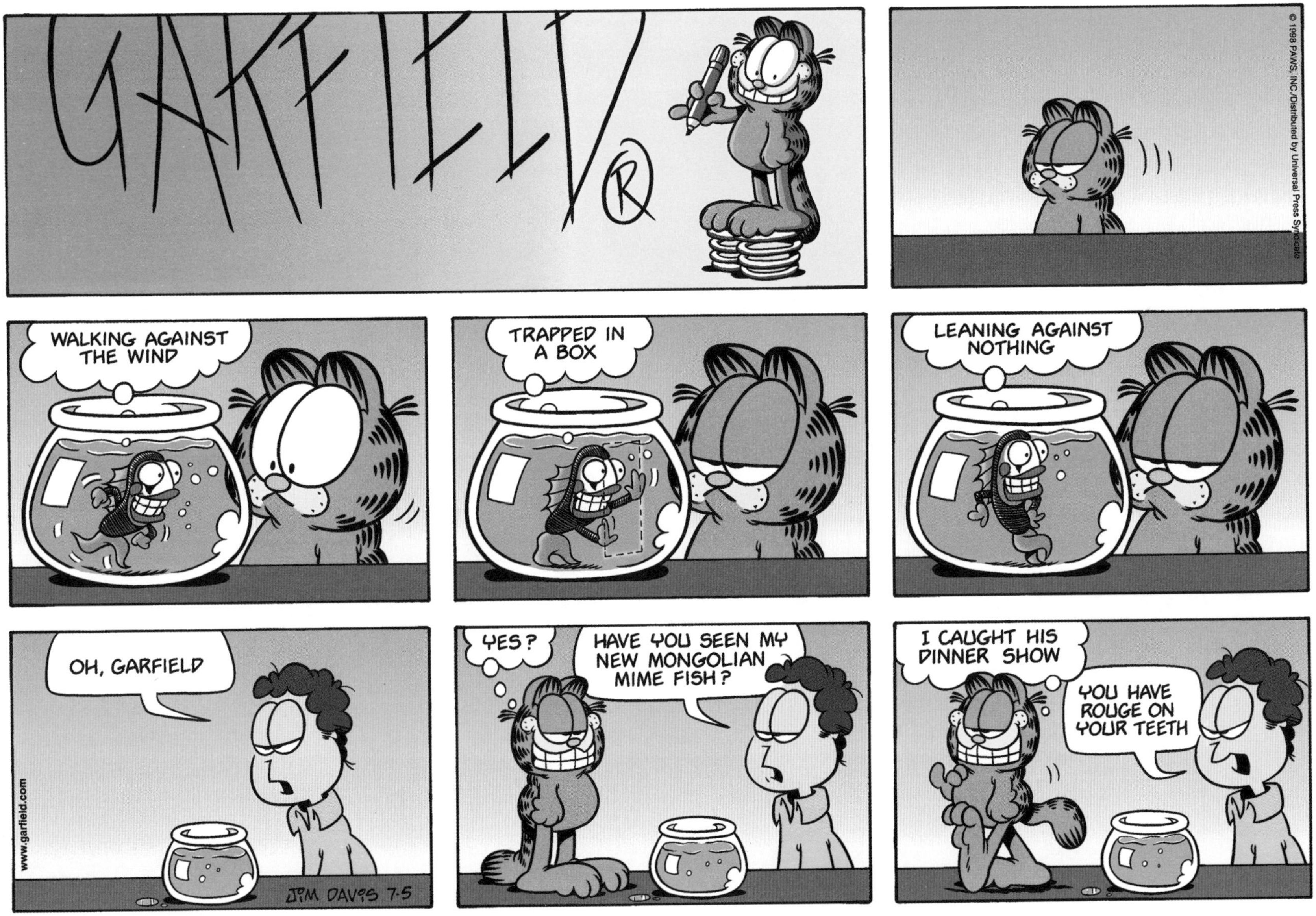
GARFIELD®
© 1998 PAWS, INC./Distributed by Universal Press Syndicate
WALKING AGAINST THE WIND
TRAPPED IN A BOX
LEANING AGAINST NOTHING
OH, GARFIELD
www.garfield.com
JIM DAVIS 7·5
YES?
HAVE YOU SEEN MY NEW MONGOLIAN MIME FISH?
I CAUGHT HIS DINNER SHOW
YOU HAVE ROUGE ON YOUR TEETH

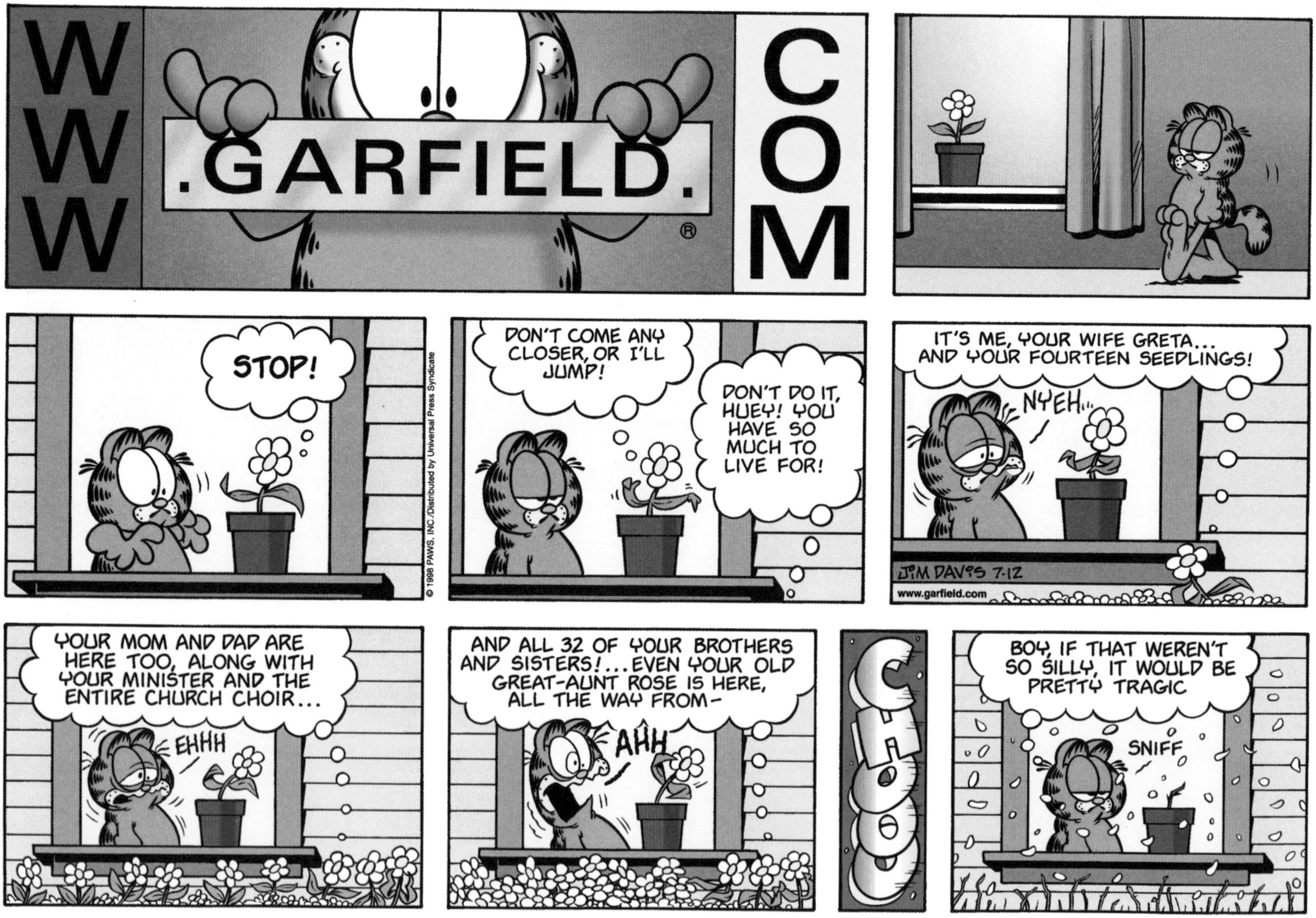

WWW .GARFIELD. COM
STOP!
DON'T COME ANY CLOSER, OR I'LL JUMP!
DON'T DO IT, HUEY! YOU HAVE SO MUCH TO LIVE FOR!
© 1998 PAWS, INC./Distributed by Universal Press Syndicate
IT'S ME, YOUR WIFE GRETA... AND YOUR FOURTEEN SEEDLINGS!
NYEH...
JIM DAVIS 7-12
www.garfield.com
YOUR MOM AND DAD ARE HERE TOO, ALONG WITH YOUR MINISTER AND THE ENTIRE CHURCH CHOIR...
EHHH
AND ALL 32 OF YOUR BROTHERS AND SISTERS!... EVEN YOUR OLD GREAT-AUNT ROSE IS HERE, ALL THE WAY FROM-
AHH
CHOOO
BOY, IF THAT WEREN'T SO SILLY, IT WOULD BE PRETTY TRAGIC
SNIFF

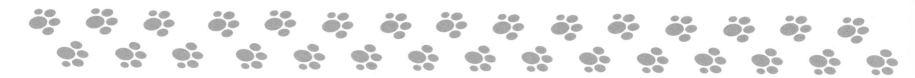

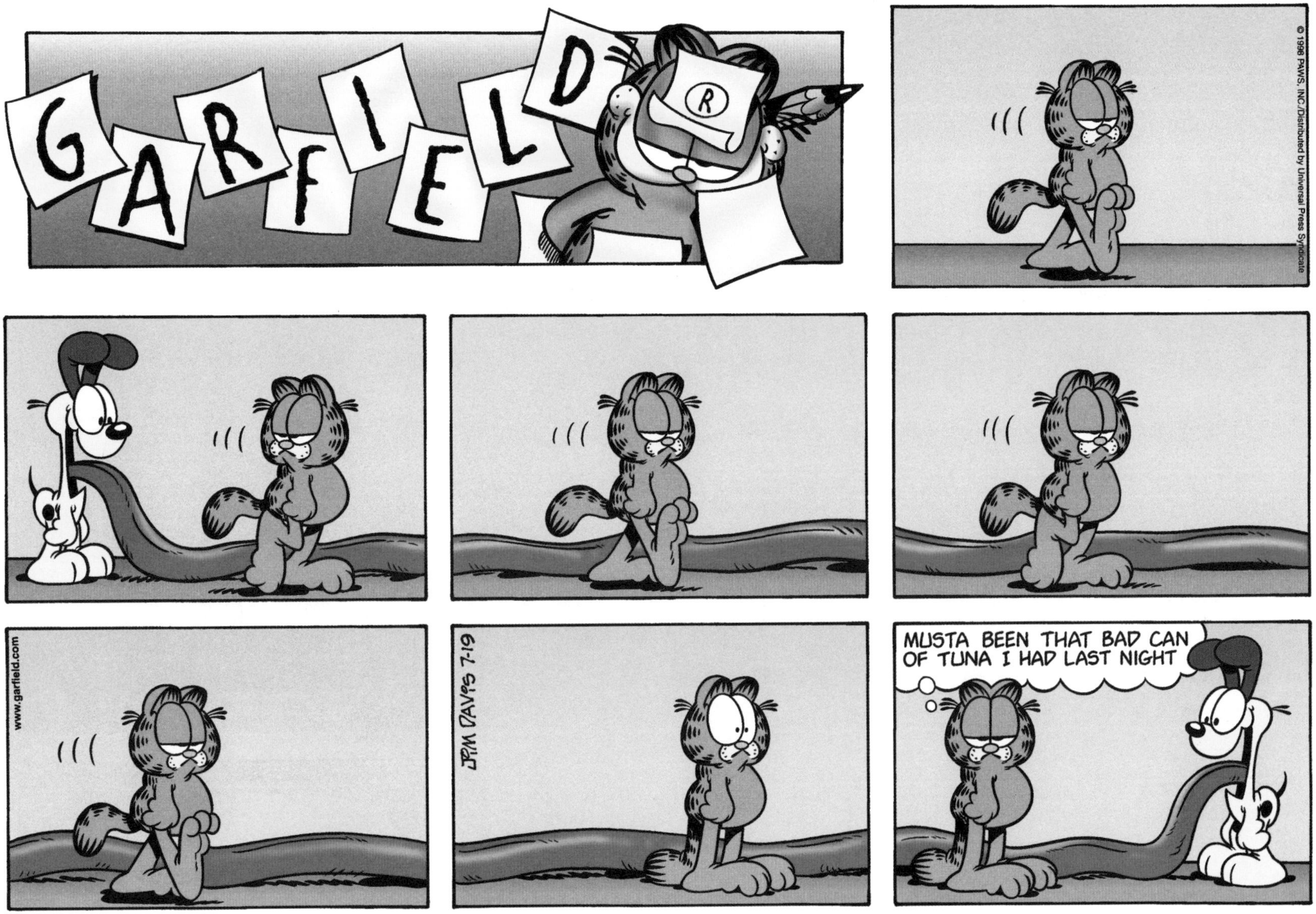
GARFIELD
© 1998 PAWS, INC./Distributed by Universal Press Syndicate
www.garfield.com
JIM DAVIS 7-19
MUSTA BEEN THAT BAD CAN OF TUNA I HAD LAST NIGHT

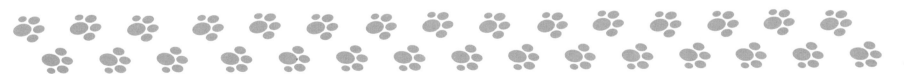

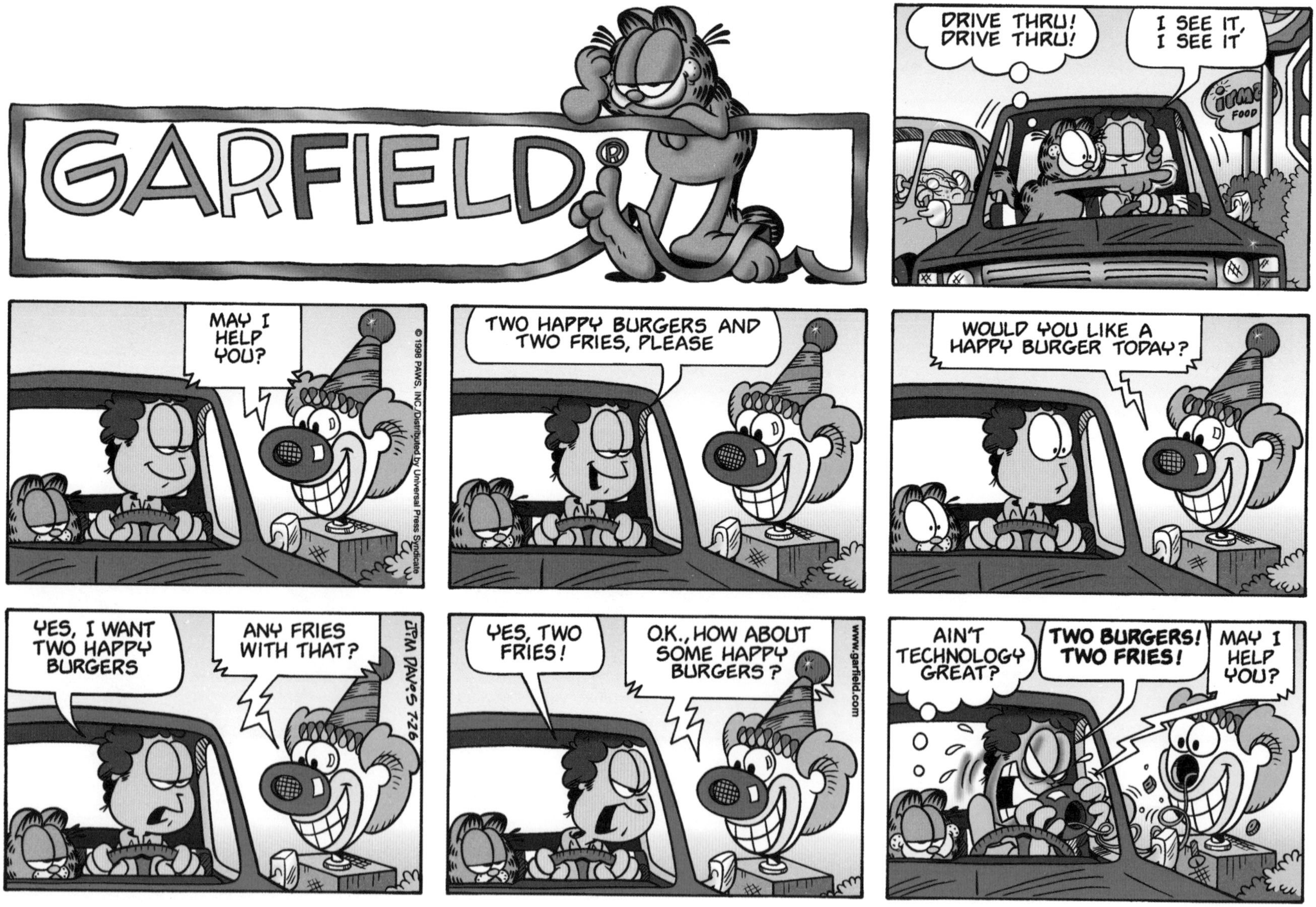
GARFIELD®
DRIVE THRU! DRIVE THRU!
I SEE IT, I SEE IT
IRMA'S FOOD
MAY I HELP YOU?
© 1998 PAWS, INC./Distributed by Universal Press Syndicate
TWO HAPPY BURGERS AND TWO FRIES, PLEASE
WOULD YOU LIKE A HAPPY BURGER TODAY?
YES, I WANT TWO HAPPY BURGERS
ANY FRIES WITH THAT?
JPM DAVIS 7-26
YES, TWO FRIES!
O.K., HOW ABOUT SOME HAPPY BURGERS?
www.garfield.com
AIN'T TECHNOLOGY GREAT?
TWO BURGERS! TWO FRIES!
MAY I HELP YOU?

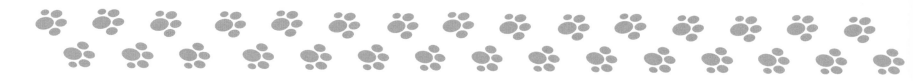

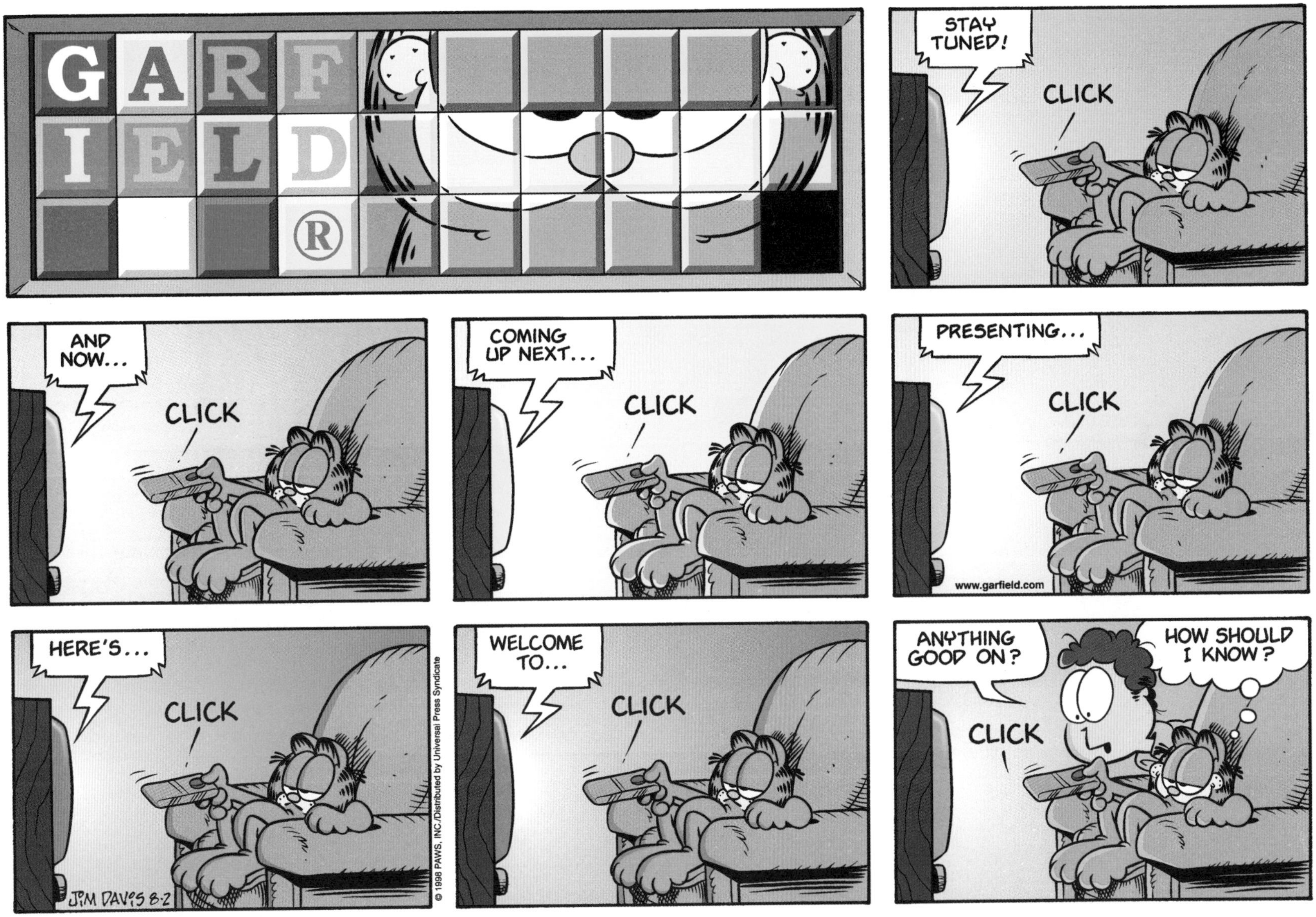
GARFIELD®
STAY TUNED!
CLICK
AND NOW...
CLICK
COMING UP NEXT...
CLICK
PRESENTING...
CLICK
www.garfield.com
HERE'S...
CLICK
JIM DAVIS 8-2
© 1998 PAWS, INC./Distributed by Universal Press Syndicate
WELCOME TO...
CLICK
ANYTHING GOOD ON?
HOW SHOULD I KNOW?
CLICK

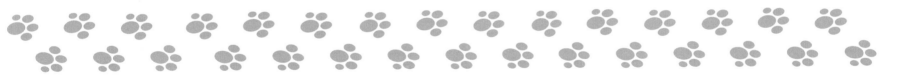

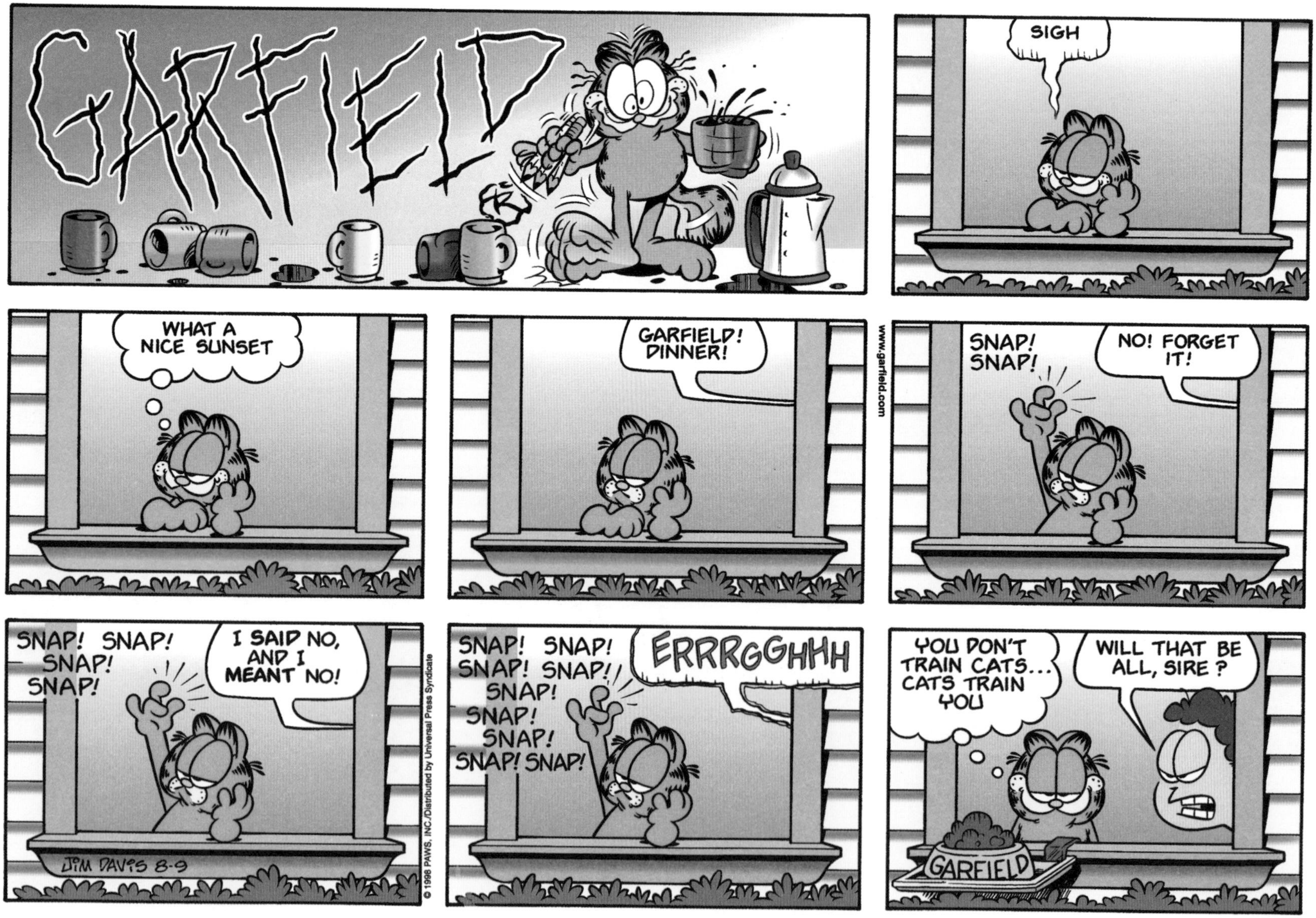
GARFIELD
SIGH
WHAT A NICE SUNSET
GARFIELD! DINNER!
SNAP! SNAP!
NO! FORGET IT!
SNAP! SNAP! SNAP! SNAP!
I SAID NO, AND I MEANT NO!
JIM DAVIS 8-9
SNAP! SNAP! SNAP! SNAP! SNAP! SNAP! SNAP! SNAP! SNAP!
ERRRGGHHH
YOU DON'T TRAIN CATS... CATS TRAIN YOU
WILL THAT BE ALL, SIRE ?
GARFIELD
www.garfield.com
© 1998 PAWS, INC./Distributed by Universal Press Syndicate

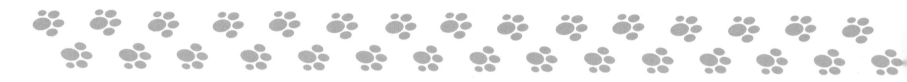

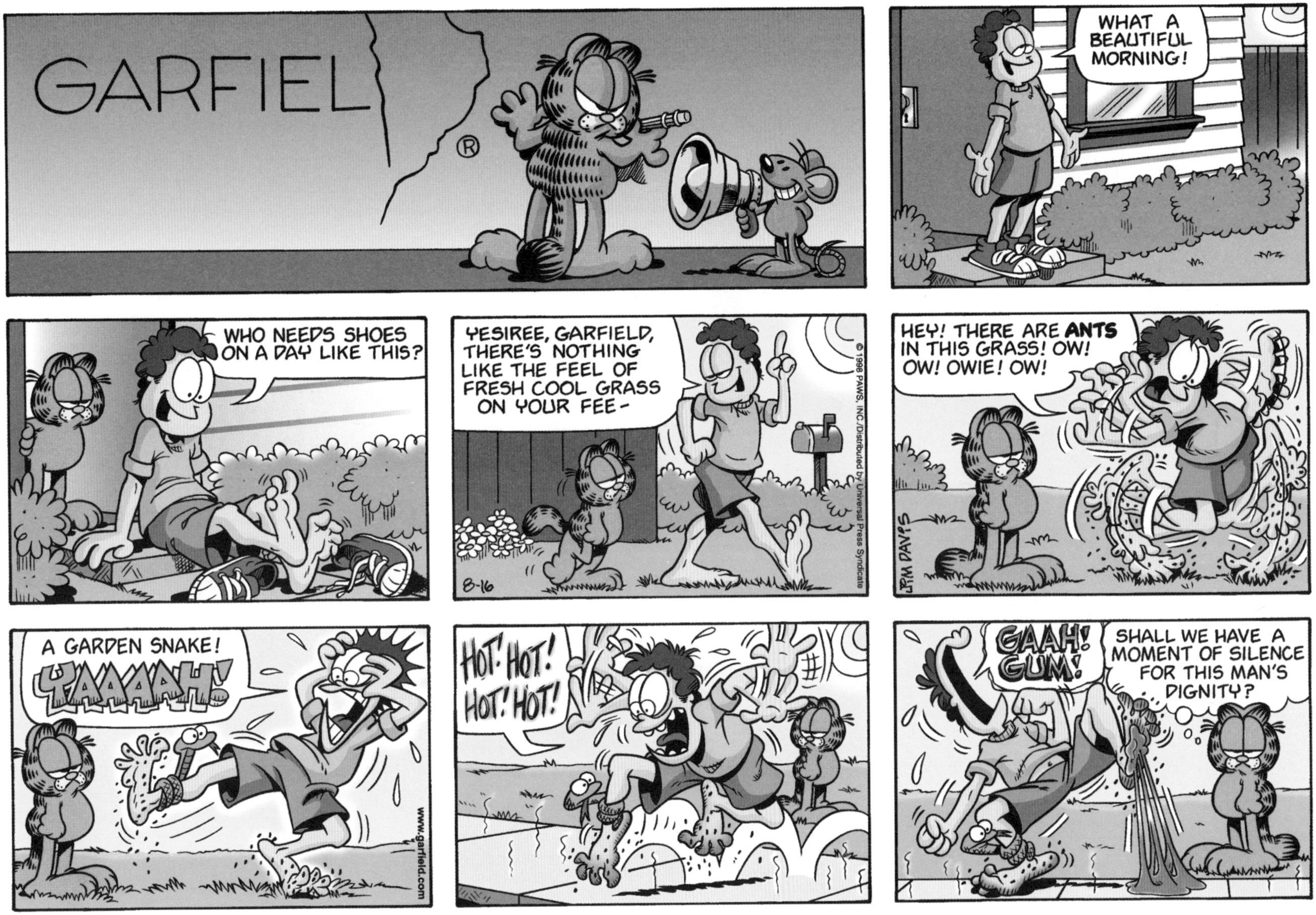
GARFIEL
®
WHAT A BEAUTIFUL MORNING!
WHO NEEDS SHOES ON A DAY LIKE THIS?
YESIREE, GARFIELD, THERE'S NOTHING LIKE THE FEEL OF FRESH COOL GRASS ON YOUR FEE-
© 1998 PAWS, INC./Distributed by Universal Press Syndicate
8-16
HEY! THERE ARE **ANTS** IN THIS GRASS! OW! OW! OWIE! OW!
JPM DAVIS
A GARDEN SNAKE!
YAAAAH!
www.garfield.com
HOT! HOT! HOT! HOT!
GAAH! GUM!
SHALL WE HAVE A MOMENT OF SILENCE FOR THIS MAN'S DIGNITY?

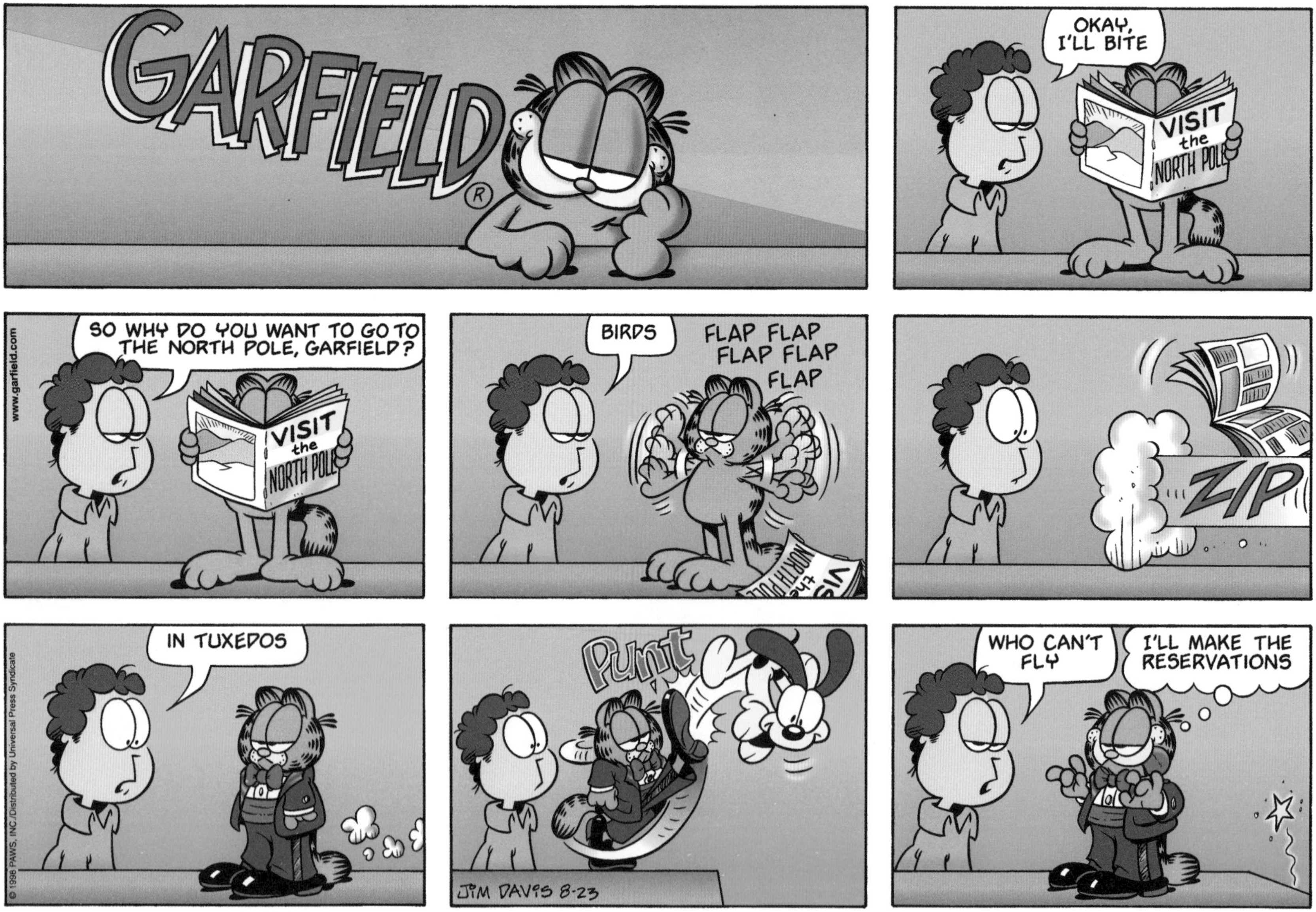
GARFIELD
OKAY, I'LL BITE
VISIT the NORTH POLE
SO WHY DO YOU WANT TO GO TO THE NORTH POLE, GARFIELD?
BIRDS
FLAP FLAP FLAP FLAP FLAP
ZIP
IN TUXEDOS
PUNT
WHO CAN'T FLY
I'LL MAKE THE RESERVATIONS
JIM DAVIS 8-23
www.garfield.com
© 1998 PAWS, INC./Distributed by Universal Press Syndicate

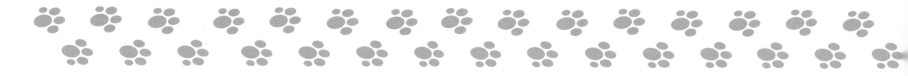

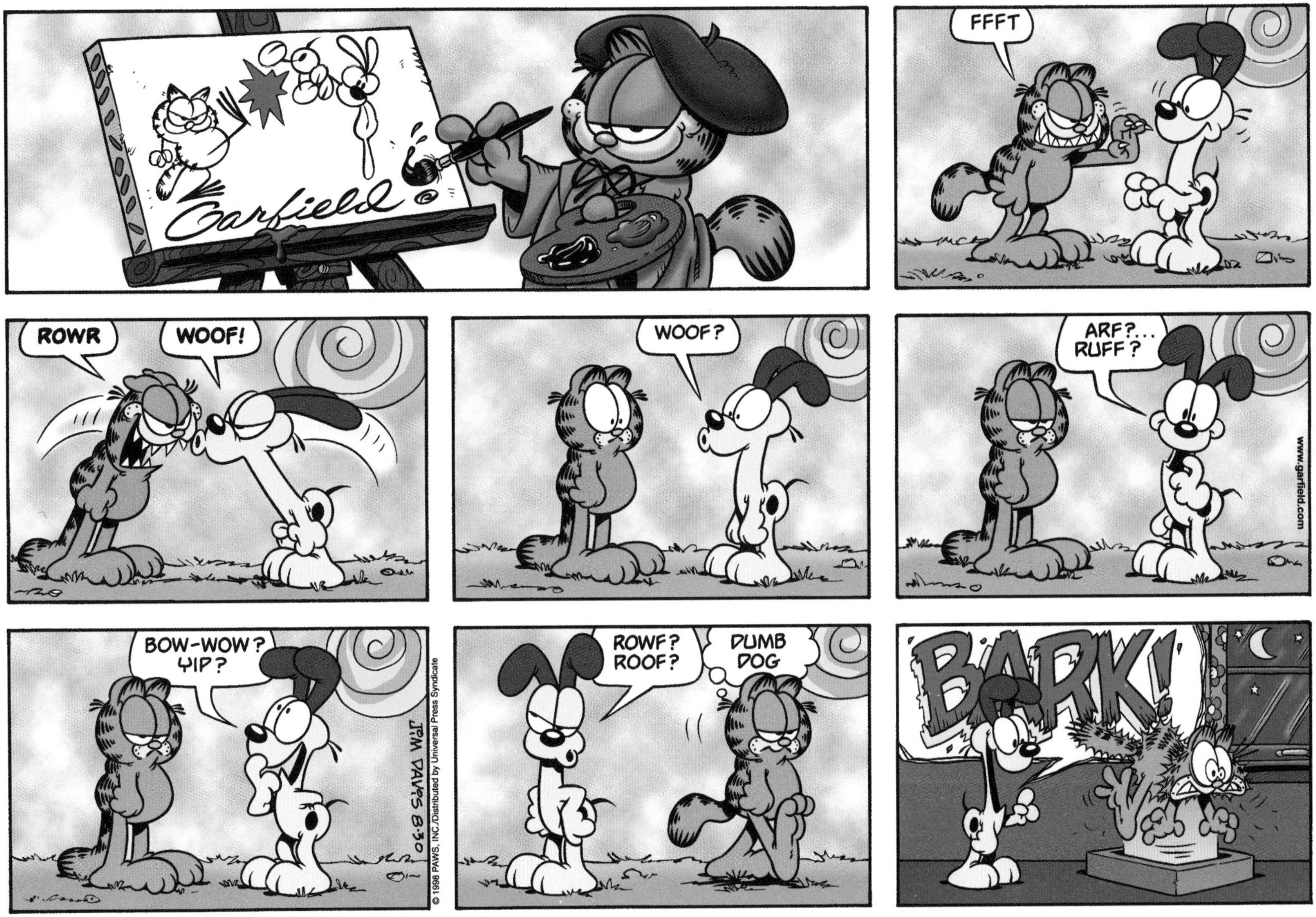
Garfield ©
FFFT
ROWR
WOOF!
WOOF?
ARF?...
RUFF?
www.garfield.com
BOW-WOW?
YIP?
JIM DAVIS 8-30
© 1998 PAWS, INC./Distributed by Universal Press Syndicate
ROWF?
ROOF?
DUMB
DOG
BARK!

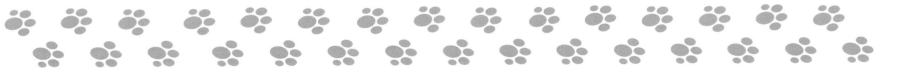

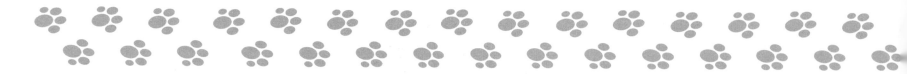

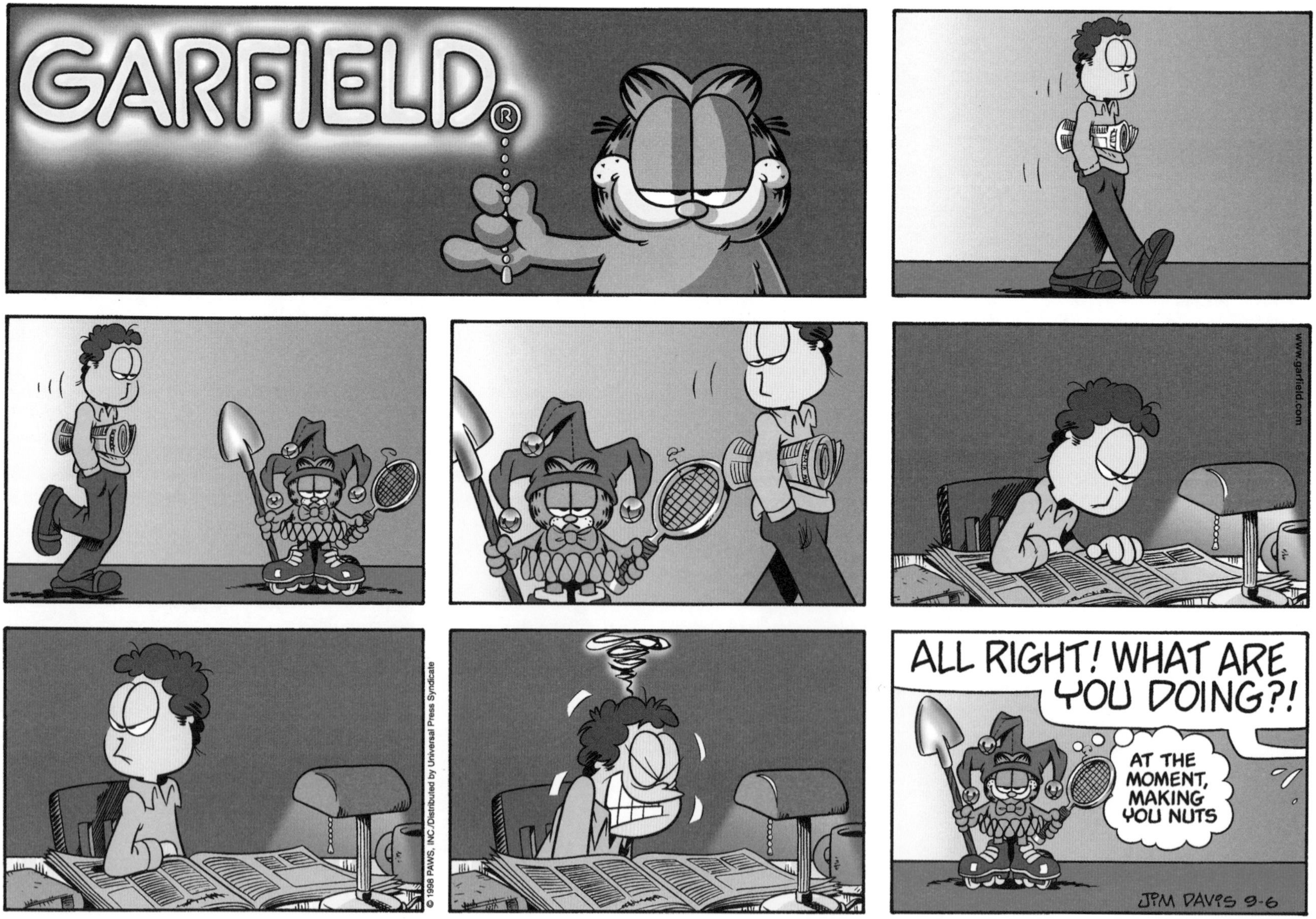
GARFIELD®
ALL RIGHT! WHAT ARE YOU DOING?!
AT THE MOMENT, MAKING YOU NUTS
JIM DAVIS 9-6
www.garfield.com

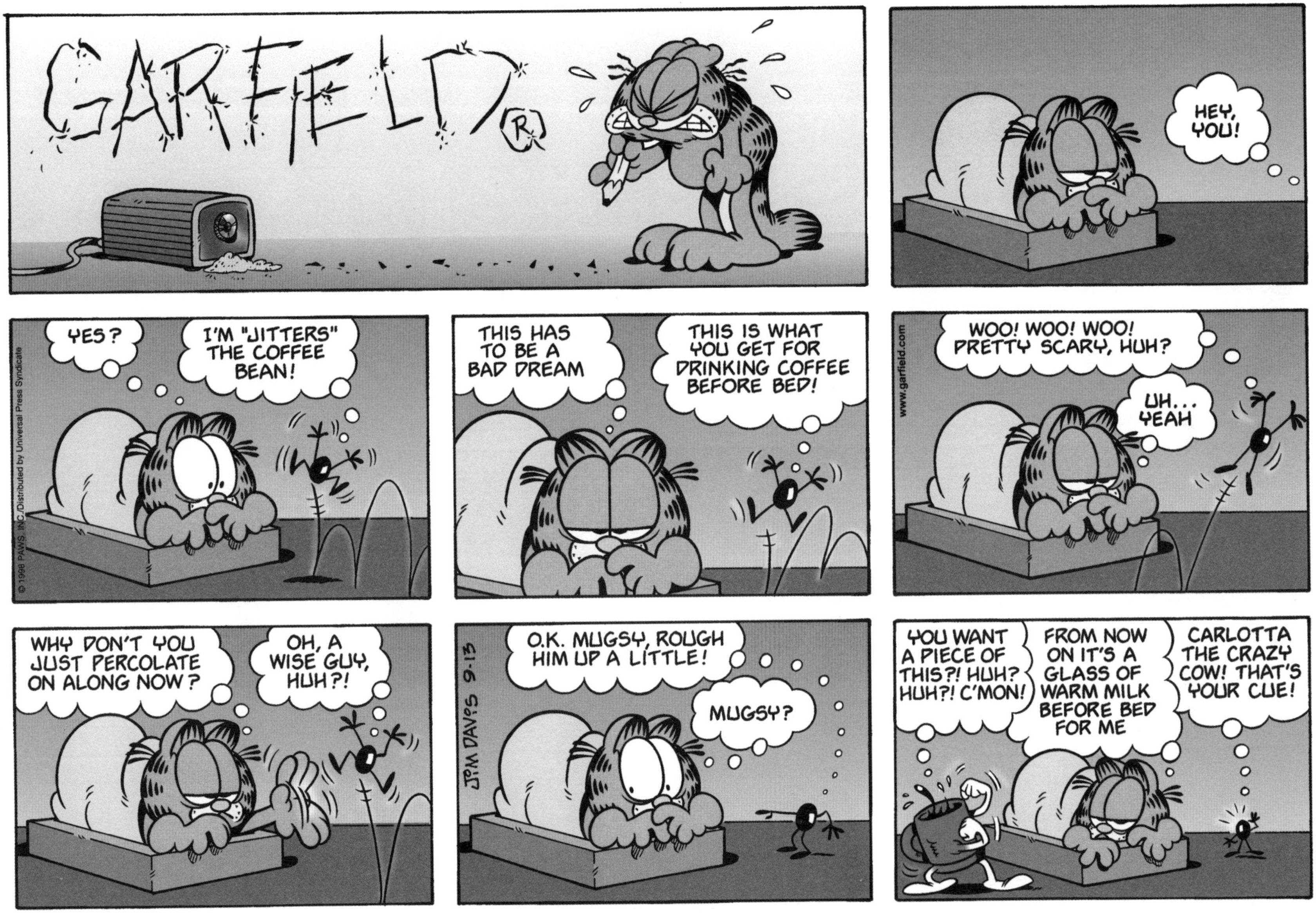
GARFIELD®
HEY, YOU!
YES?
I'M "JITTERS" THE COFFEE BEAN!
© 1998 PAWS, INC./Distributed by Universal Press Syndicate
THIS HAS TO BE A BAD DREAM
THIS IS WHAT YOU GET FOR DRINKING COFFEE BEFORE BED!
www.garfield.com
WOO! WOO! WOO! PRETTY SCARY, HUH?
UH... YEAH
WHY DON'T YOU JUST PERCOLATE ON ALONG NOW?
OH, A WISE GUY, HUH?!
JIM DAVIS 9-13
O.K. MUGSY, ROUGH HIM UP A LITTLE!
MUGSY?
YOU WANT A PIECE OF THIS?! HUH? HUH?! C'MON!
FROM NOW ON IT'S A GLASS OF WARM MILK BEFORE BED FOR ME
CARLOTTA THE CRAZY COW! THAT'S YOUR CUE!

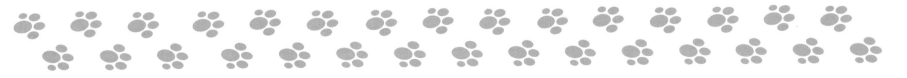

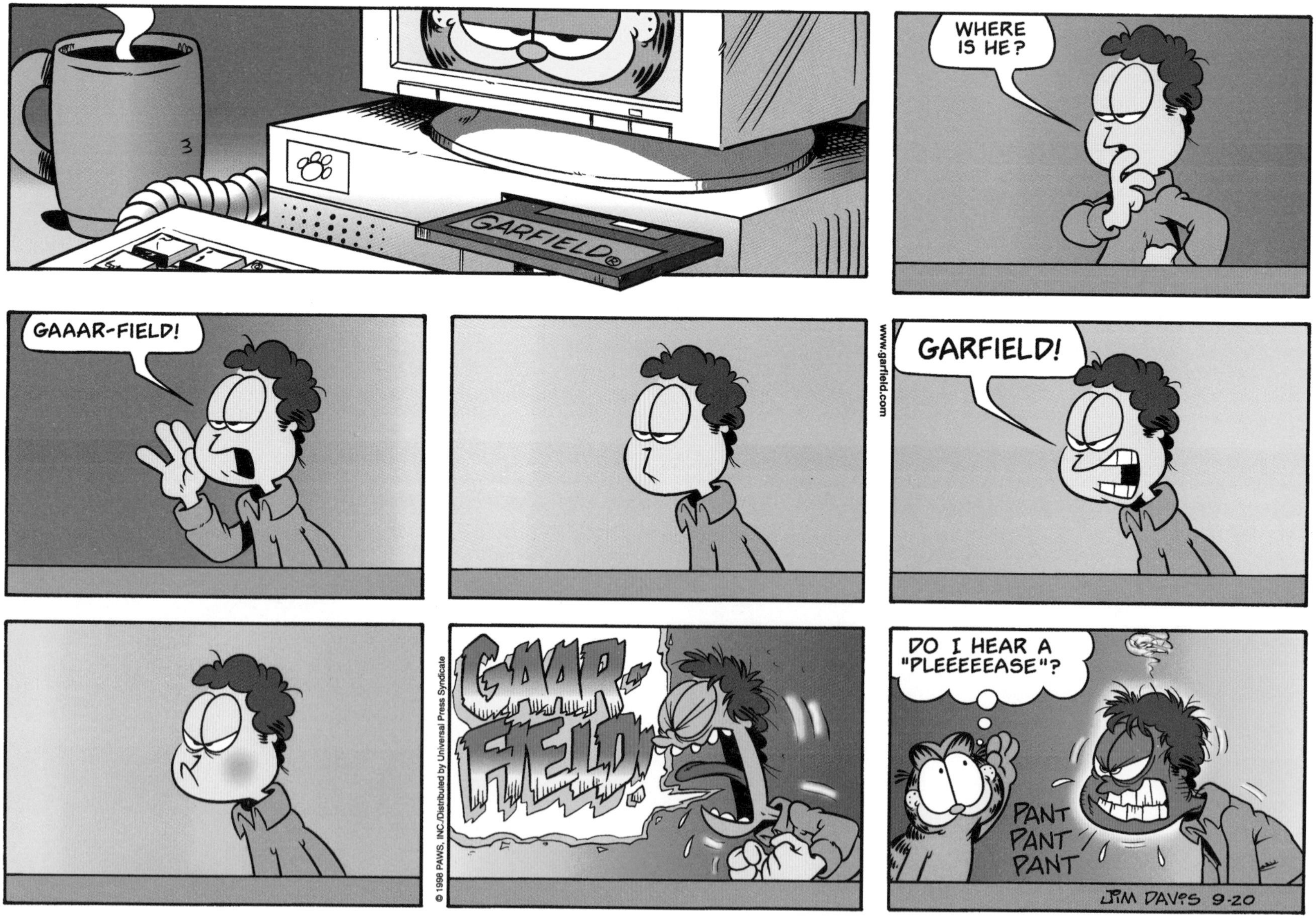
GARFIELD®
WHERE IS HE?
GAAAR-FIELD!
www.garfield.com
GARFIELD!
© 1998 PAWS, INC./Distributed by Universal Press Syndicate
GAAR-FIELD!
DO I HEAR A "PLEEEEEASE"?
PANT PANT PANT
JIM DAVIS 9-20

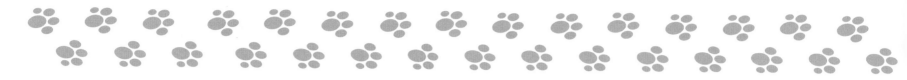

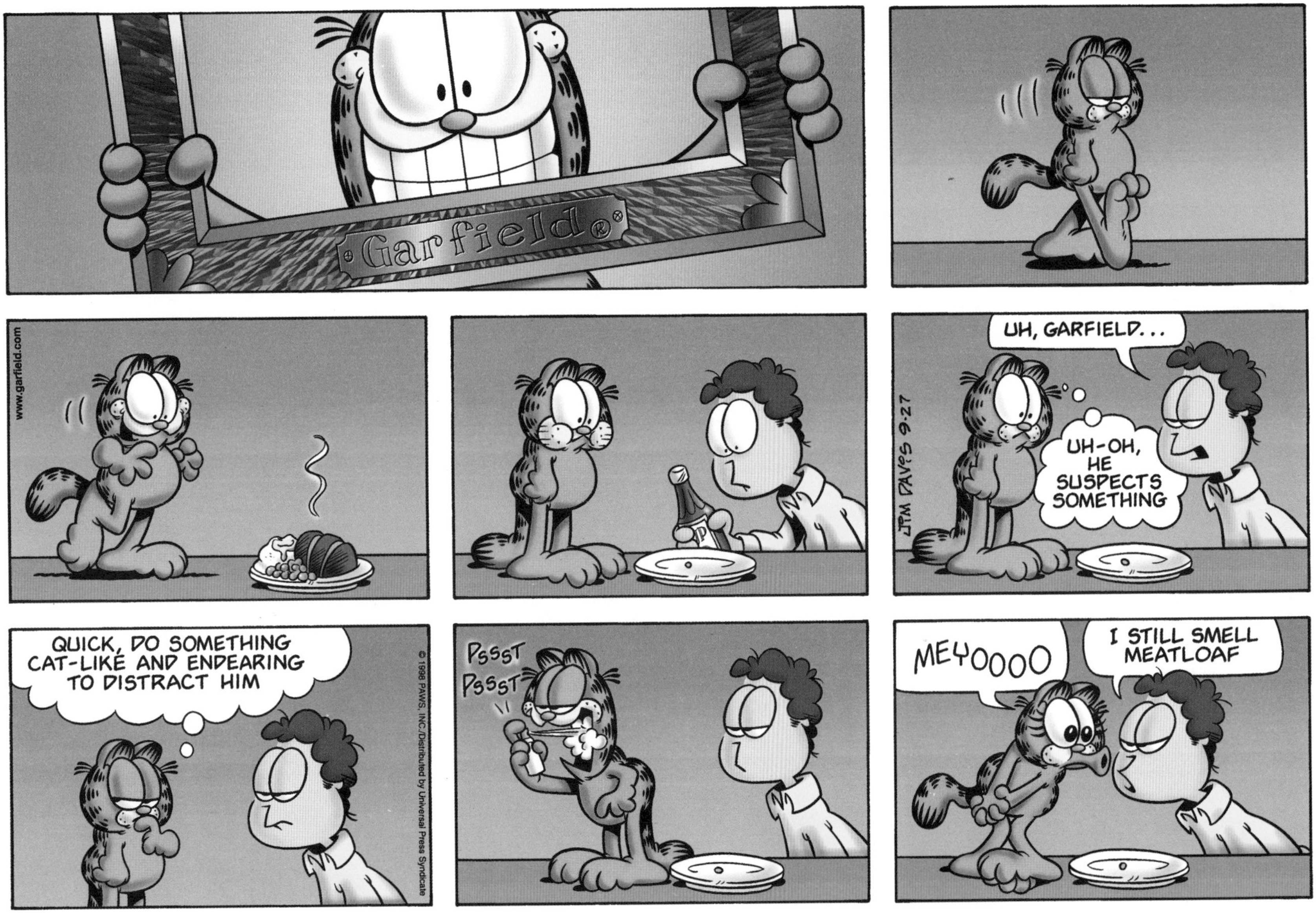
Garfield®
www.garfield.com
UH, GARFIELD...
UH-OH, HE SUSPECTS SOMETHING
JPM DAVIS 9-27
QUICK, DO SOMETHING CAT-LIKE AND ENDEARING TO DISTRACT HIM
© 1998 PAWS, INC./Distributed by Universal Press Syndicate
PSSST PSSST
MEYOOOO
I STILL SMELL MEATLOAF

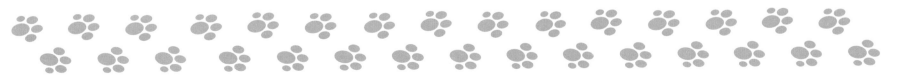

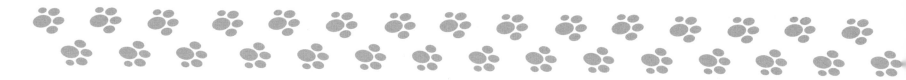

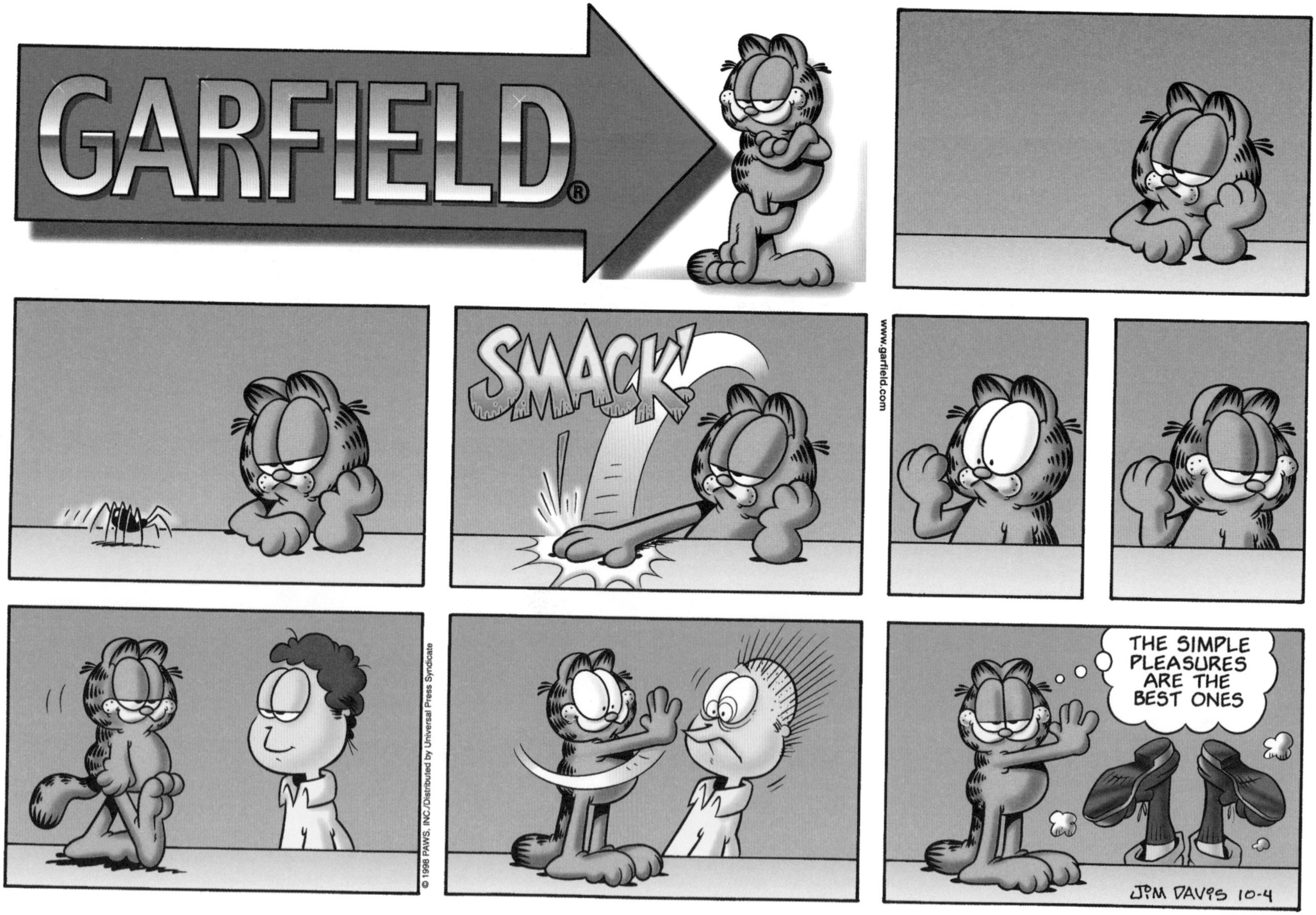
GARFIELD®
SMACK!
THE SIMPLE PLEASURES ARE THE BEST ONES
JIM DAVIS 10-4
www.garfield.com
© 1998 PAWS, INC./Distributed by Universal Press Syndicate

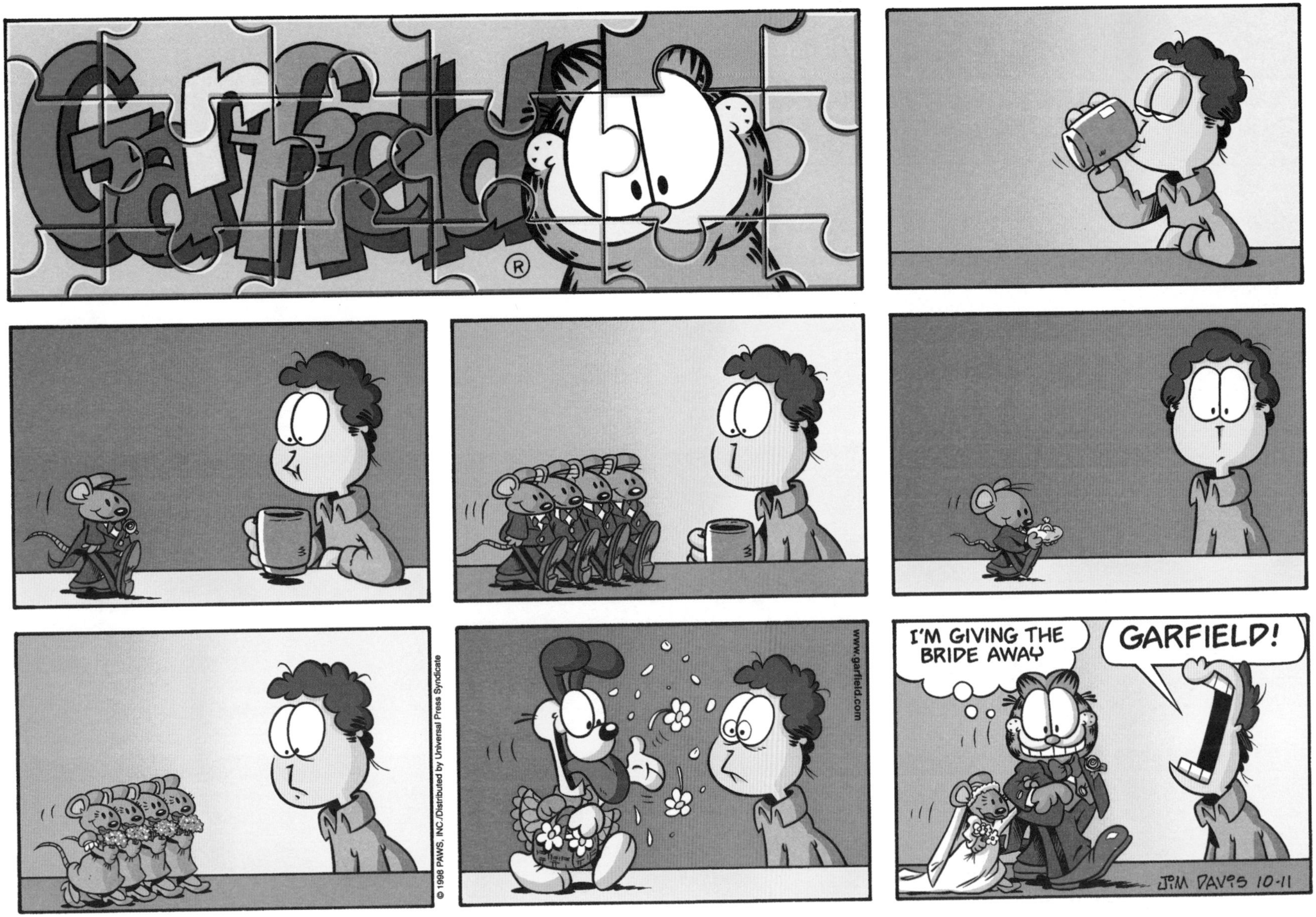
Garfield®
© 1998 PAWS, INC./Distributed by Universal Press Syndicate
www.garfield.com
I'M GIVING THE BRIDE AWAY
GARFIELD!
JIM DAVIS 10-11

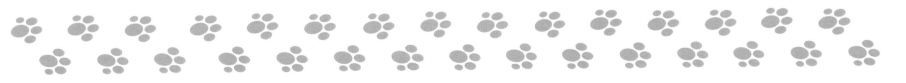

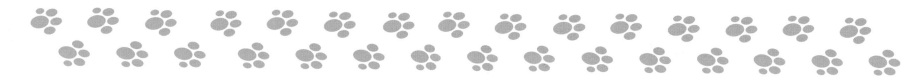

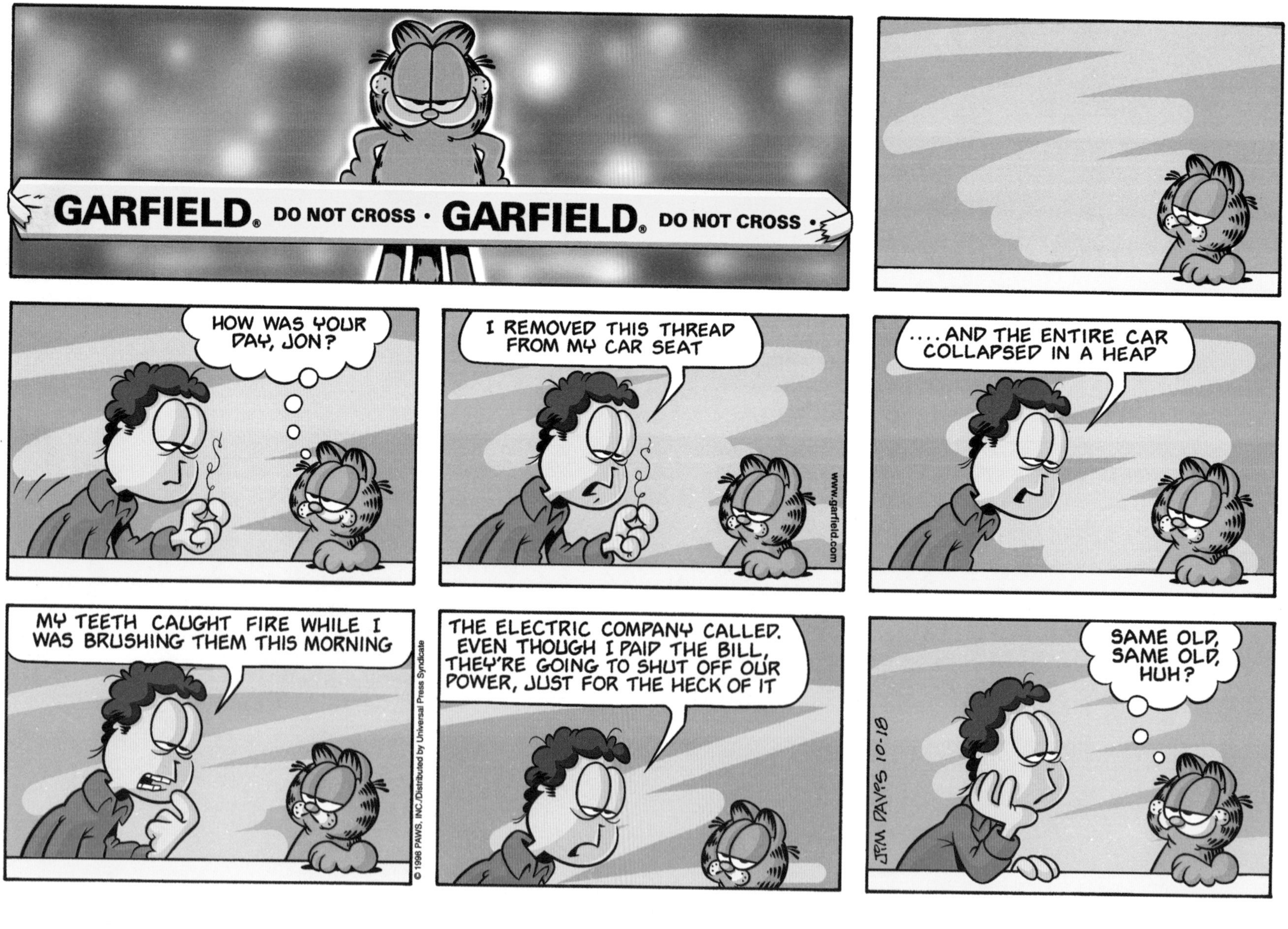
GARFIELD® DO NOT CROSS · GARFIELD® DO NOT CROSS ·
HOW WAS YOUR DAY, JON?
I REMOVED THIS THREAD FROM MY CAR SEAT
www.garfield.com
....AND THE ENTIRE CAR COLLAPSED IN A HEAP
MY TEETH CAUGHT FIRE WHILE I WAS BRUSHING THEM THIS MORNING
© 1998 PAWS, INC./Distributed by Universal Press Syndicate
THE ELECTRIC COMPANY CALLED. EVEN THOUGH I PAID THE BILL, THEY'RE GOING TO SHUT OFF OUR POWER, JUST FOR THE HECK OF IT
JIM DAVIS 10-18
SAME OLD, SAME OLD, HUH?

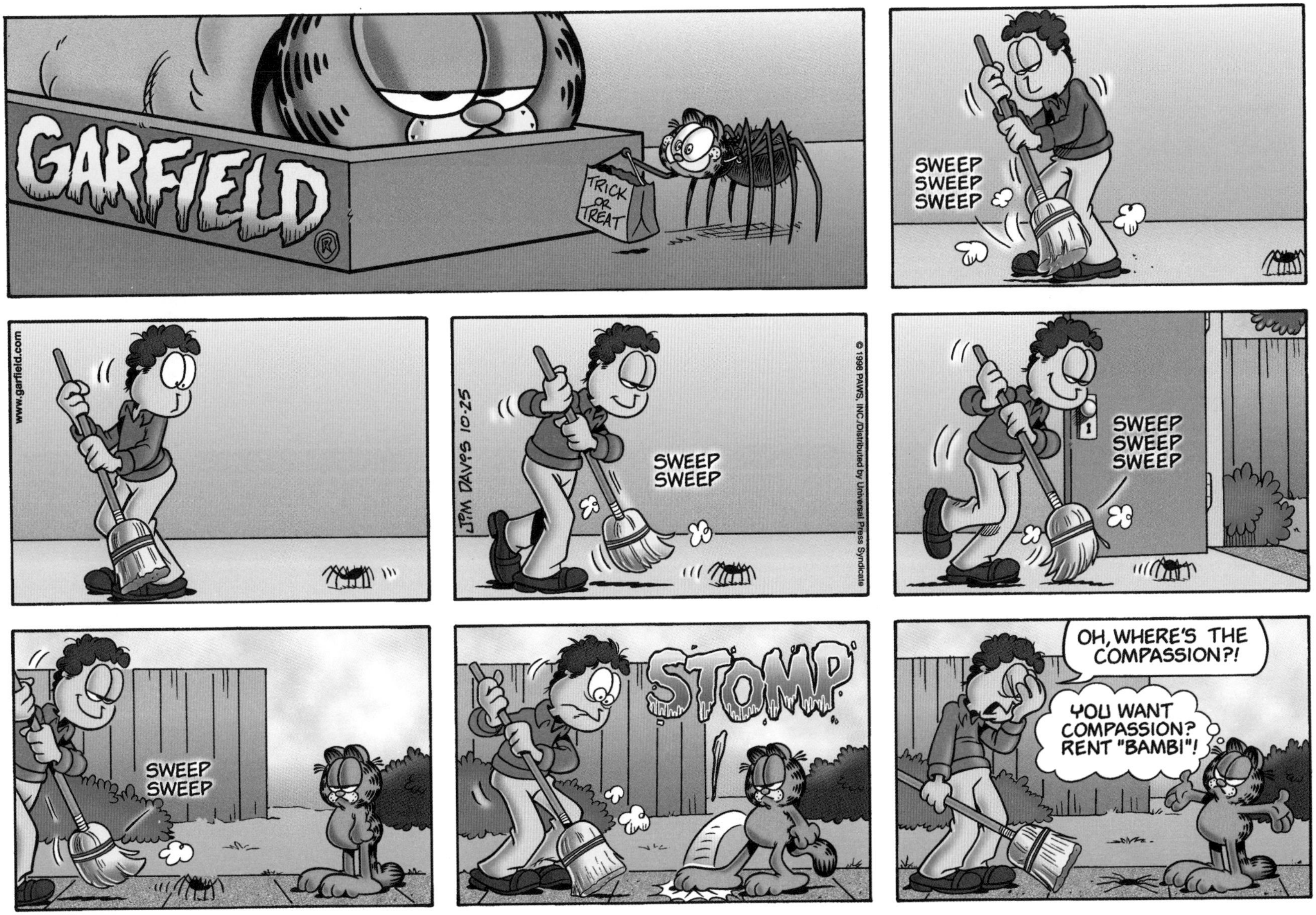
GARFIELD
TRICK OR TREAT
SWEEP SWEEP SWEEP
www.garfield.com
JPM DAVPS 10-25
SWEEP SWEEP
© 1998 PAWS, INC./Distributed by Universal Press Syndicate
SWEEP SWEEP SWEEP
SWEEP SWEEP
STOMP
OH, WHERE'S THE COMPASSION?!
YOU WANT COMPASSION? RENT "BAMBI"!

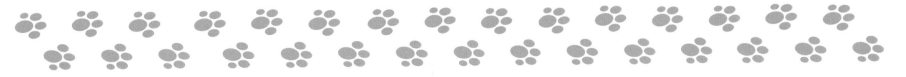

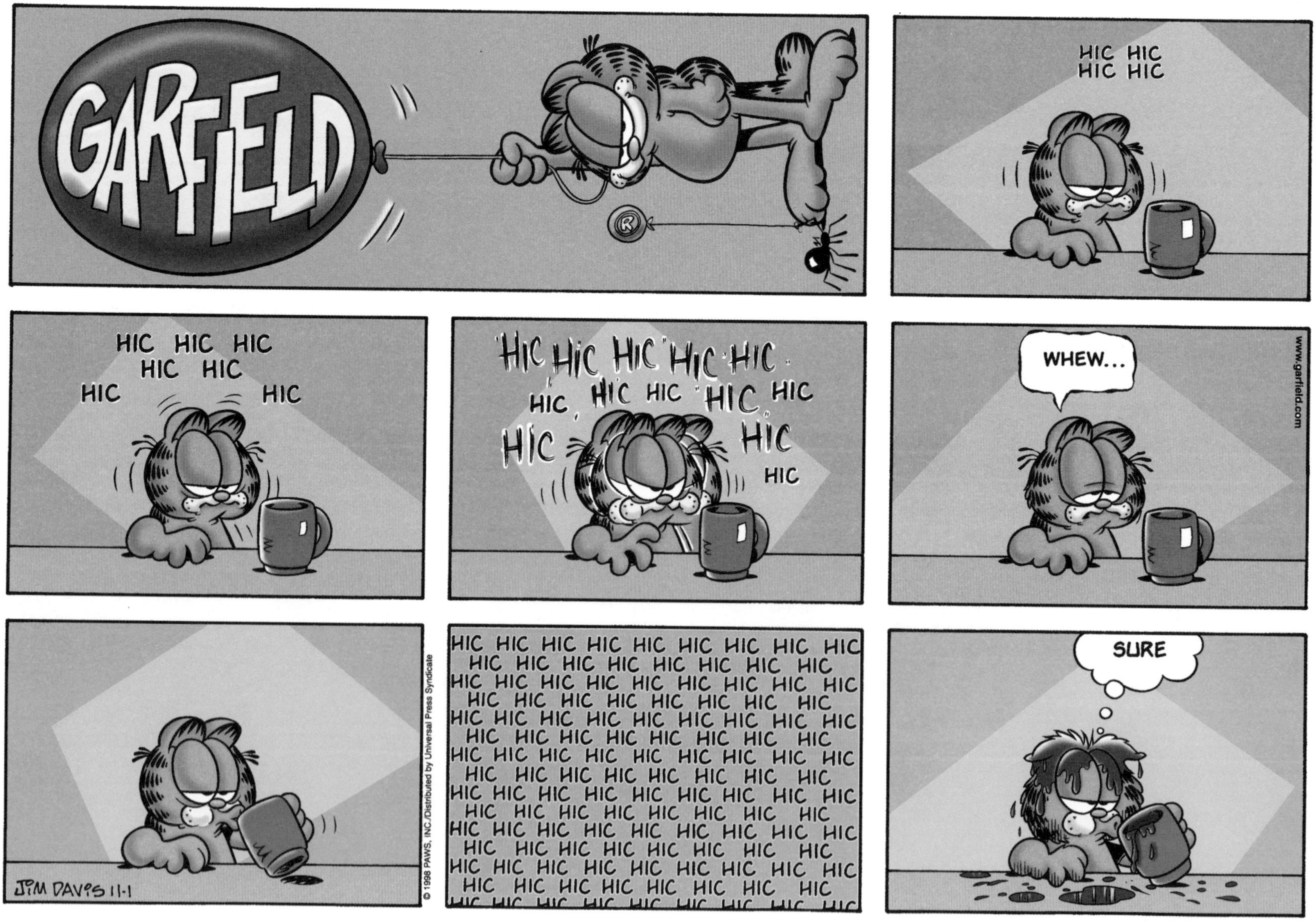
GARFIELD
HIC HIC
HIC HIC
HIC HIC HIC
HIC HIC
HIC HIC
HIC HIC HIC HIC HIC
HIC HIC HIC HIC HIC
HIC HIC
HIC
WHEW...
www.garfield.com
JIM DAVIS 11-1
© 1998 PAWS, INC./Distributed by Universal Press Syndicate
HIC HIC HIC HIC HIC HIC HIC HIC HIC
HIC HIC HIC HIC HIC HIC HIC HIC
HIC HIC HIC HIC HIC HIC HIC HIC HIC
HIC HIC HIC HIC HIC HIC HIC HIC
HIC HIC HIC HIC HIC HIC HIC HIC HIC
HIC HIC HIC HIC HIC HIC HIC HIC
HIC HIC HIC HIC HIC HIC HIC HIC HIC
HIC HIC HIC HIC HIC HIC HIC HIC
HIC HIC HIC HIC HIC HIC HIC HIC HIC
HIC HIC HIC HIC HIC HIC HIC HIC
HIC HIC HIC HIC HIC HIC HIC HIC HIC
HIC HIC HIC HIC HIC HIC HIC HIC
HIC HIC HIC HIC HIC HIC HIC HIC HIC
HIC HIC HIC HIC HIC HIC HIC HIC
SURE

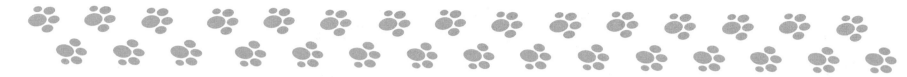

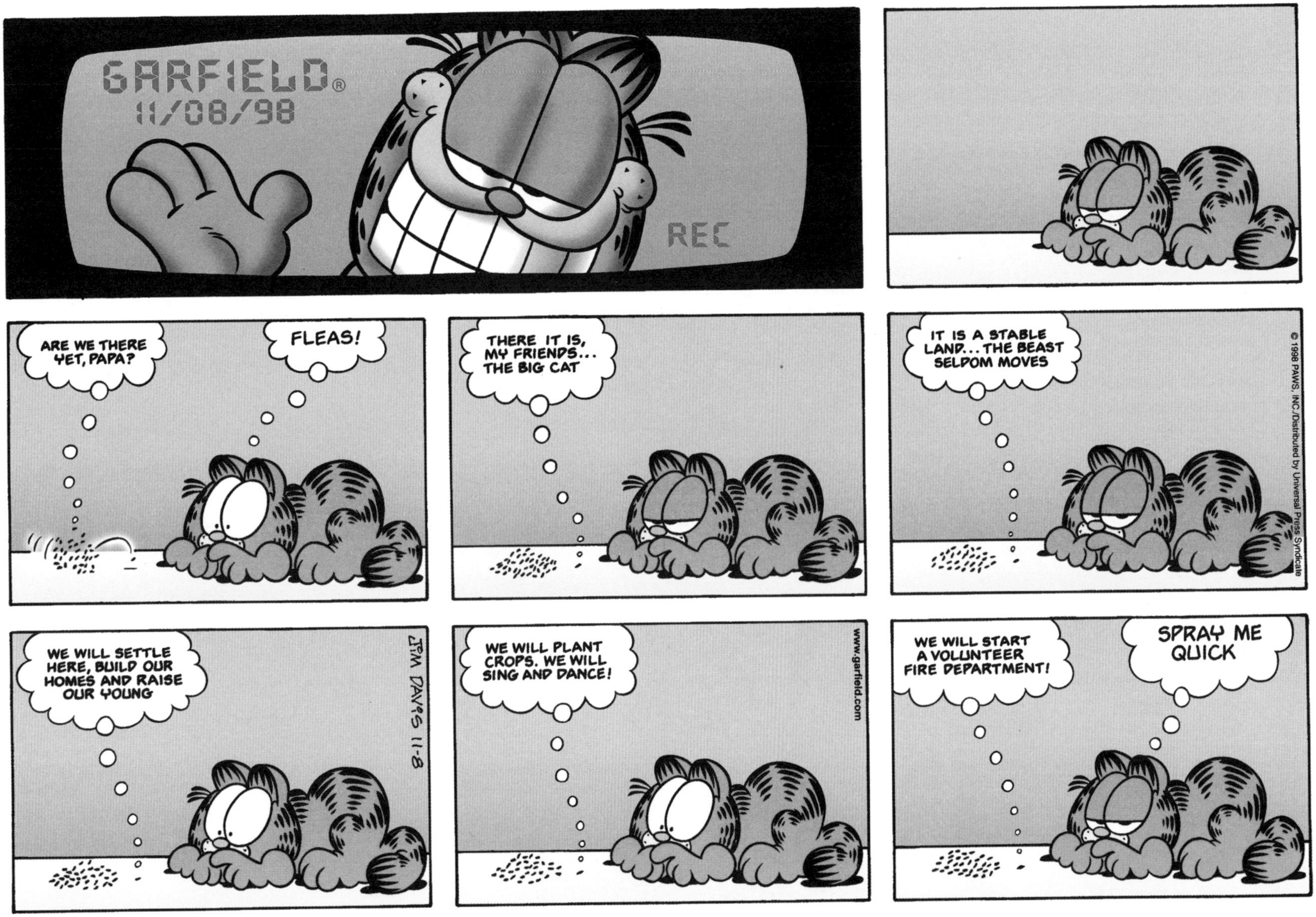
GARFIELD®
11/08/98
REC
ARE WE THERE YET, PAPA?
FLEAS!
THERE IT IS, MY FRIENDS... THE BIG CAT
IT IS A STABLE LAND... THE BEAST SELDOM MOVES
© 1998 PAWS, INC./Distributed by Universal Press Syndicate
WE WILL SETTLE HERE, BUILD OUR HOMES AND RAISE OUR YOUNG
JIM DAVIS 11-8
WE WILL PLANT CROPS. WE WILL SING AND DANCE!
www.garfield.com
WE WILL START A VOLUNTEER FIRE DEPARTMENT!
SPRAY ME QUICK

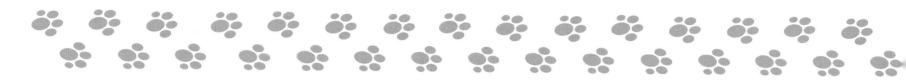

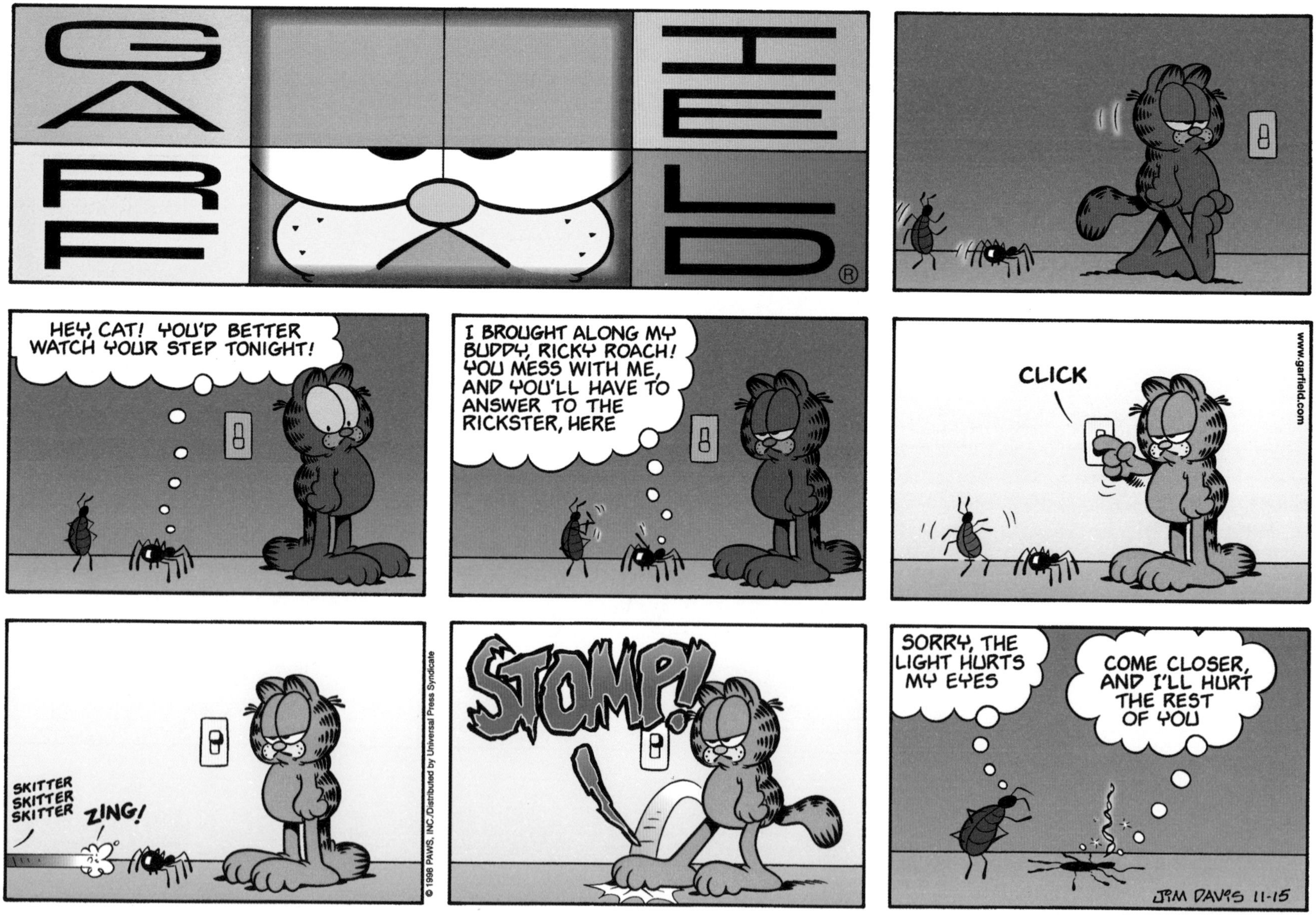
GARFIELD®
HEY, CAT! YOU'D BETTER WATCH YOUR STEP TONIGHT!
I BROUGHT ALONG MY BUDDY, RICKY ROACH! YOU MESS WITH ME, AND YOU'LL HAVE TO ANSWER TO THE RICKSTER, HERE
CLICK
www.garfield.com
SKITTER SKITTER SKITTER
ZING!
© 1998 PAWS, INC./Distributed by Universal Press Syndicate
STOMP!
SORRY, THE LIGHT HURTS MY EYES
COME CLOSER, AND I'LL HURT THE REST OF YOU
JIM DAVIS 11-15

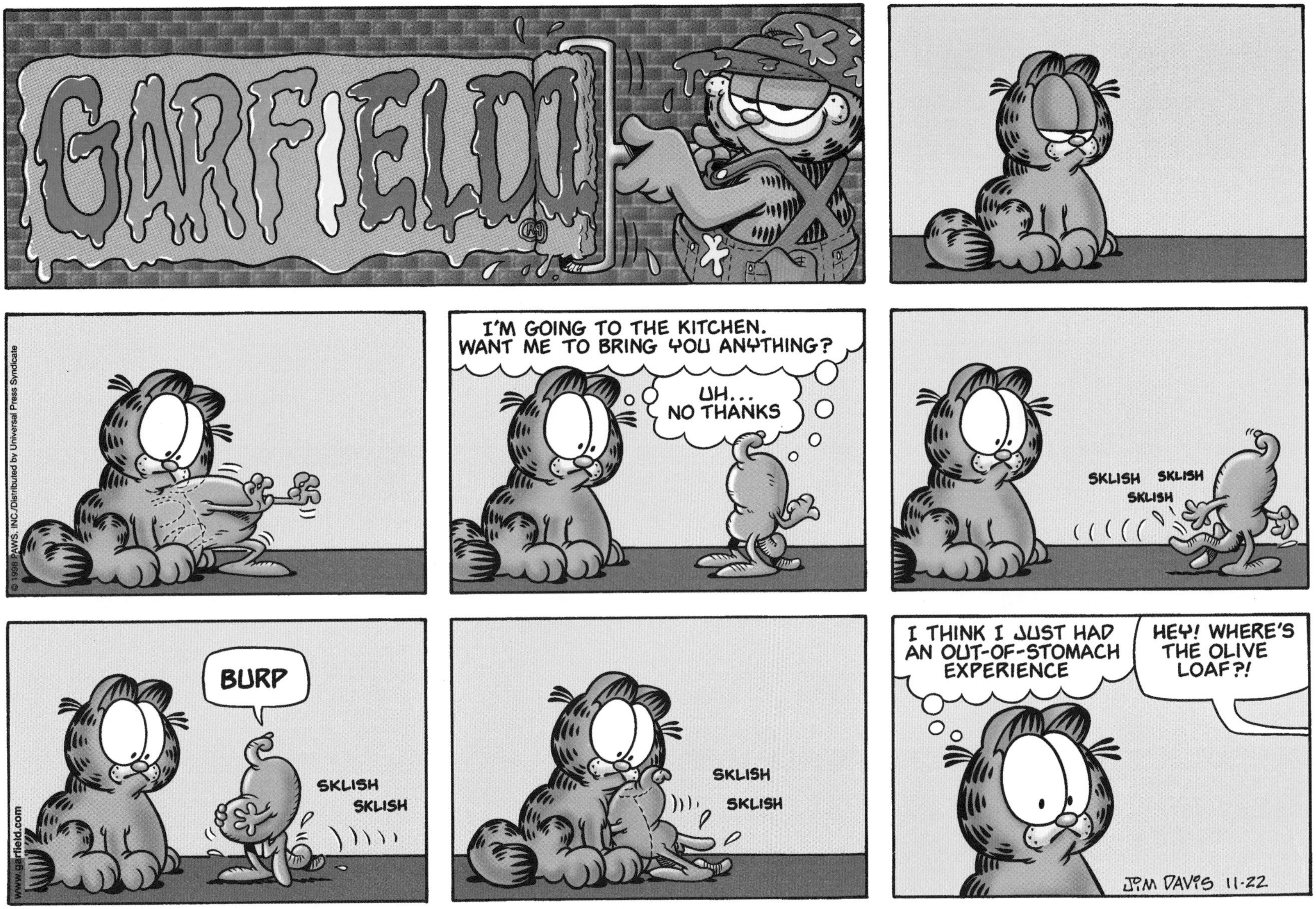
GARFIELD
© 1998 PAWS, INC./Distributed by Universal Press Syndicate
I'M GOING TO THE KITCHEN. WANT ME TO BRING YOU ANYTHING?
UH... NO THANKS
SKLISH SKLISH
SKLISH
www.garfield.com
BURP
SKLISH
SKLISH
SKLISH
SKLISH
I THINK I JUST HAD AN OUT-OF-STOMACH EXPERIENCE
HEY! WHERE'S THE OLIVE LOAF?!
JIM DAVIS 11-22

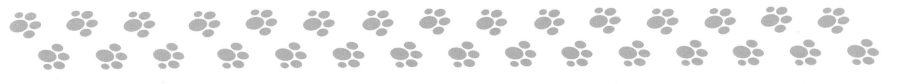

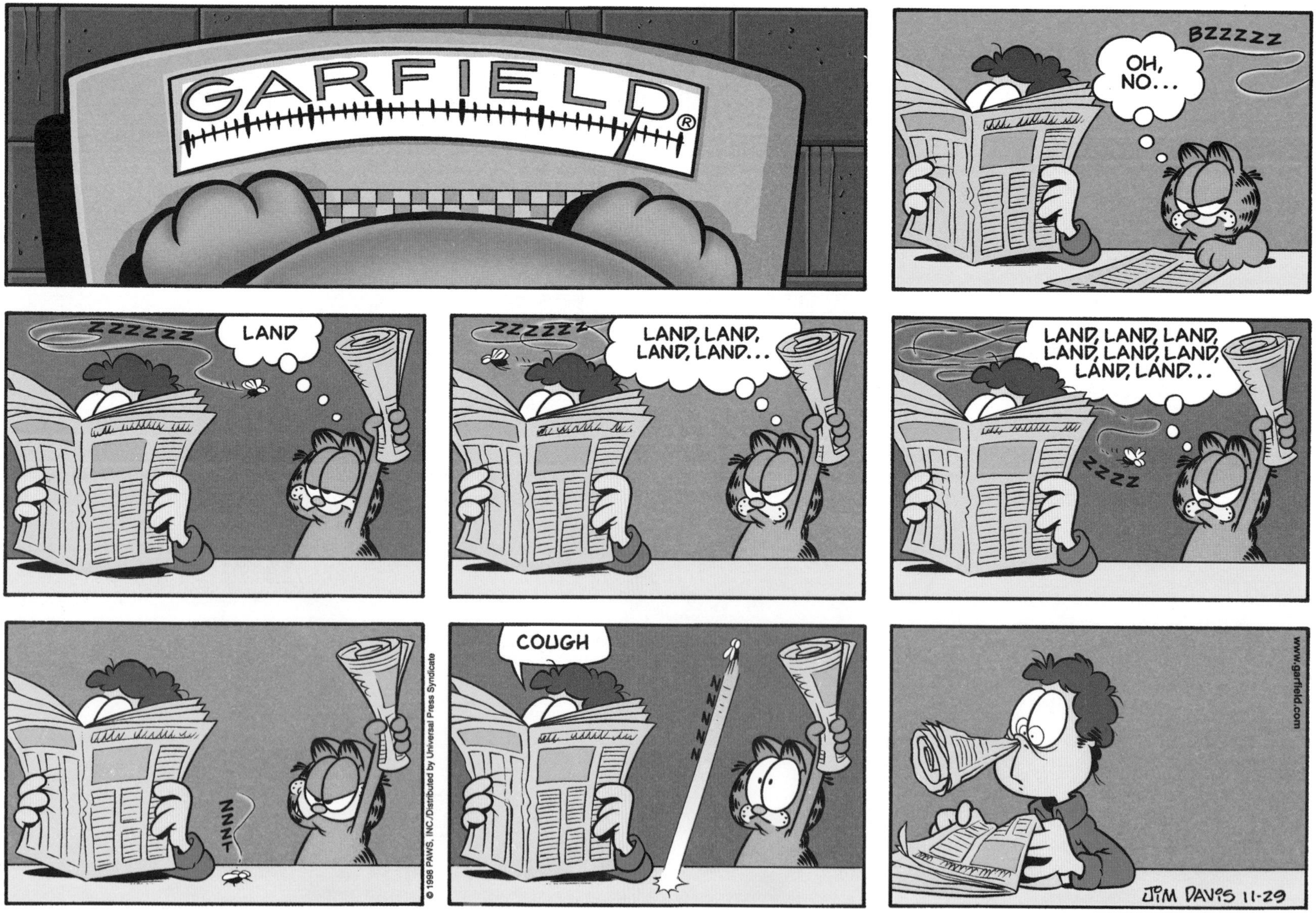
GARFIELD®
OH, NO...
BZZZZZ
ZZZZZZ
LAND
LAND, LAND, LAND, LAND...
LAND, LAND, LAND, LAND, LAND, LAND, LAND, LAND...
ZZZZ
COUGH
JIM DAVIS 11-29
© 1998 PAWS, INC./Distributed by Universal Press Syndicate
www.garfield.com

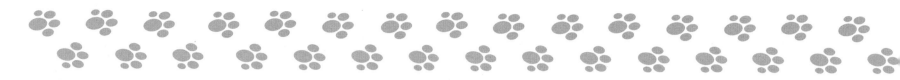

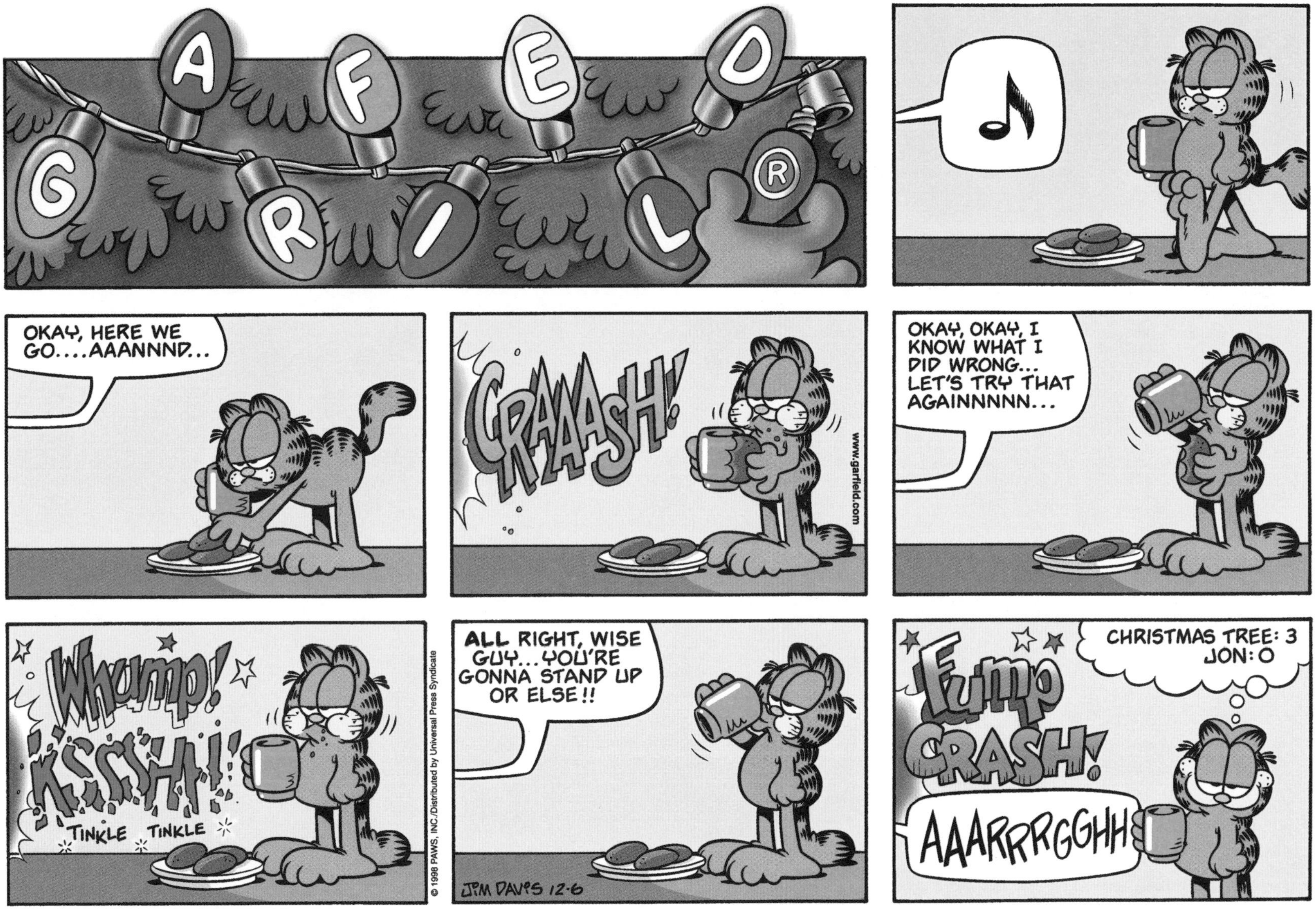
GARFIELD®
OKAY, HERE WE GO....AAANNND...
CRAAASH!
www.garfield.com
OKAY, OKAY, I KNOW WHAT I DID WRONG... LET'S TRY THAT AGAINNNNN...
Whump!
KSSSH!!
TINKLE TINKLE
© 1998 PAWS, INC./Distributed by Universal Press Syndicate
ALL RIGHT, WISE GUY...YOU'RE GONNA STAND UP OR ELSE!!
JIM DAVIS 12-6
Fump
CRASH!
AAARRRGGHH
CHRISTMAS TREE: 3
JON: 0

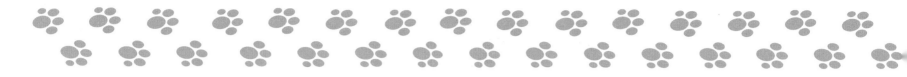

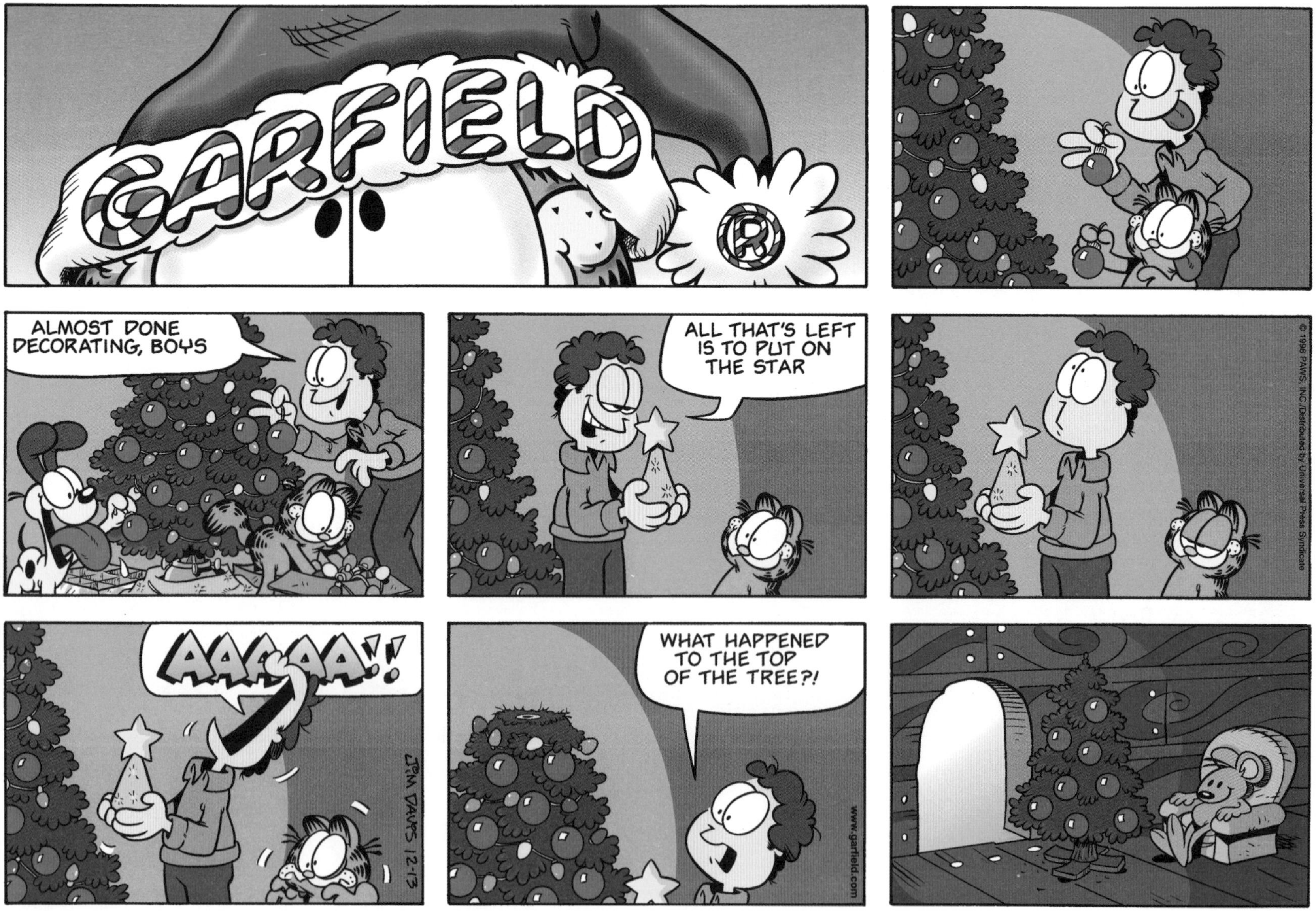
GARFIELD ®
ALMOST DONE DECORATING, BOYS
ALL THAT'S LEFT IS TO PUT ON THE STAR
© 1996 PAWS, INC./Distributed by Universal Press Syndicate
AAAAA!!
JIM DAVIS 12-13
WHAT HAPPENED TO THE TOP OF THE TREE?!
www.garfield.com

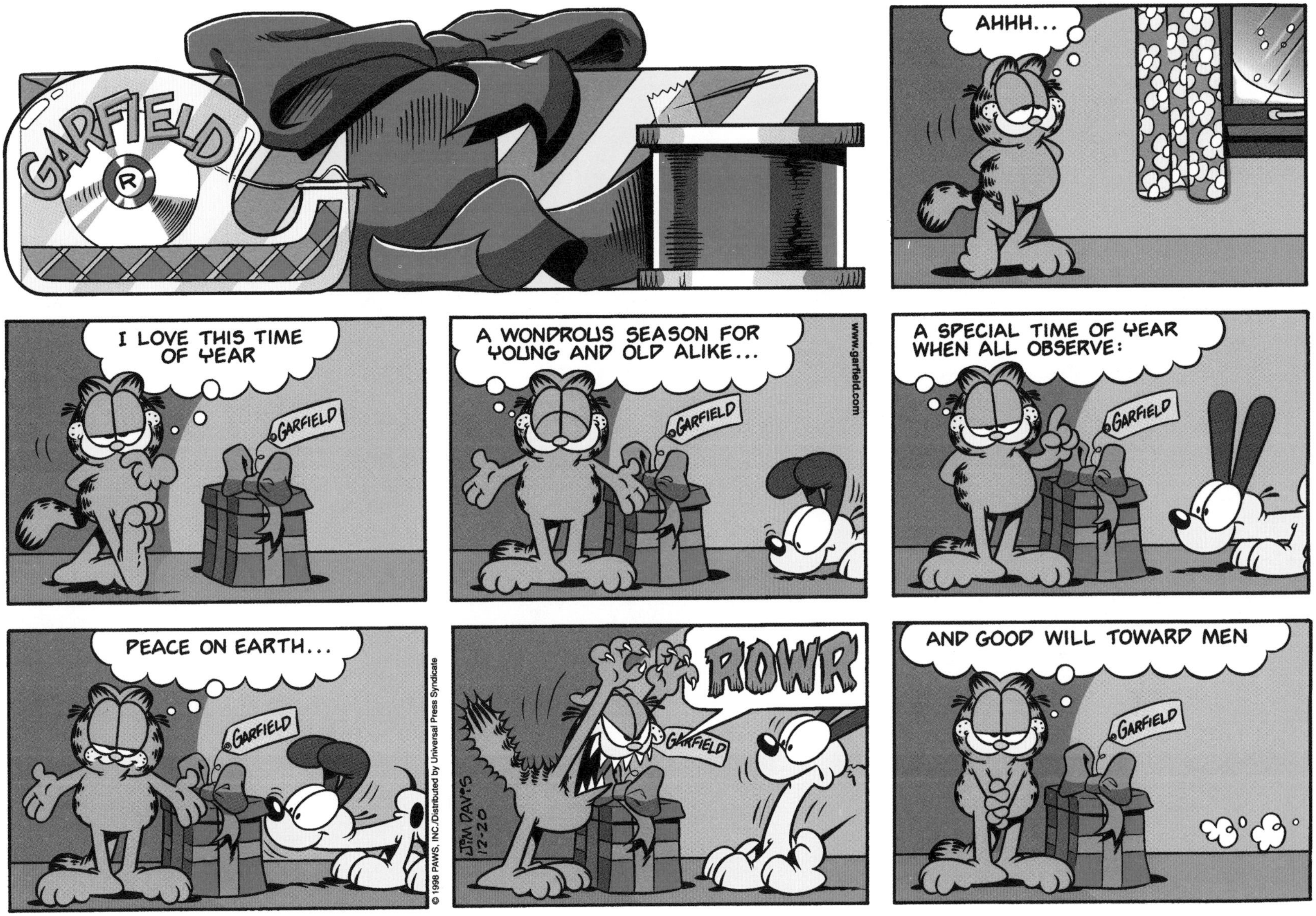
GARFIELD
AHHH...
I LOVE THIS TIME OF YEAR
GARFIELD
A WONDROUS SEASON FOR YOUNG AND OLD ALIKE...
GARFIELD
www.garfield.com
A SPECIAL TIME OF YEAR WHEN ALL OBSERVE:
GARFIELD
PEACE ON EARTH...
GARFIELD
© 1998 PAWS, INC./Distributed by Universal Press Syndicate
JIM DAVIS 12-20
ROWR
GARFIELD
AND GOOD WILL TOWARD MEN
GARFIELD

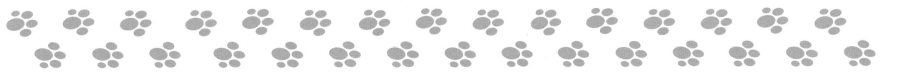

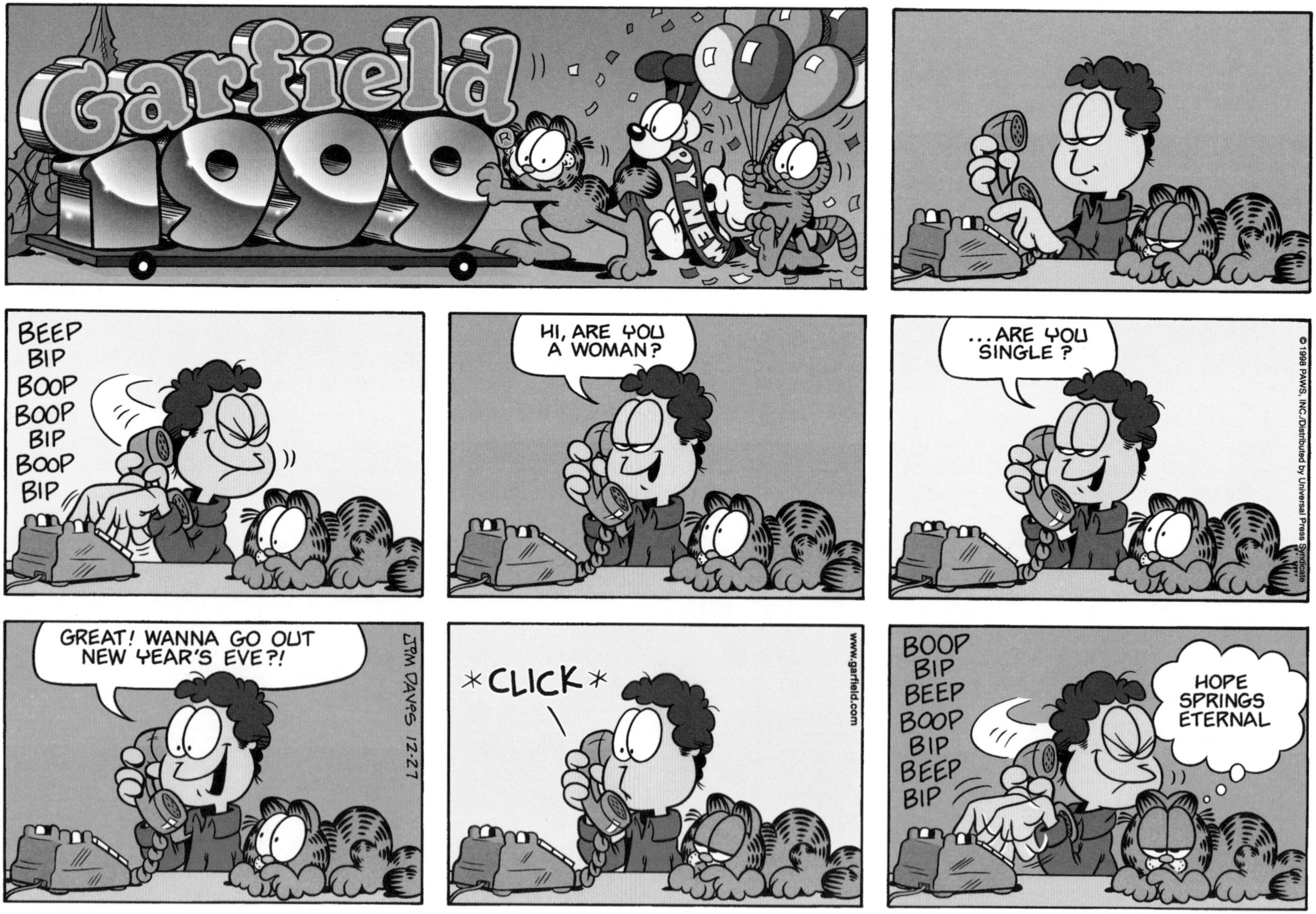
Garfield
1999
BEEP BIP BOOP BOOP BIP BOOP BIP
HI, ARE YOU A WOMAN?
...ARE YOU SINGLE?
© 1998 PAWS, INC./Distributed by Universal Press Syndicate
GREAT! WANNA GO OUT NEW YEAR'S EVE?!
JIM DAVIS 12-27
CLICK
www.garfield.com
BOOP BIP BEEP BOOP BIP BEEP BIP
HOPE SPRINGS ETERNAL

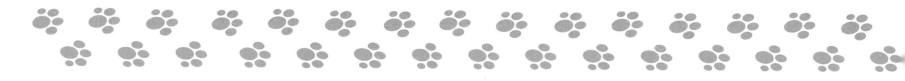

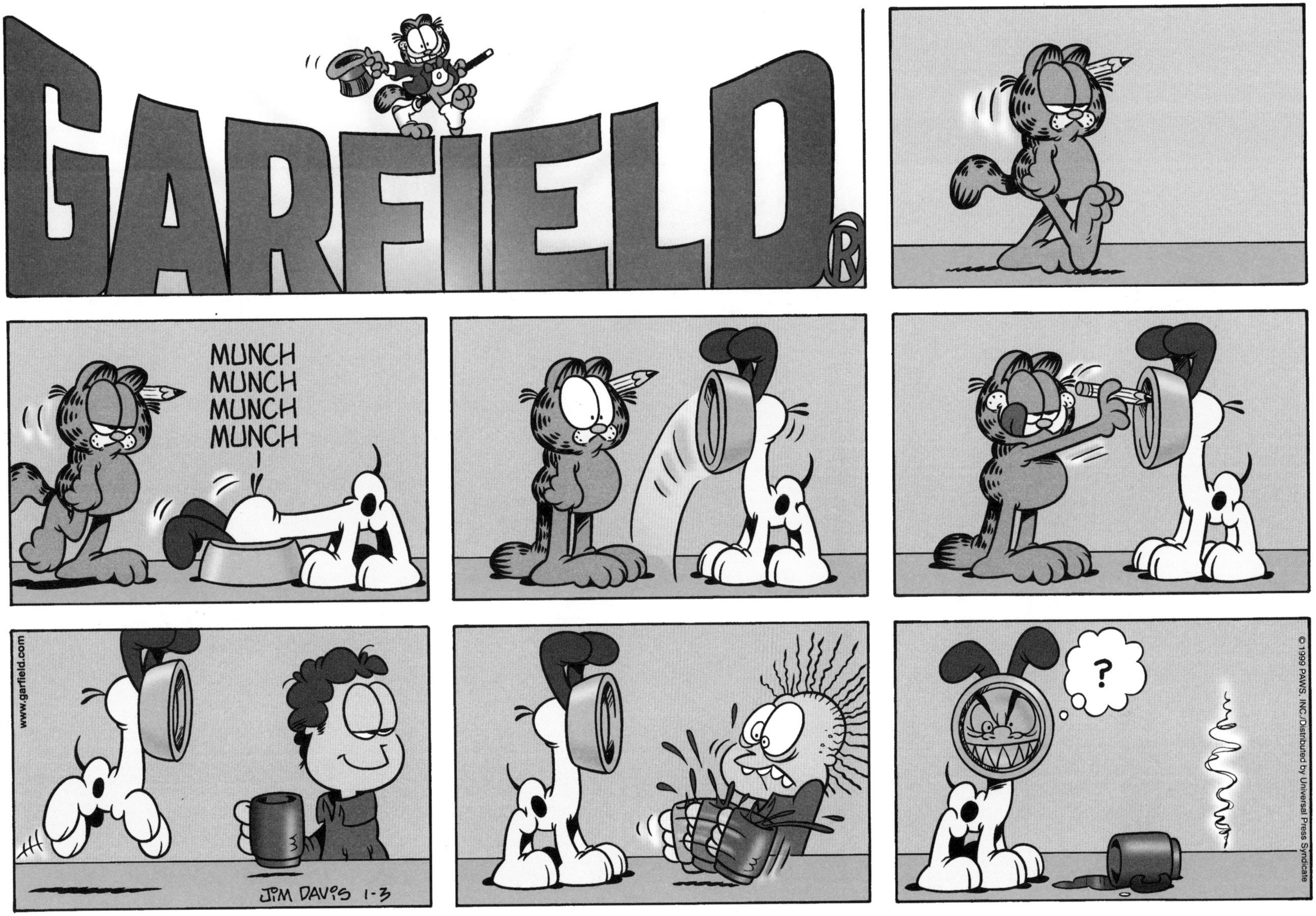
GARFIELD®
MUNCH
MUNCH
MUNCH
MUNCH
www.garfield.com
JIM DAVIS 1-3
?
© 1999 PAWS, INC./Distributed by Universal Press Syndicate

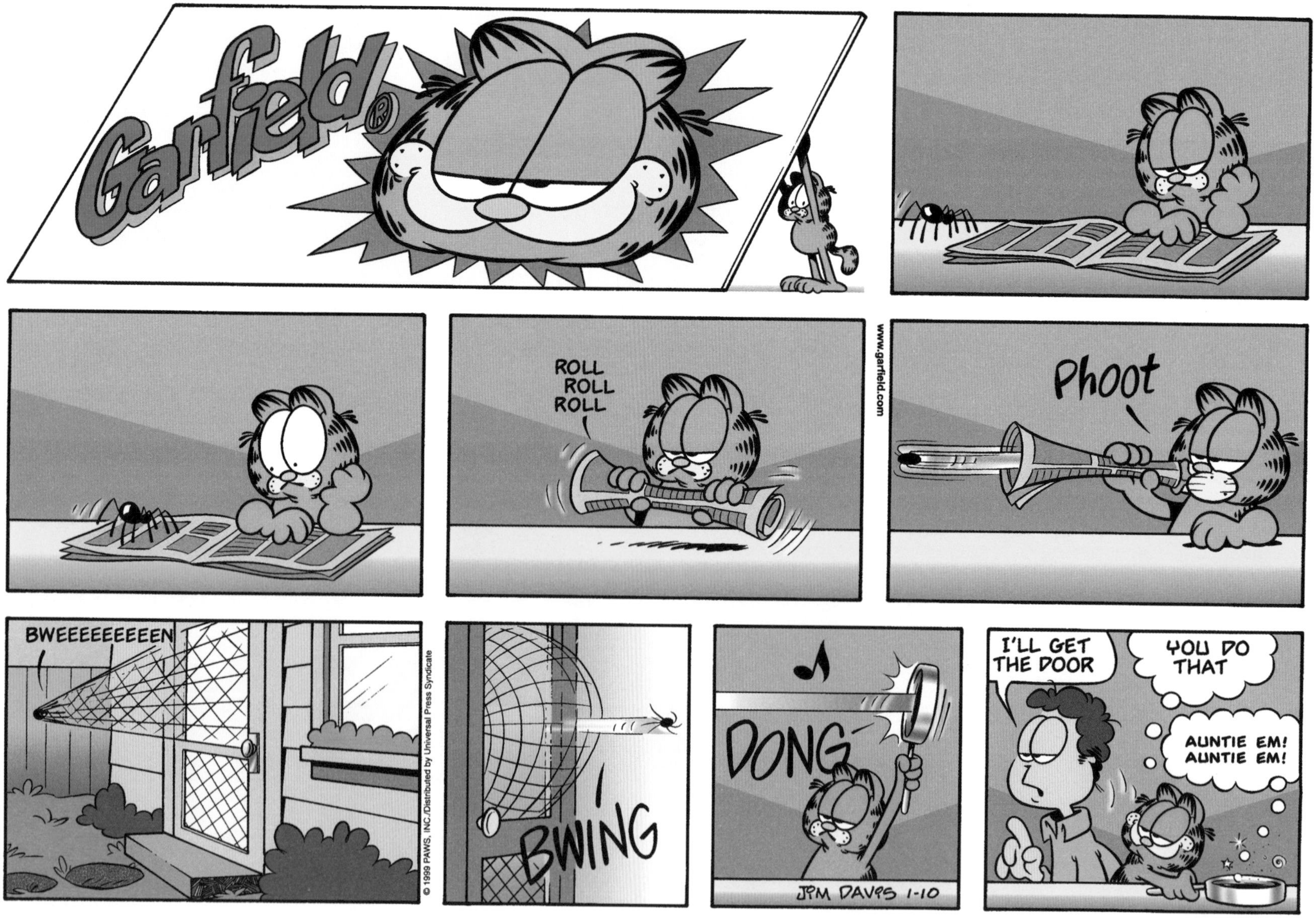

Garfield®
ROLL
ROLL
ROLL
Phoot
www.garfield.com
BWEEEEEEEEEN
© 1999 PAWS, INC./Distributed by Universal Press Syndicate
BWING
DONG
JIM DAVIS 1-10
I'LL GET THE DOOR
YOU DO THAT
AUNTIE EM! AUNTIE EM!

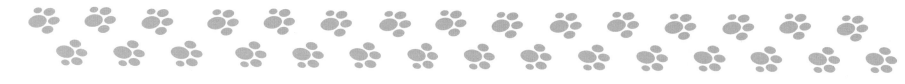

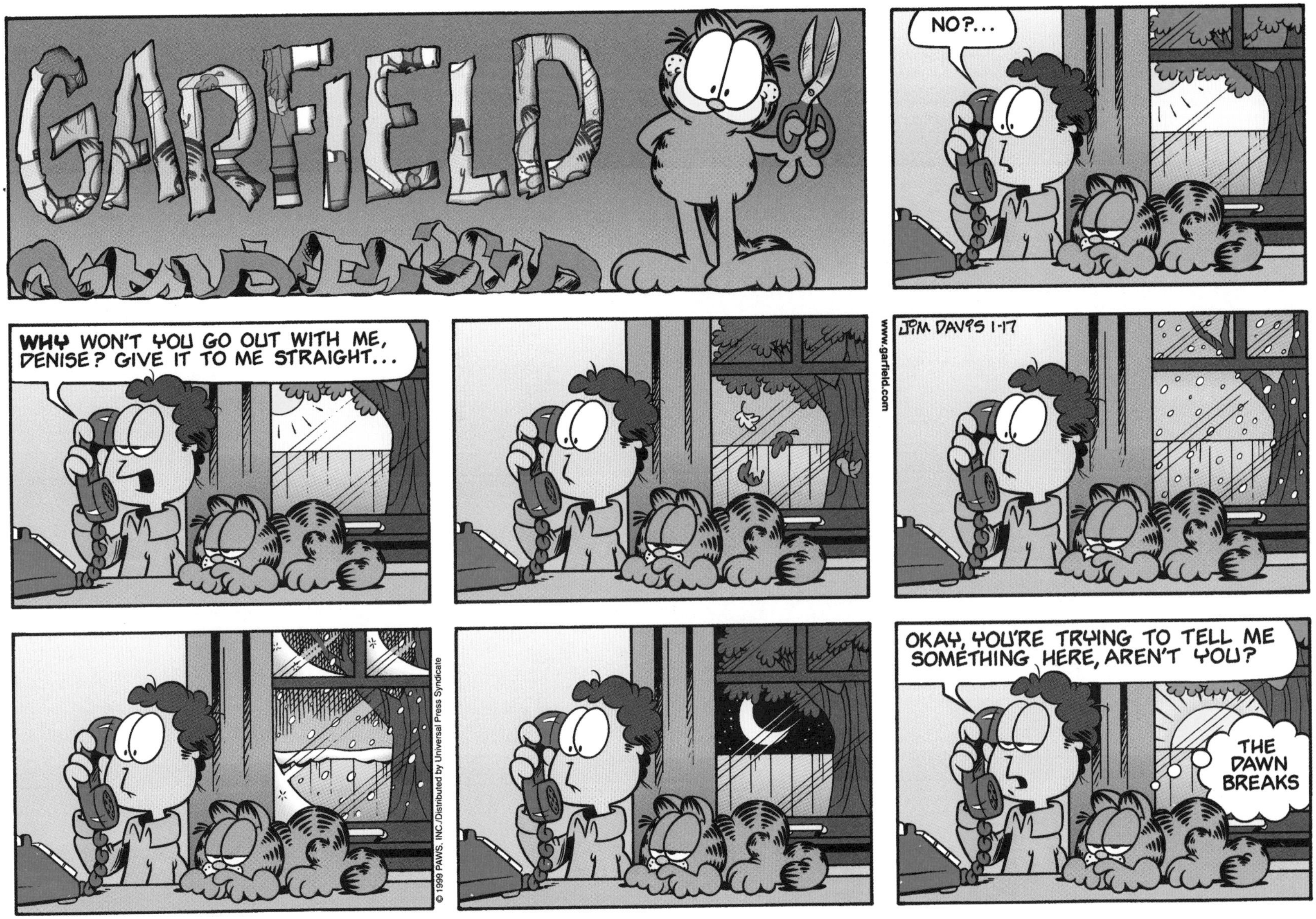
GARFIELD
NO?...
WHY WON'T YOU GO OUT WITH ME, DENISE? GIVE IT TO ME STRAIGHT...
JIM DAVIS 1-17
www.garfield.com
© 1999 PAWS, INC./Distributed by Universal Press Syndicate
OKAY, YOU'RE TRYING TO TELL ME SOMETHING HERE, AREN'T YOU?
THE DAWN BREAKS

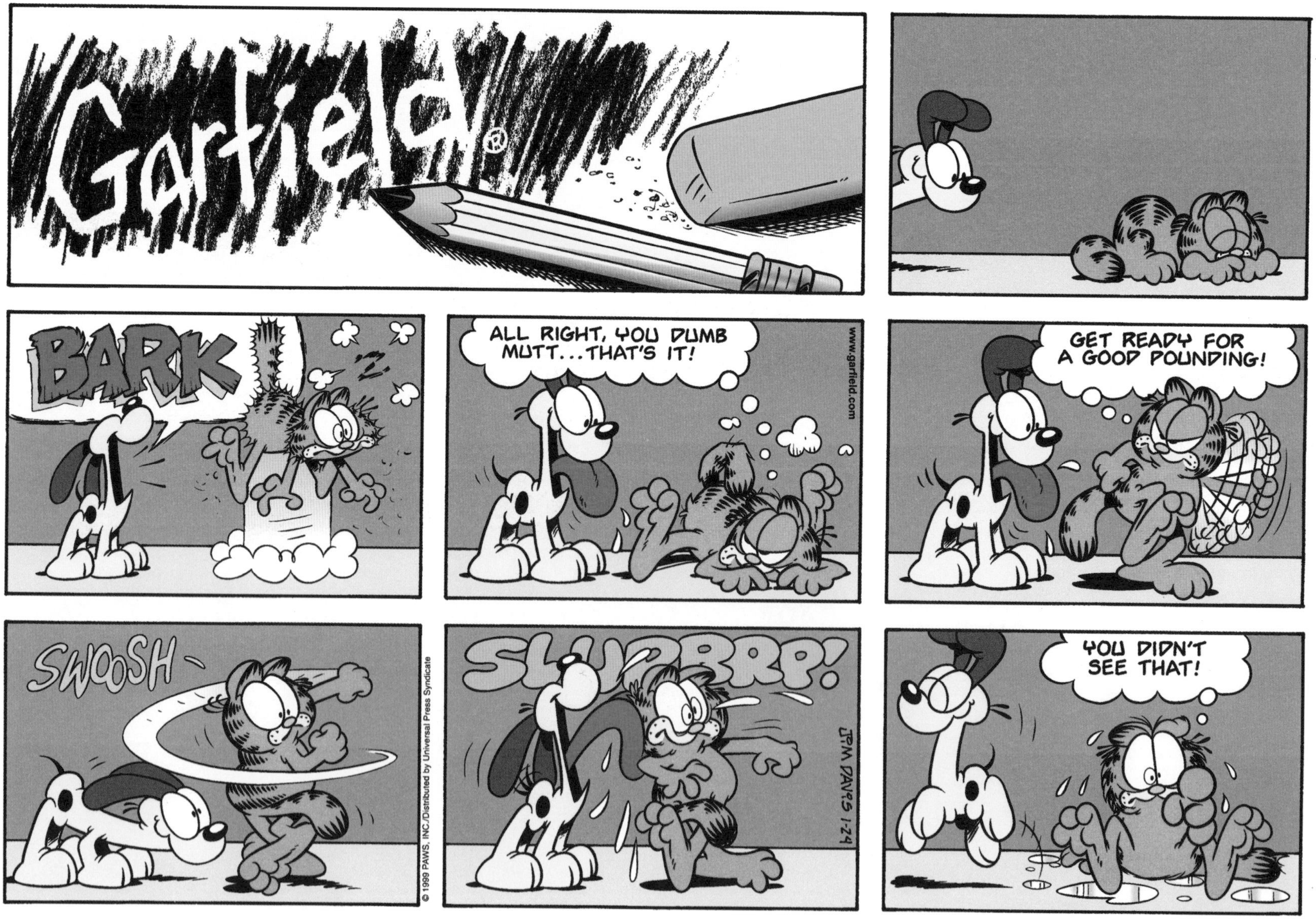
Garfield®
BARK
ALL RIGHT, YOU DUMB MUTT...THAT'S IT!
www.garfield.com
GET READY FOR A GOOD POUNDING!
SWOOSH-
© 1999 PAWS, INC./Distributed by Universal Press Syndicate
JIM DAVIS 1-24
YOU DIDN'T SEE THAT!

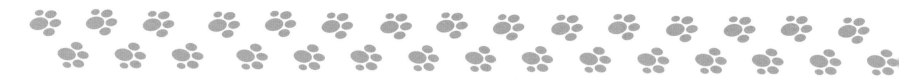

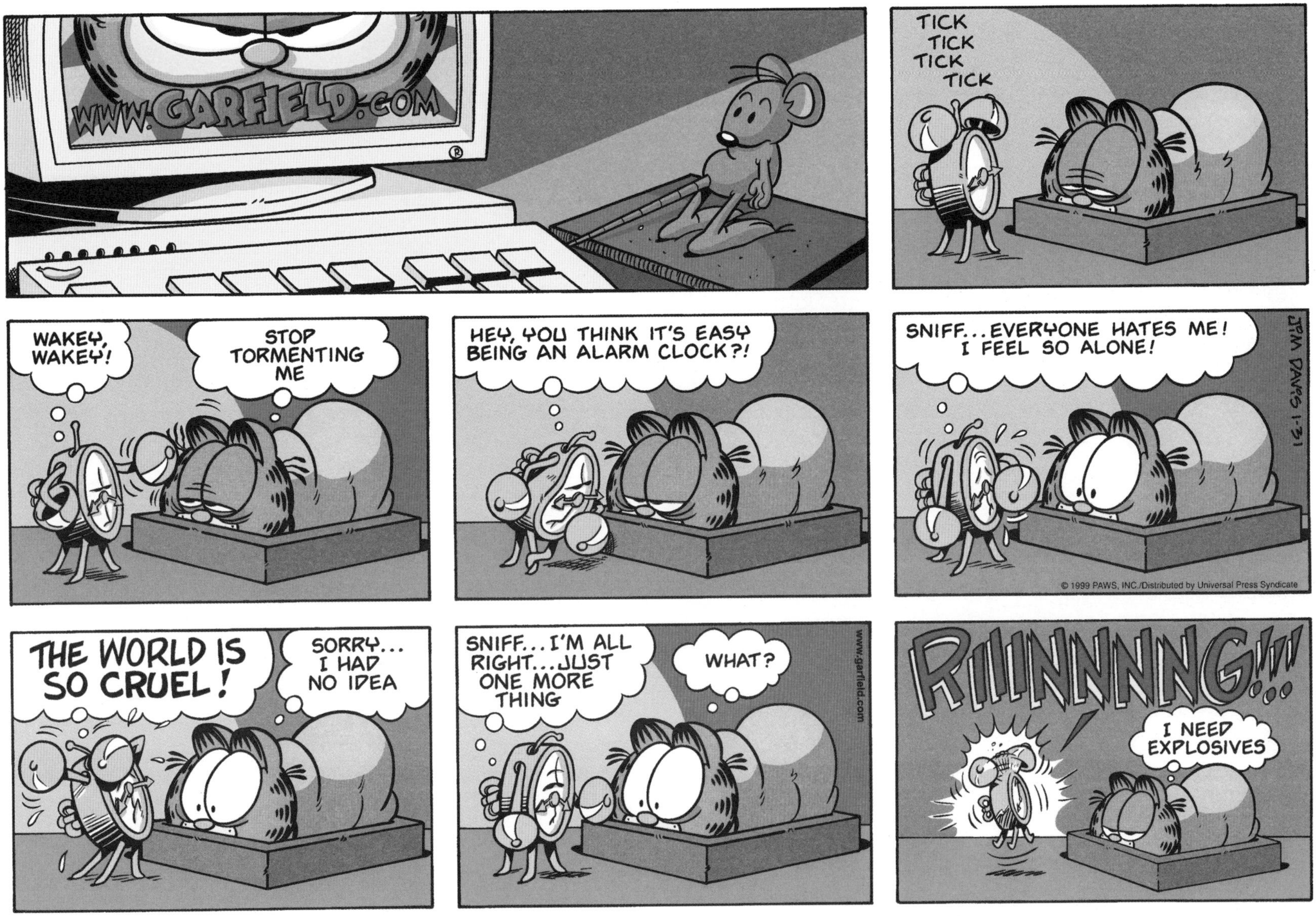
WWW.GARFIELD.COM
TICK TICK TICK TICK
WAKEY, WAKEY!
STOP TORMENTING ME
HEY, YOU THINK IT'S EASY BEING AN ALARM CLOCK?!
JPM DAVIS 1-31
SNIFF...EVERYONE HATES ME! I FEEL SO ALONE!
© 1999 PAWS, INC./Distributed by Universal Press Syndicate
THE WORLD IS SO CRUEL!
SORRY... I HAD NO IDEA
www.garfield.com
SNIFF... I'M ALL RIGHT... JUST ONE MORE THING
WHAT?
RIIINNNNG!!!
I NEED EXPLOSIVES

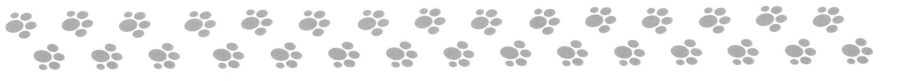

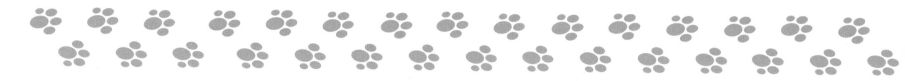

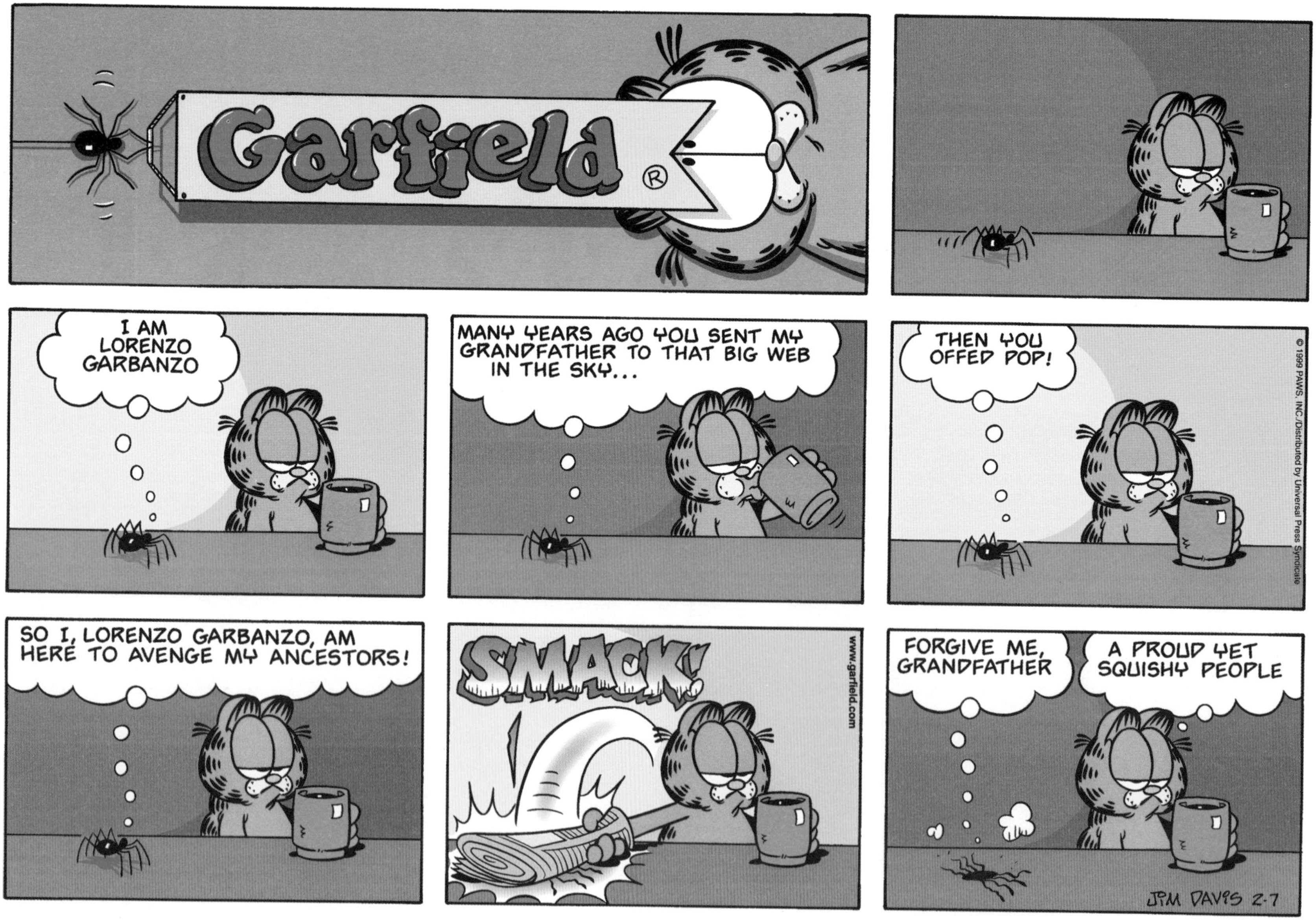
Garfield ®
I AM LORENZO GARBANZO
MANY YEARS AGO YOU SENT MY GRANDFATHER TO THAT BIG WEB IN THE SKY...
THEN YOU OFFED POP!
© 1999 PAWS, INC./Distributed by Universal Press Syndicate
SO I, LORENZO GARBANZO, AM HERE TO AVENGE MY ANCESTORS!
SMACK!
www.garfield.com
FORGIVE ME, GRANDFATHER
A PROUD YET SQUISHY PEOPLE
JIM DAVIS 2-7

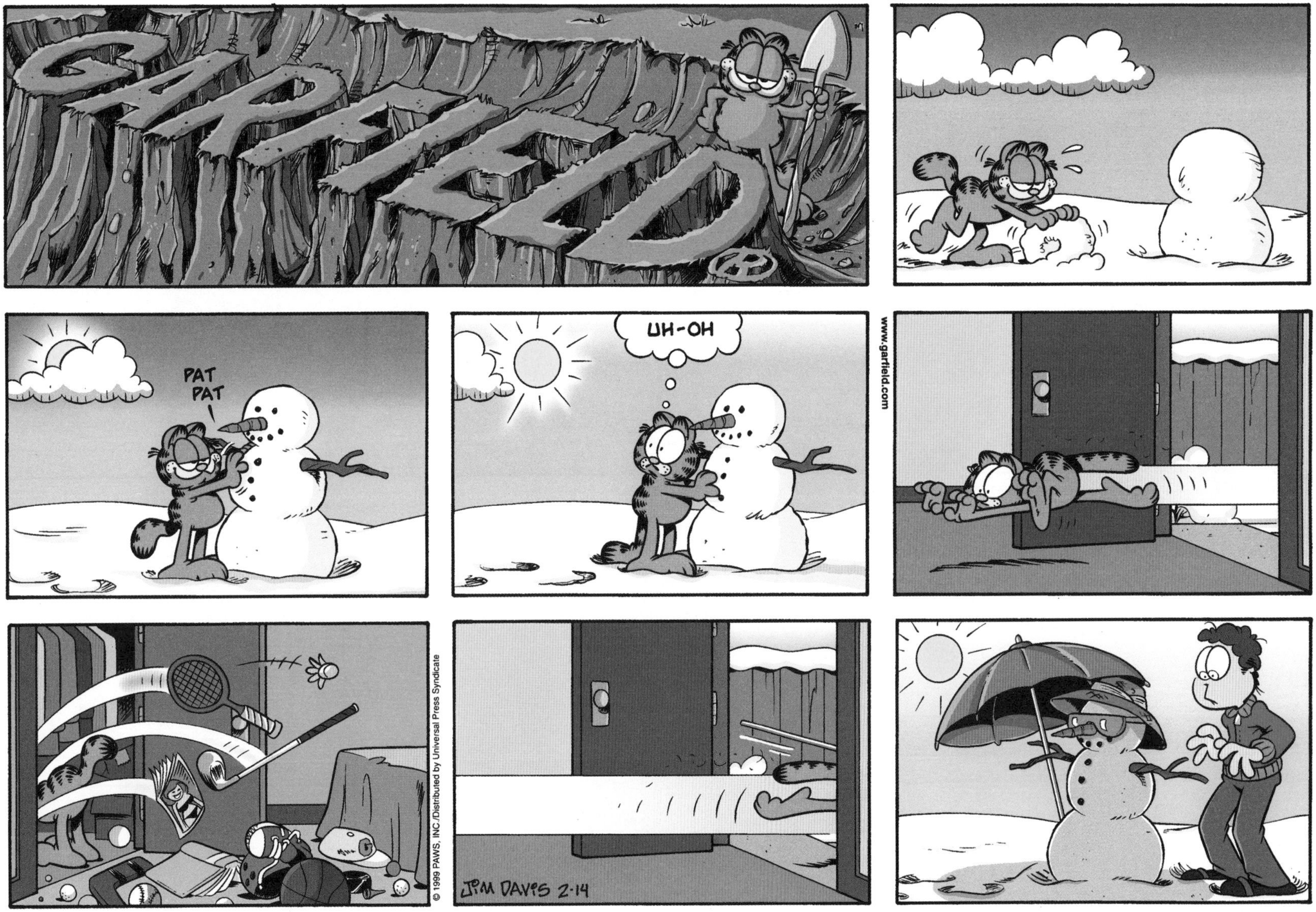
GARFIELD
PAT PAT
UH-OH
www.garfield.com
© 1999 PAWS, INC./Distributed by Universal Press Syndicate
JIM DAVIS 2-14

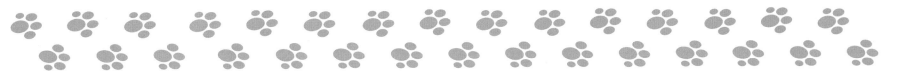

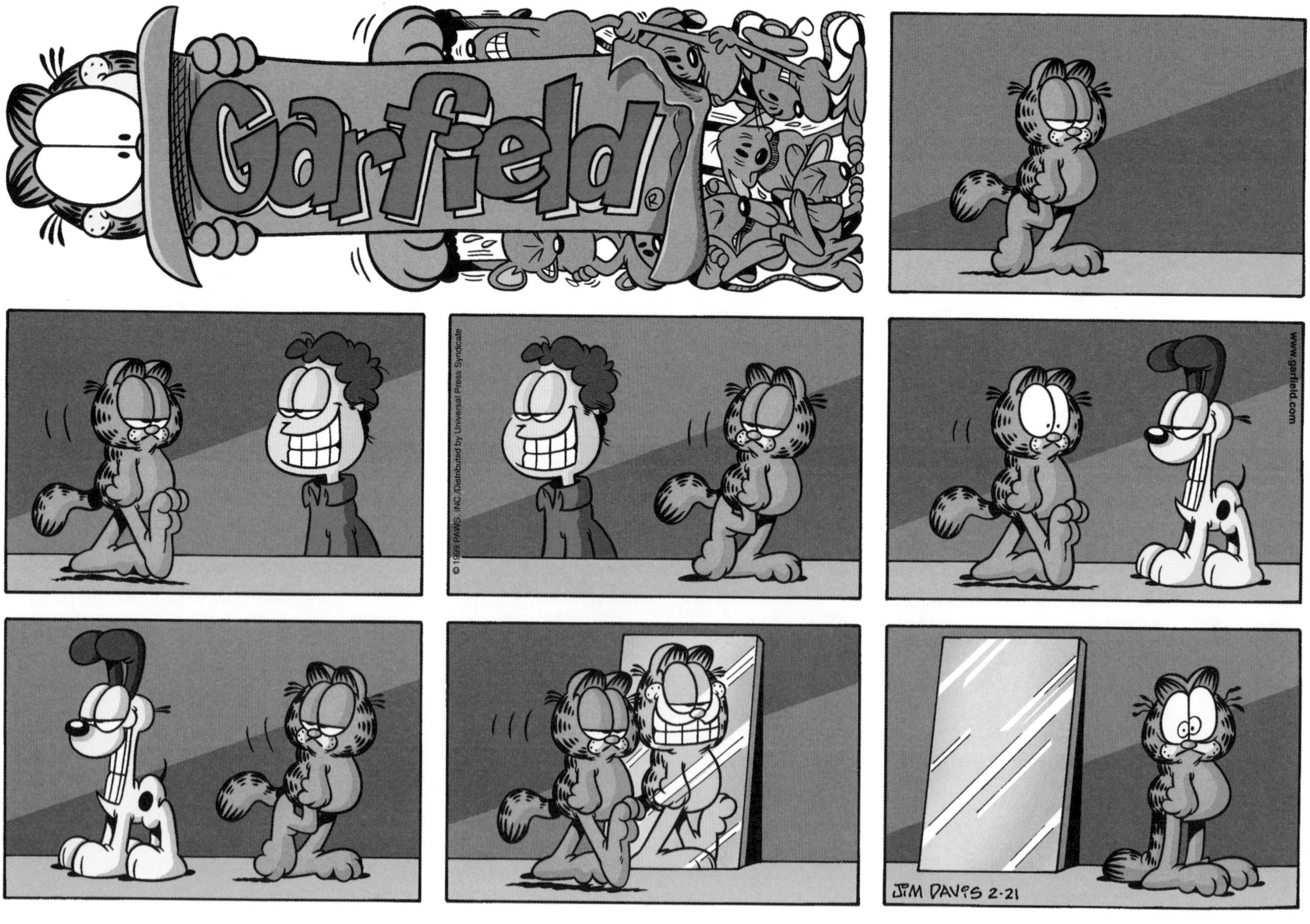
Garfield®
© 1999 PAWS, INC./Distributed by Universal Press Syndicate
www.garfield.com
JIM DAVIS 2-21

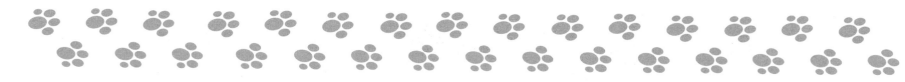

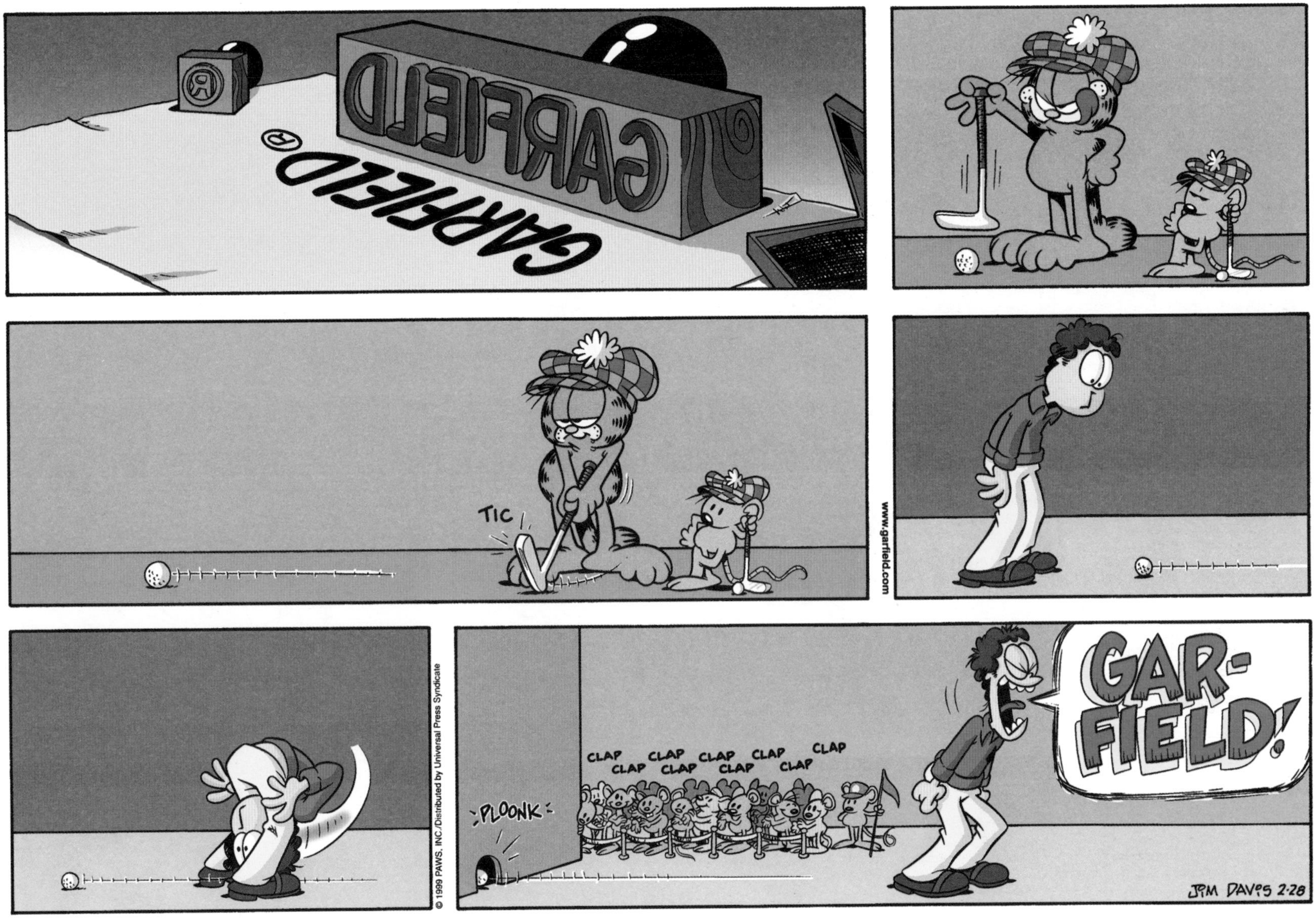

GARFIELD®
www.garfield.com
TIC
© 1999 PAWS, INC./Distributed by Universal Press Syndicate
PLOONK
CLAP CLAP CLAP CLAP CLAP CLAP CLAP CLAP CLAP
GAR-FIELD!
JIM DAVIS 2·28

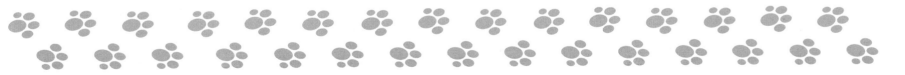

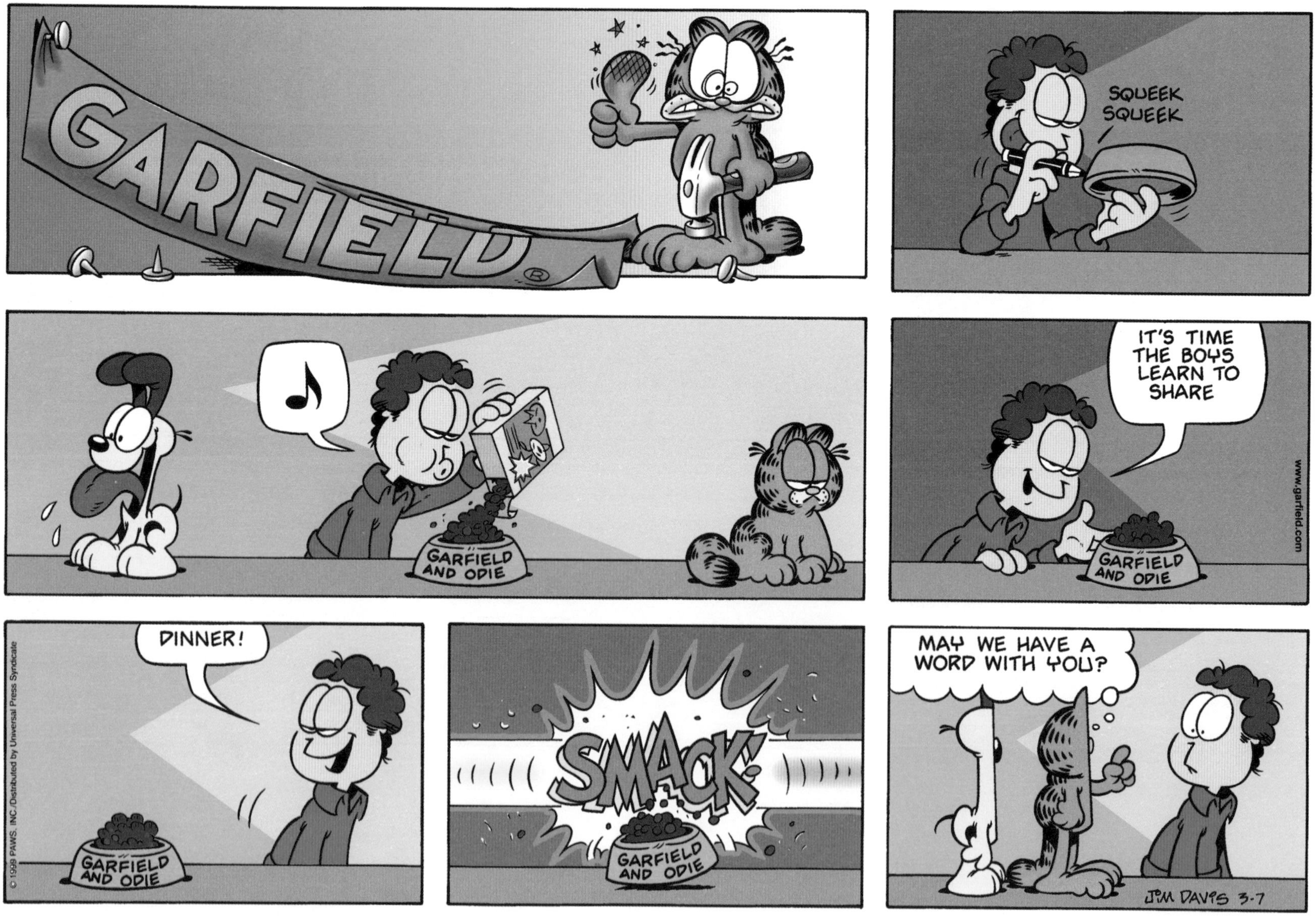
GARFIELD®
SQUEEK SQUEEK
IT'S TIME THE BOYS LEARN TO SHARE
GARFIELD AND ODIE
www.garfield.com
© 1999 PAWS, INC./Distributed by Universal Press Syndicate
DINNER!
GARFIELD AND ODIE
SMACK!
GARFIELD AND ODIE
MAY WE HAVE A WORD WITH YOU?
JIM DAVIS 3-7

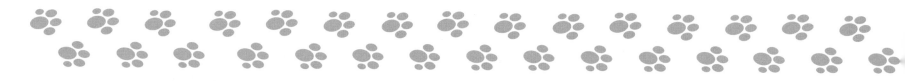

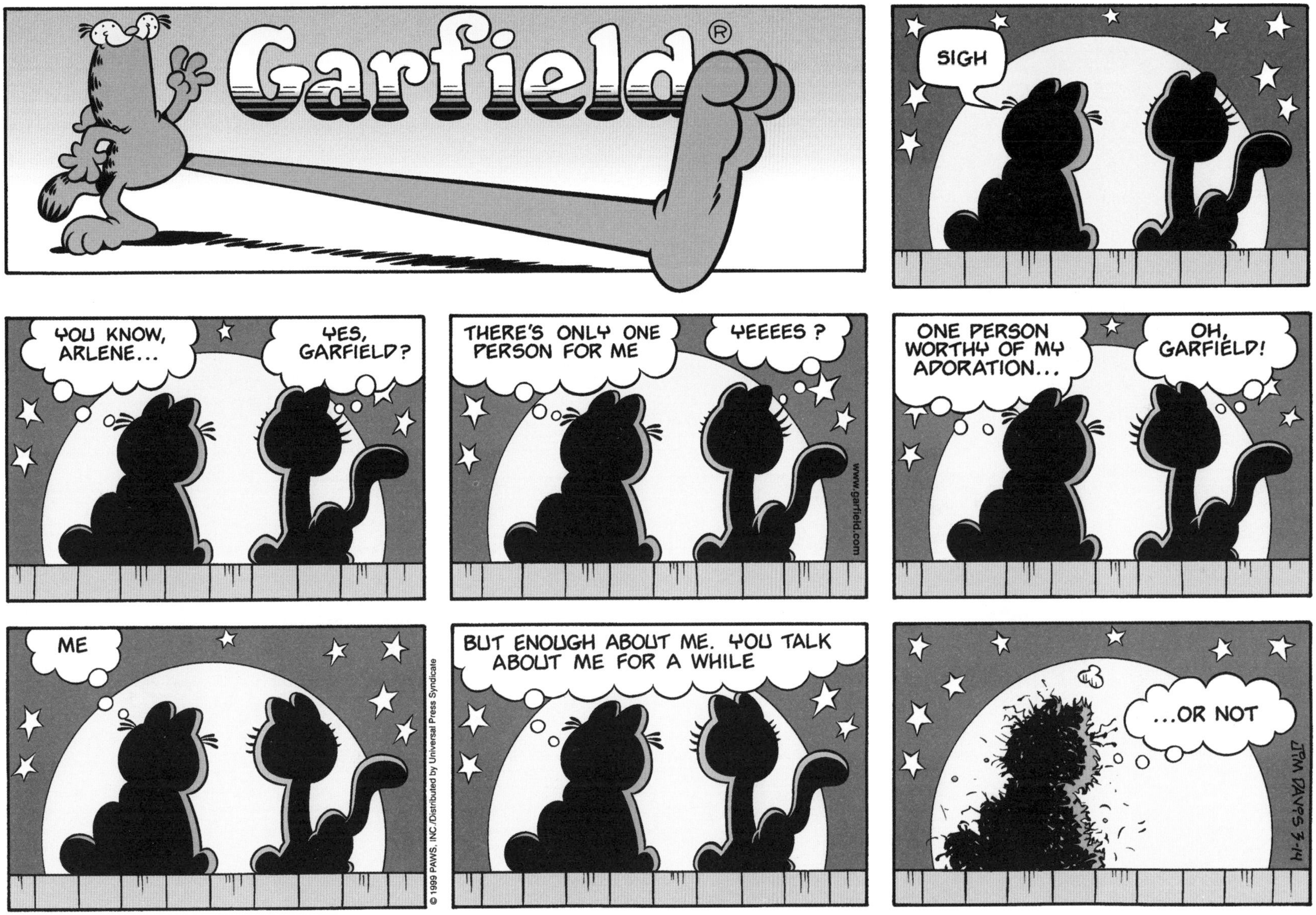
Garfield®
SIGH
YOU KNOW, ARLENE...
YES, GARFIELD?
THERE'S ONLY ONE PERSON FOR ME
YEEEES ?
www.garfield.com
ONE PERSON WORTHY OF MY ADORATION...
OH, GARFIELD!
ME
© 1999 PAWS. INC./Distributed by Universal Press Syndicate
BUT ENOUGH ABOUT ME. YOU TALK ABOUT ME FOR A WHILE
...OR NOT
JIM DAVIS 3-14

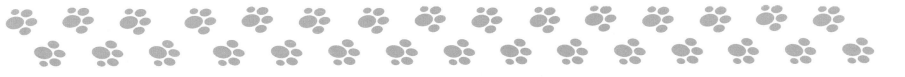

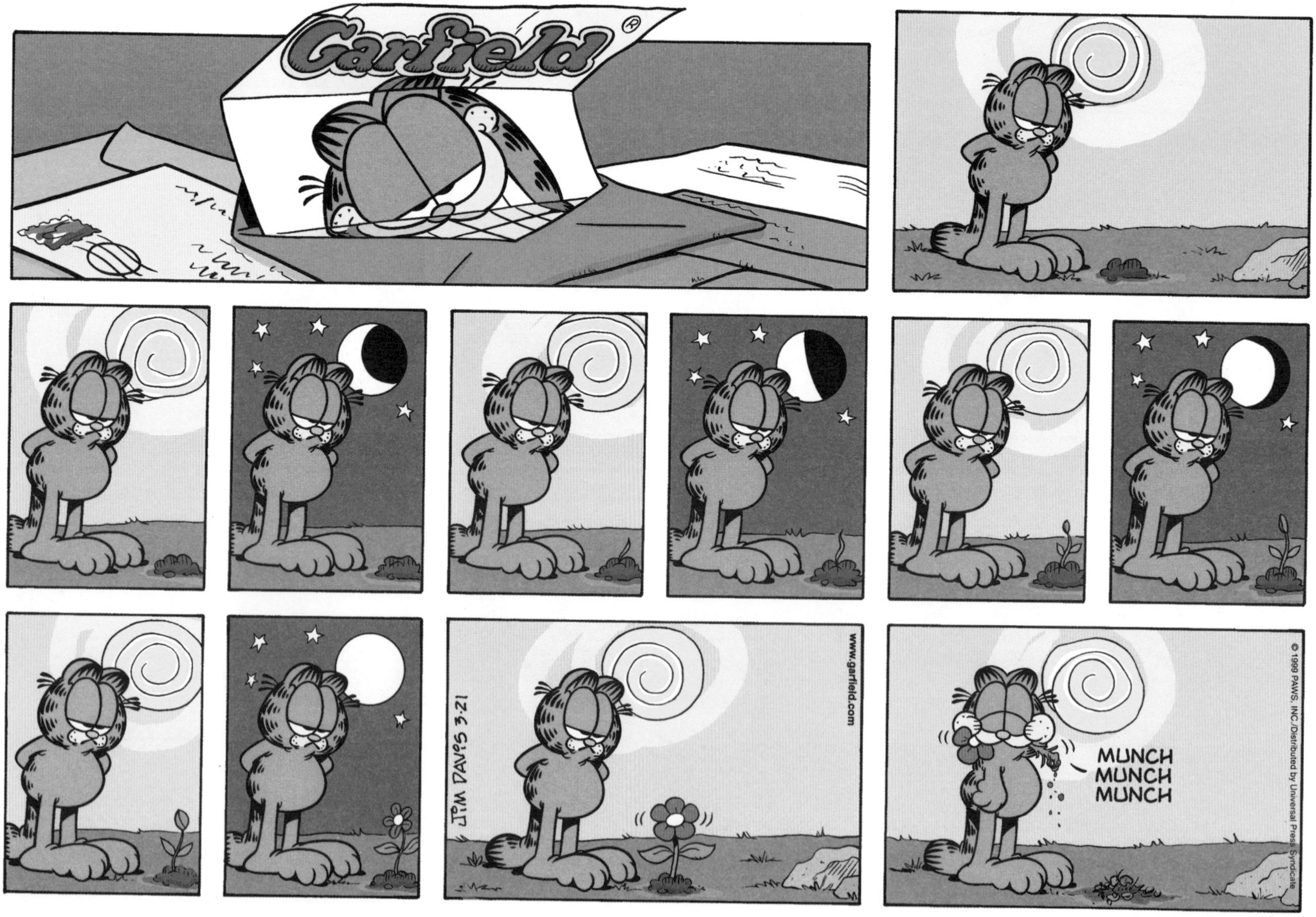
Garfield
JIM DAVIS 3-21
www.garfield.com
MUNCH
MUNCH
MUNCH
© 1999 PAWS, INC./Distributed by Universal Press Syndicate

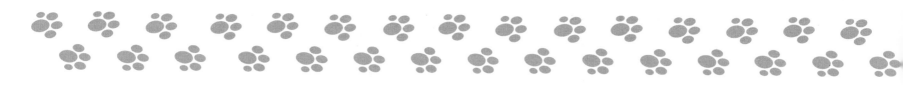

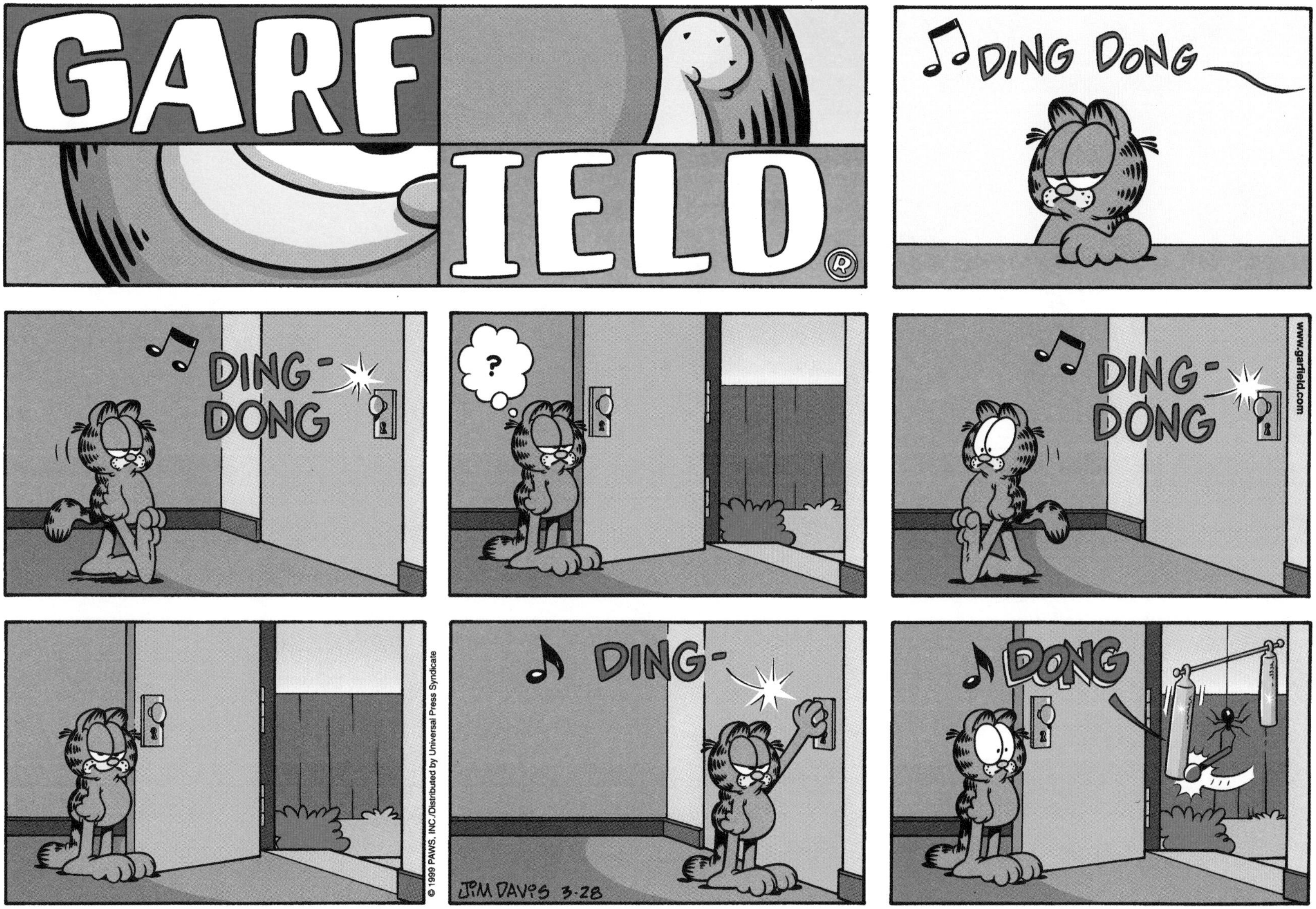
GARFIELD®
DING DONG
DING-DONG
?
DING-DONG
www.garfield.com
© 1999 PAWS, INC./Distributed by Universal Press Syndicate
DING-
JIM DAVIS 3-28
DONG

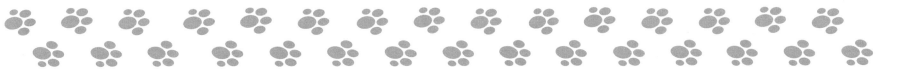

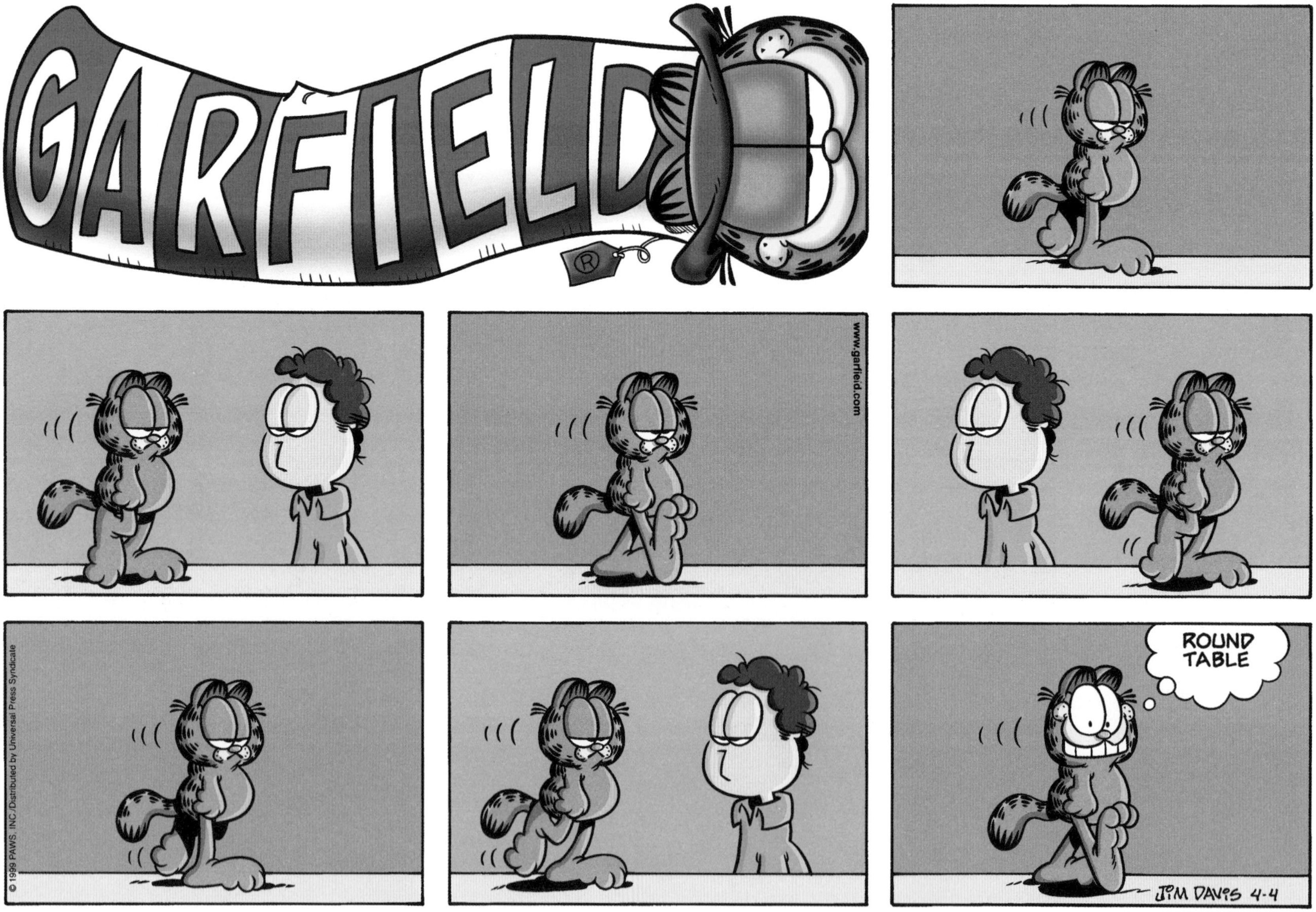
GARFIELD
www.garfield.com
© 1999 PAWS, INC./Distributed by Universal Press Syndicate
ROUND TABLE
JIM DAVIS 4-4

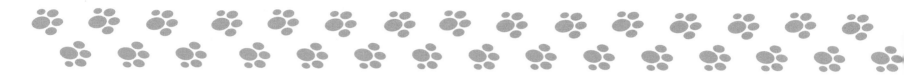

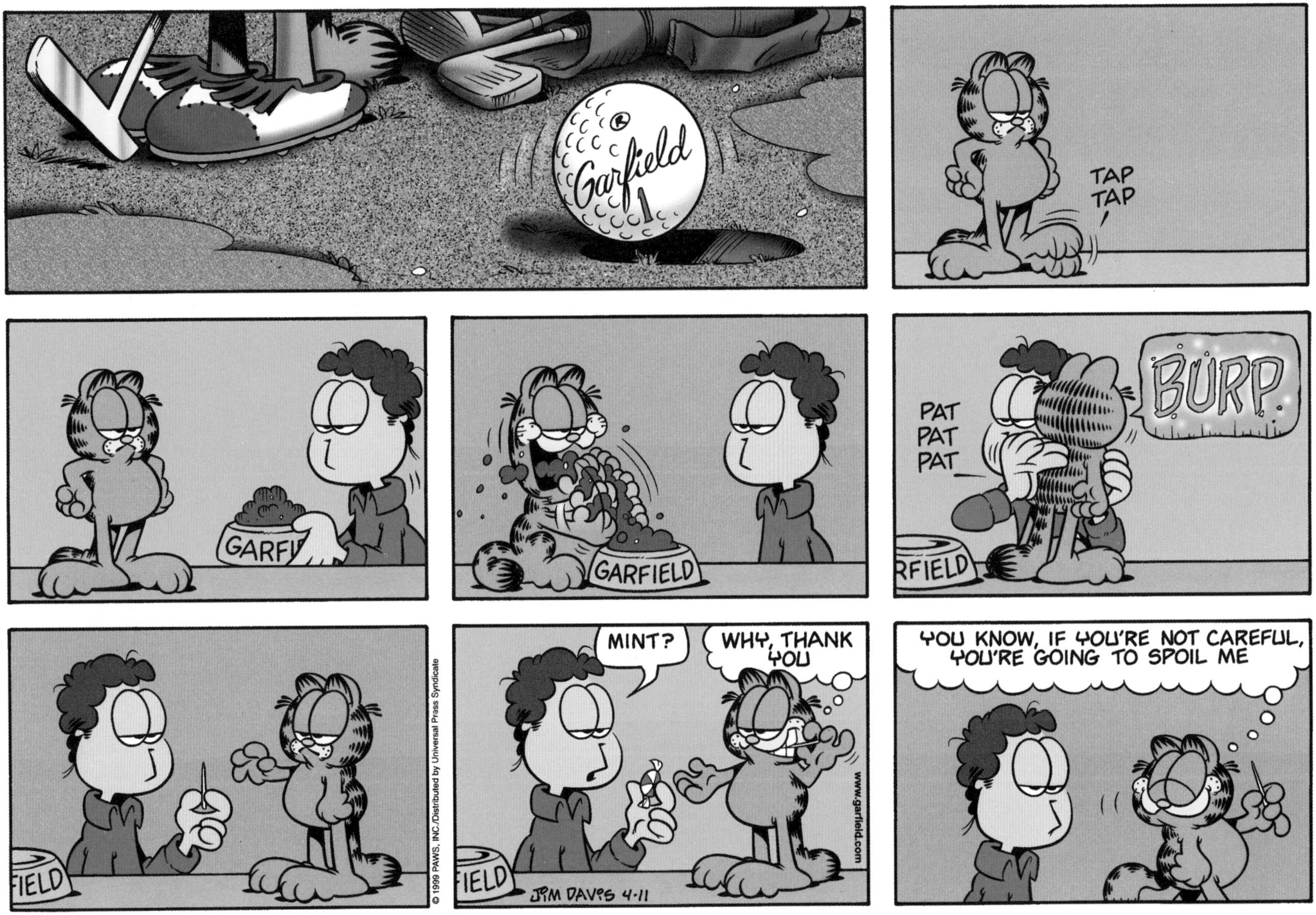

Garfield
TAP
TAP
GARFI
GARFIELD
PAT
PAT
PAT
BURP
RFIELD
FIELD
© 1999 PAWS, INC./Distributed by Universal Press Syndicate
MINT?
WHY, THANK YOU
www.garfield.com
IELD
JIM DAVIS 4-11
YOU KNOW, IF YOU'RE NOT CAREFUL, YOU'RE GOING TO SPOIL ME

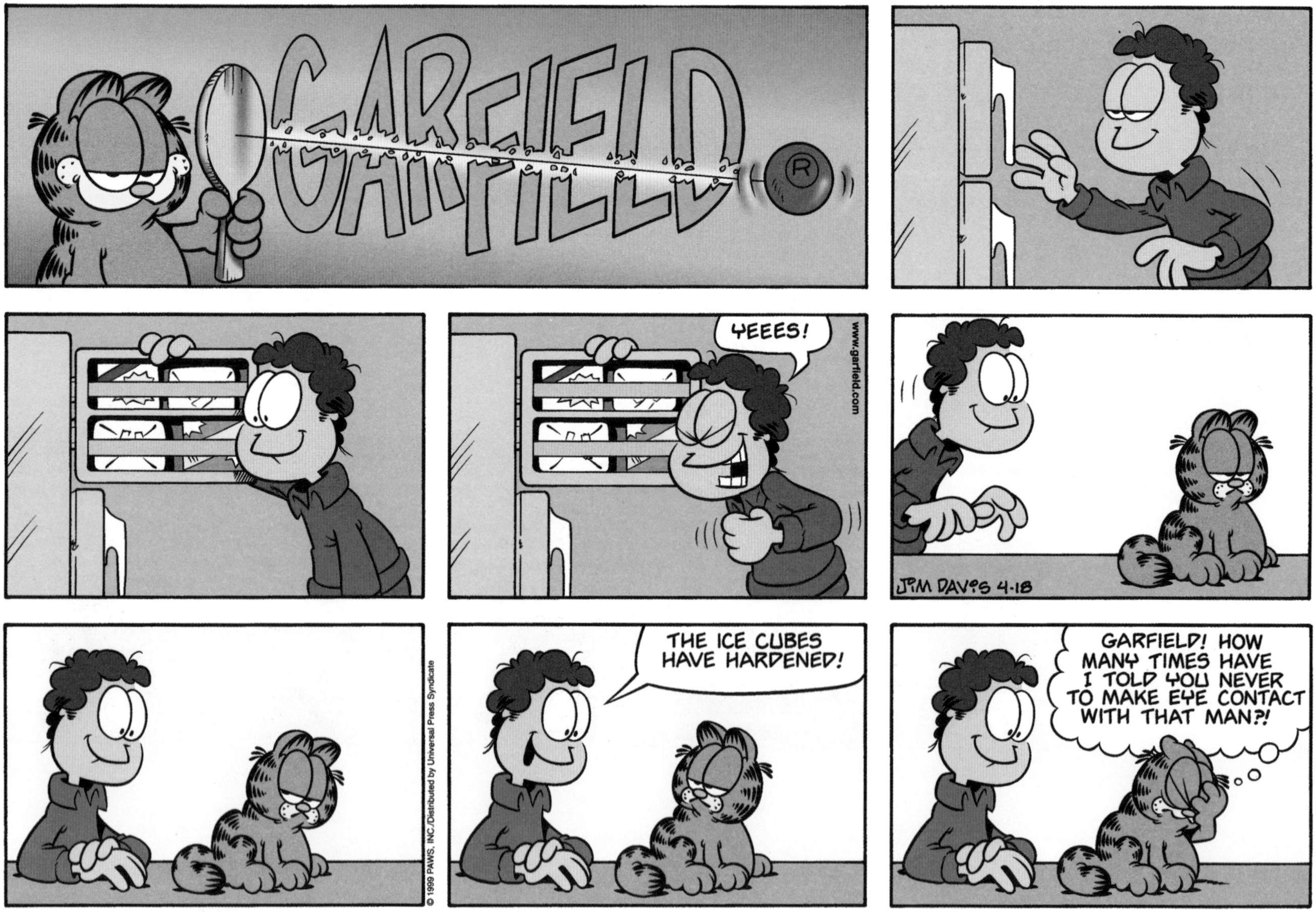
GARFIELD
YEEES!
www.garfield.com
JIM DAVIS 4-18
© 1999 PAWS, INC./Distributed by Universal Press Syndicate
THE ICE CUBES HAVE HARDENED!
GARFIELD! HOW MANY TIMES HAVE I TOLD YOU NEVER TO MAKE EYE CONTACT WITH THAT MAN?!

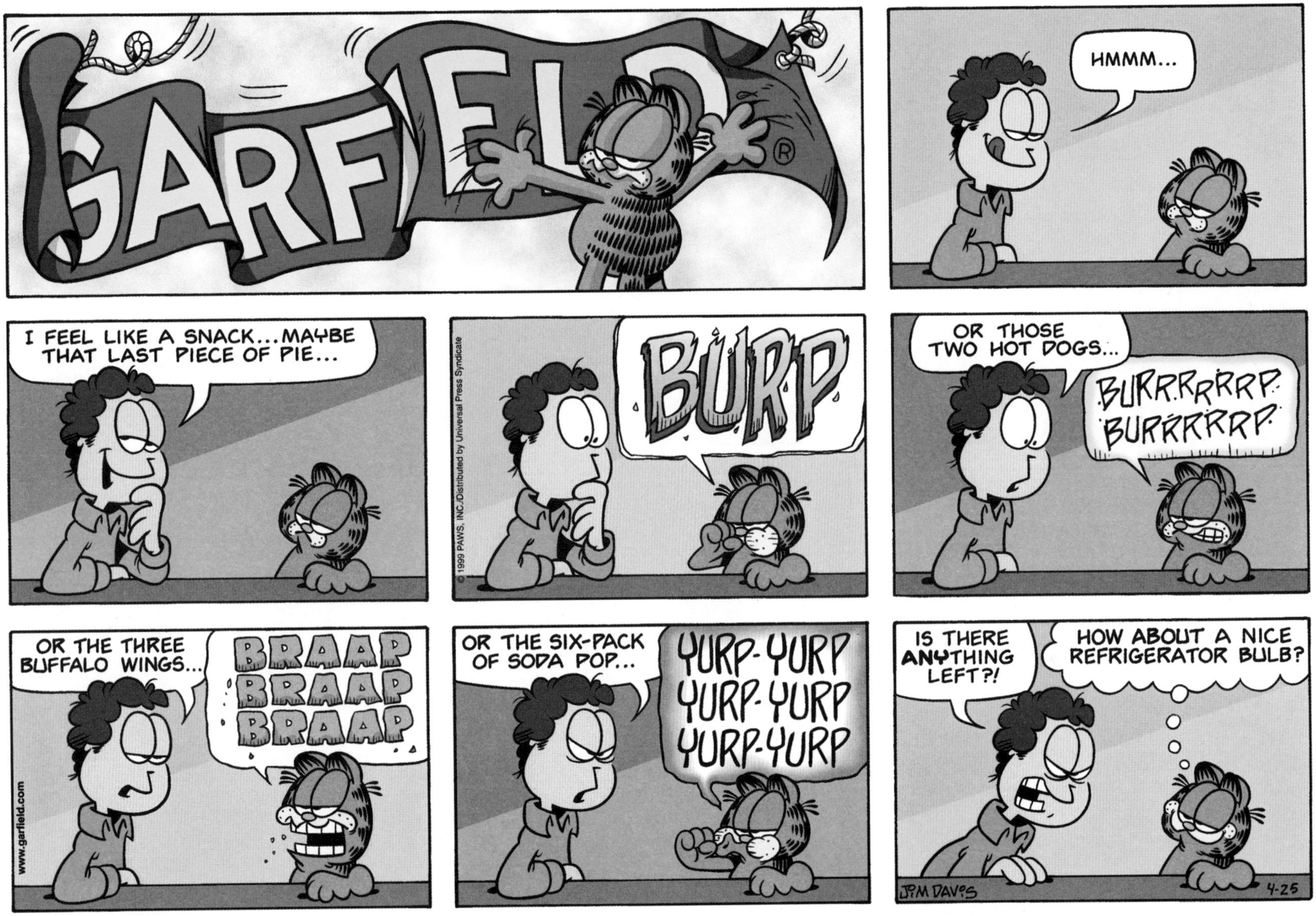
GARFIELD®
HMMM...
I FEEL LIKE A SNACK... MAYBE THAT LAST PIECE OF PIE...
© 1999 PAWS, INC./Distributed by Universal Press Syndicate
BURP
OR THOSE TWO HOT DOGS...
BURRRRRRP BURRRRRP
OR THE THREE BUFFALO WINGS...
BRAAP BRAAP BRAAP
www.garfield.com
OR THE SIX-PACK OF SODA POP...
YURP-YURP YURP-YURP YURP-YURP
IS THERE ANYTHING LEFT?!
HOW ABOUT A NICE REFRIGERATOR BULB?
JIM DAVIS
4-25

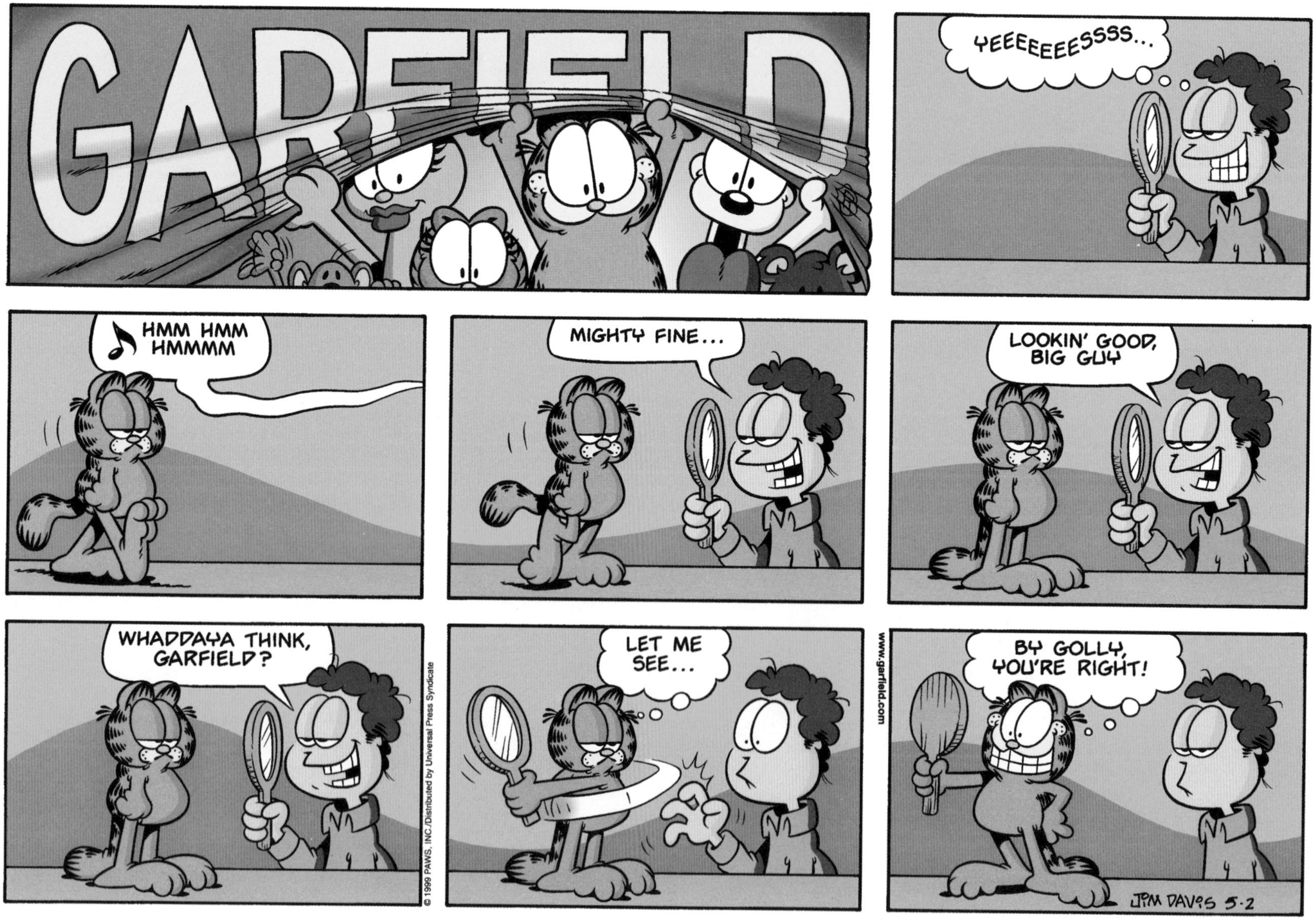
GARFIELD
YEEEEEEEESSSS...
HMM HMM HMMMM
MIGHTY FINE...
LOOKIN' GOOD, BIG GUY
WHADDAYA THINK, GARFIELD?
LET ME SEE...
BY GOLLY, YOU'RE RIGHT!
© 1999 PAWS, INC./Distributed by Universal Press Syndicate
www.garfield.com
JIM DAVIS 5-2

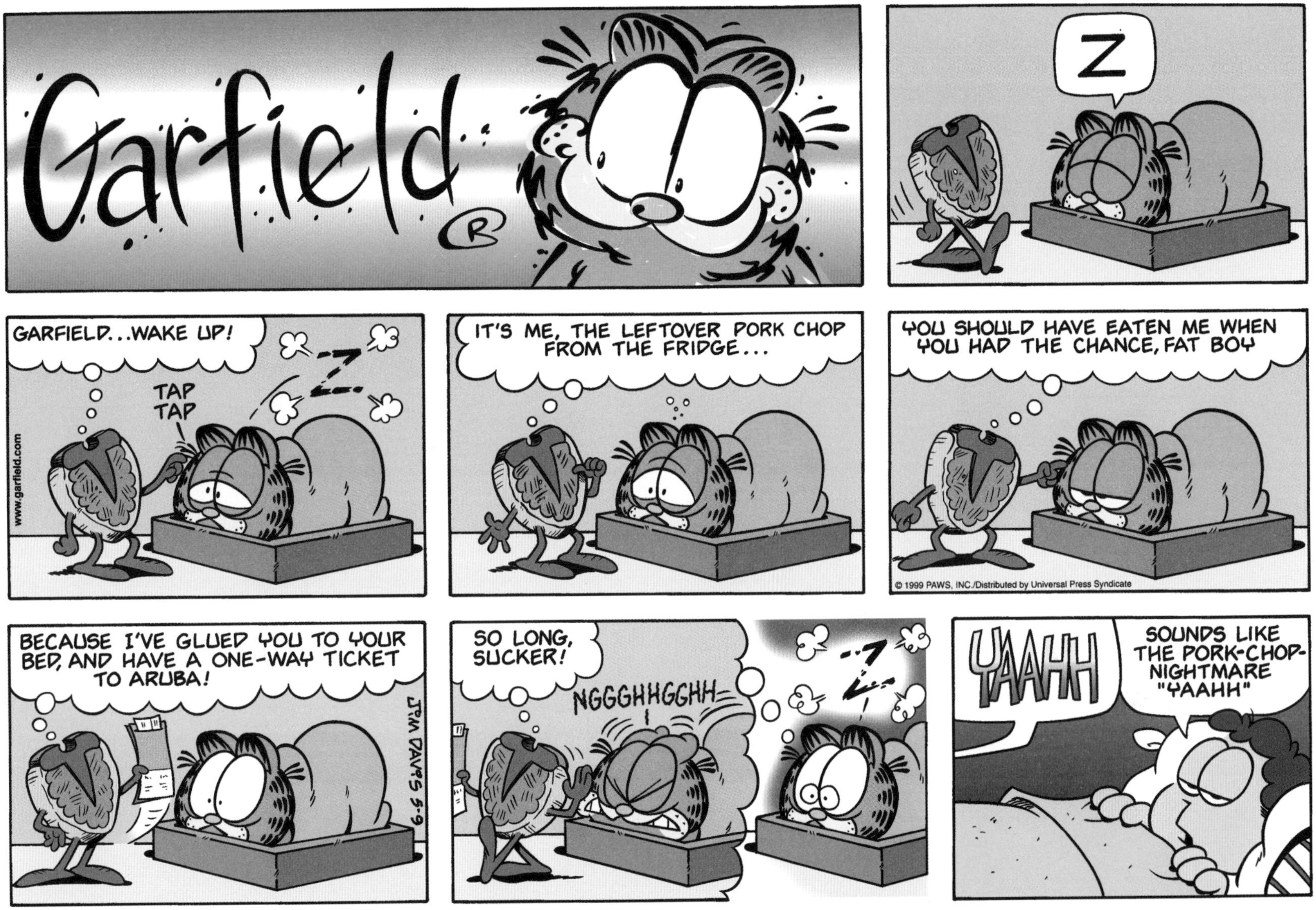
Garfield®
Z
GARFIELD...WAKE UP!
TAP TAP
www.garfield.com
IT'S ME, THE LEFTOVER PORK CHOP FROM THE FRIDGE...
YOU SHOULD HAVE EATEN ME WHEN YOU HAD THE CHANCE, FAT BOY
© 1999 PAWS, INC./Distributed by Universal Press Syndicate
BECAUSE I'VE GLUED YOU TO YOUR BED, AND HAVE A ONE-WAY TICKET TO ARUBA!
JIM DAVIS 5-9
SO LONG, SUCKER!
NGGGHHGGHH
YAAHH
SOUNDS LIKE THE PORK-CHOP-NIGHTMARE "YAAHH"

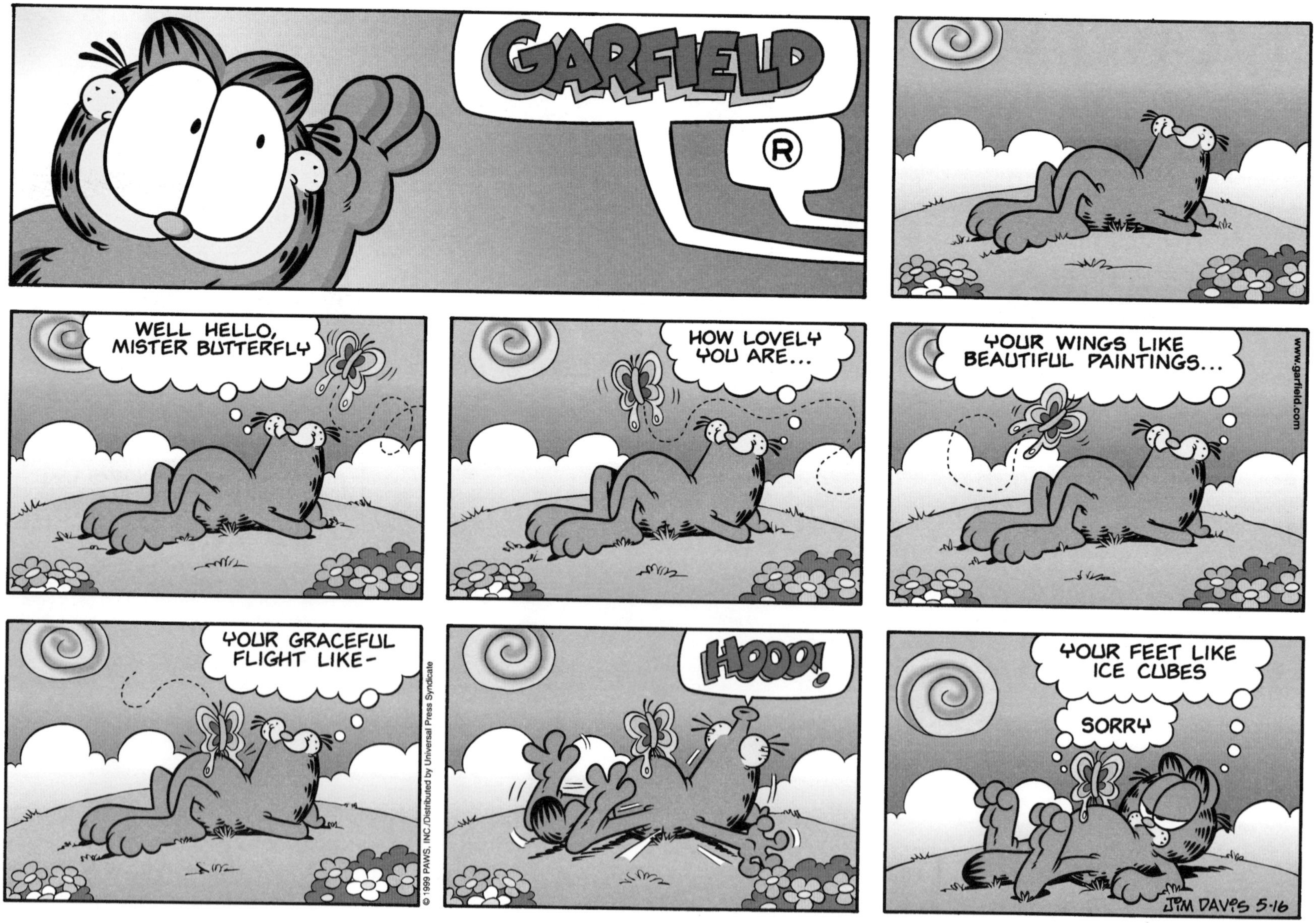
GARFIELD ®
WELL HELLO, MISTER BUTTERFLY
HOW LOVELY YOU ARE...
YOUR WINGS LIKE BEAUTIFUL PAINTINGS...
www.garfield.com
YOUR GRACEFUL FLIGHT LIKE-
© 1999 PAWS, INC./Distributed by Universal Press Syndicate
HOOO!
YOUR FEET LIKE ICE CUBES
SORRY
JIM DAVIS 5-16

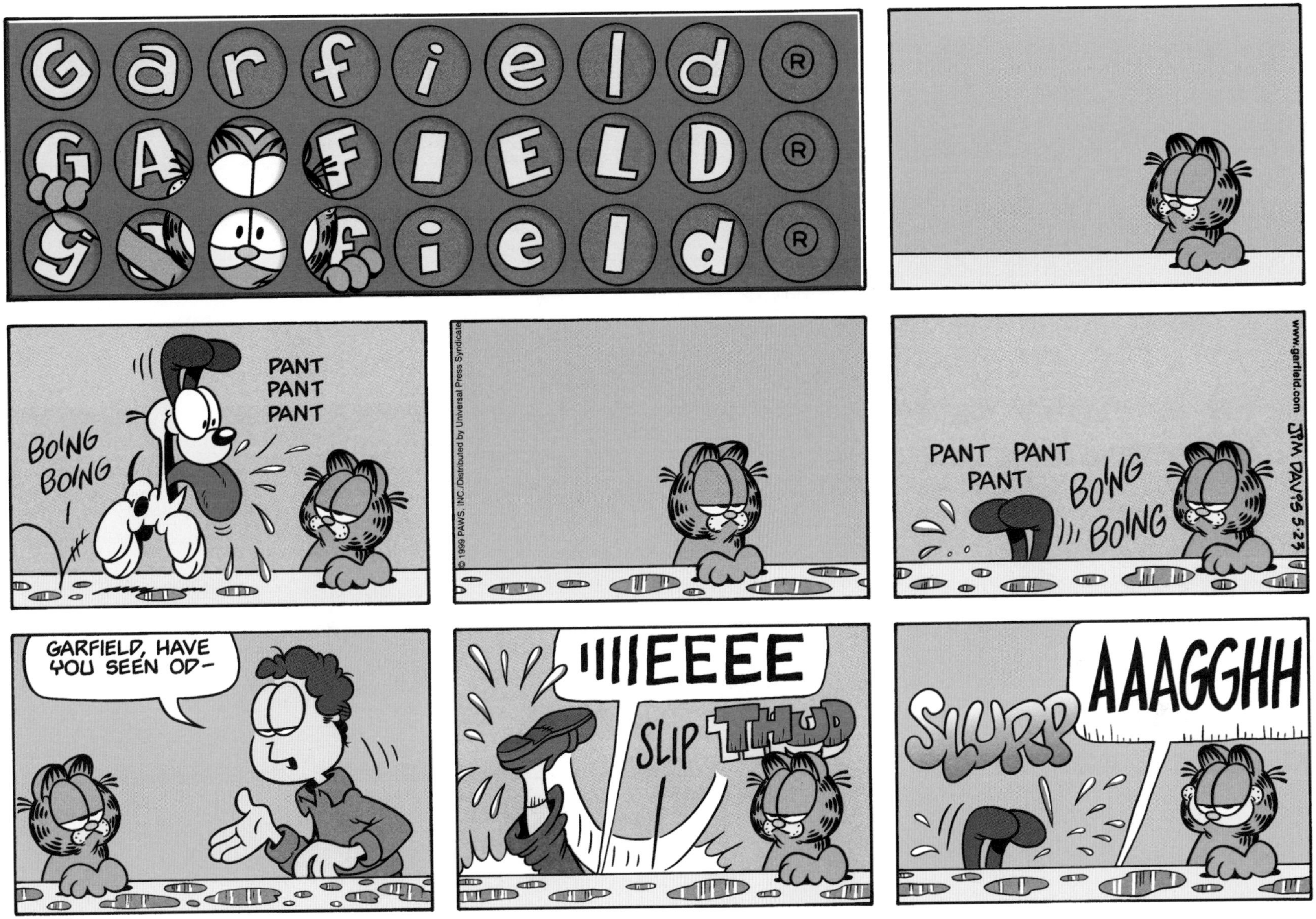
Garfield®
GARFIELD®
garfield®
BOING BOING
PANT PANT PANT
© 1999 PAWS, INC./Distributed by Universal Press Syndicate
PANT PANT PANT
BOING BOING
JPM DAVIS 5-23
www.garfield.com
GARFIELD, HAVE YOU SEEN OD-
IIIIEEEE
SLIP THUD
SLURP
AAAGGHH

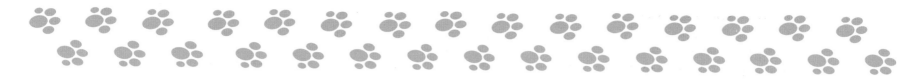

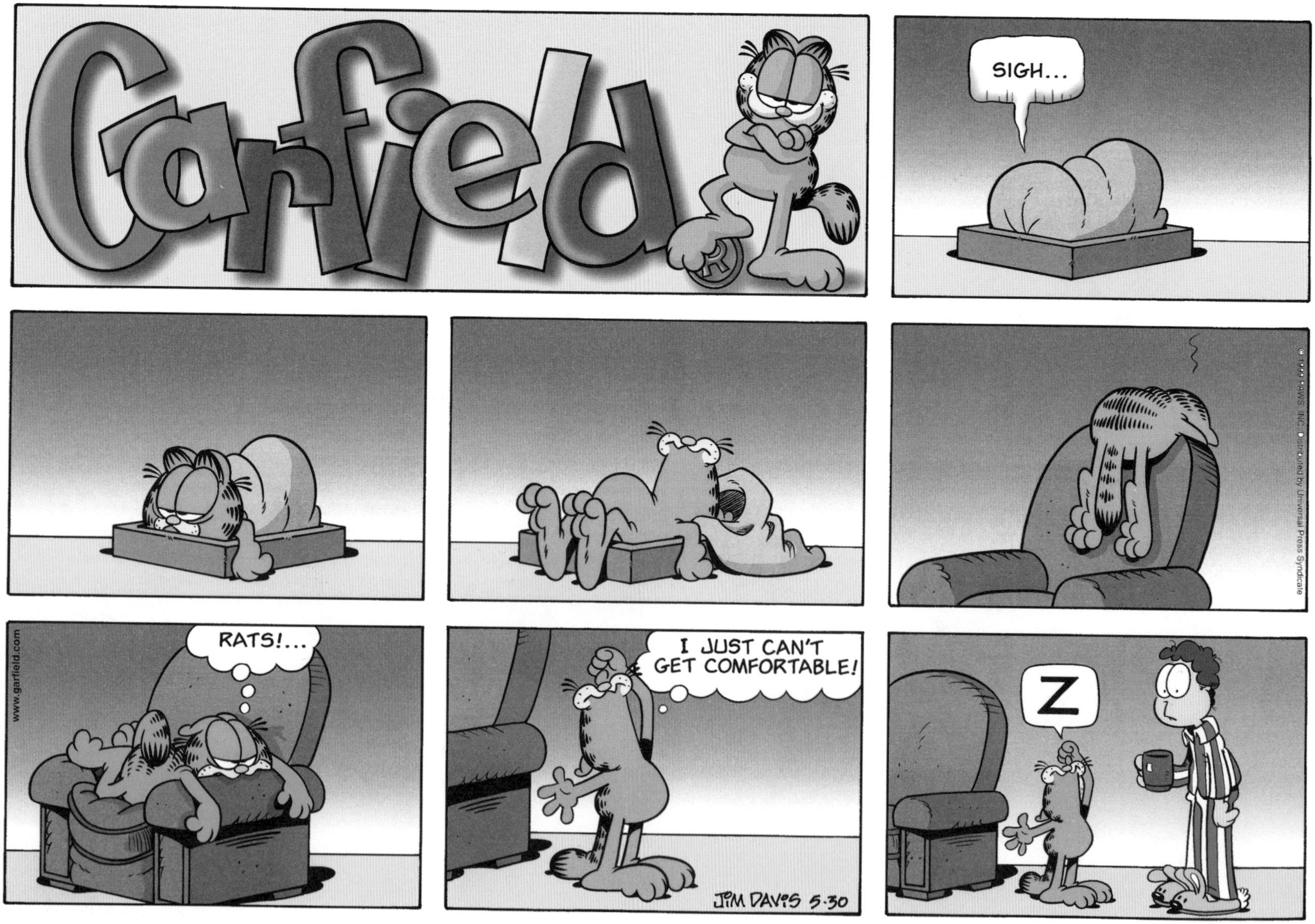
Garfield
SIGH...
RATS!...
I JUST CAN'T GET COMFORTABLE!
Z
JIM DAVIS 5-30
www.garfield.com
PAWS, INC. Distributed by Universal Press Syndicate

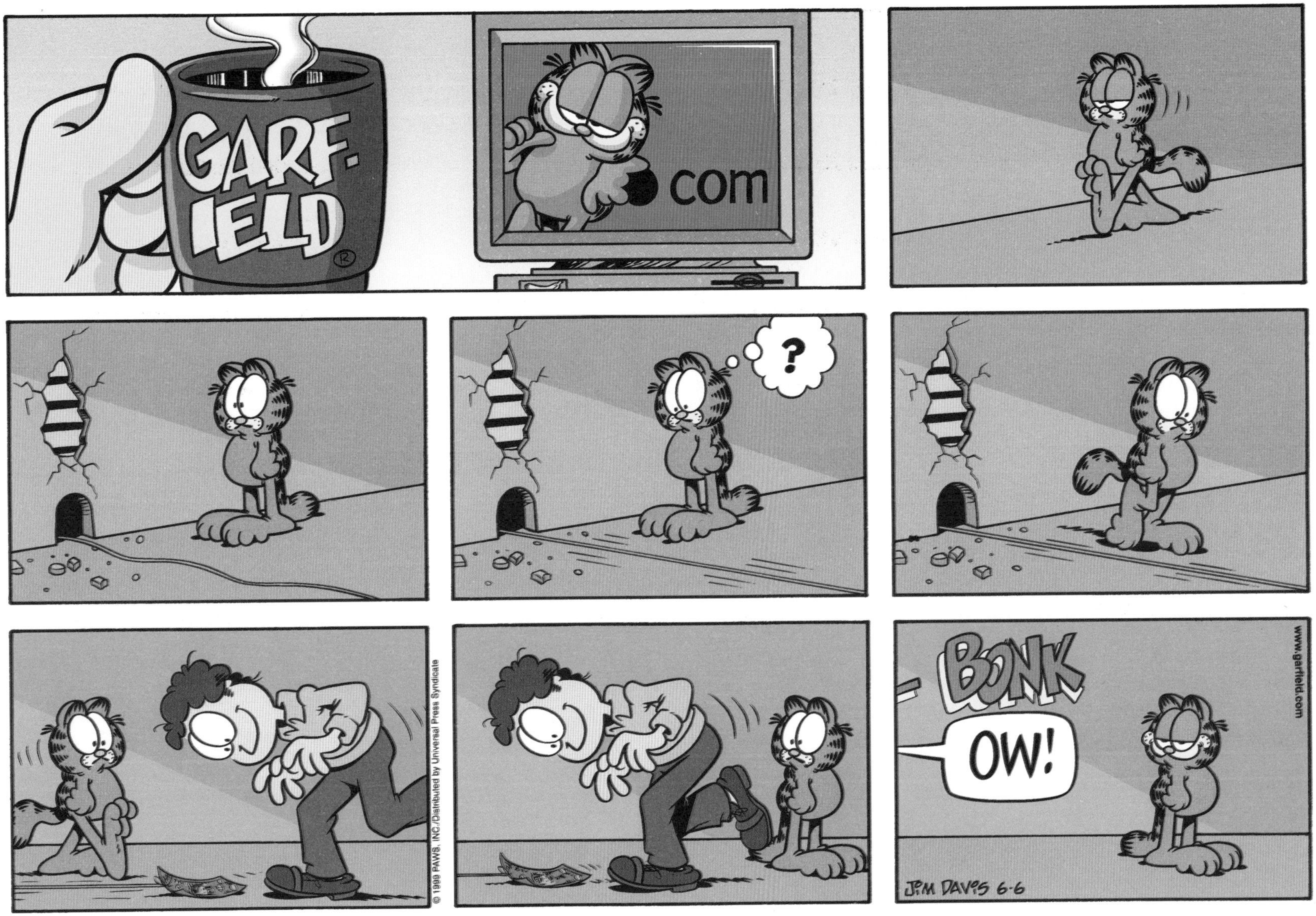
GARF-
IELD
com
?
BONK
OW!
© 1999 PAWS, INC./Distributed by Universal Press Syndicate
www.garfield.com
JIM DAVIS 6-6

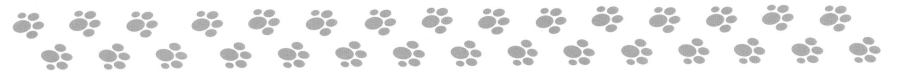

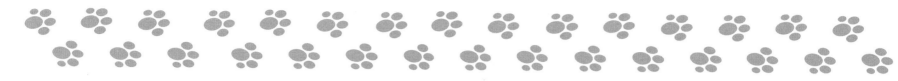

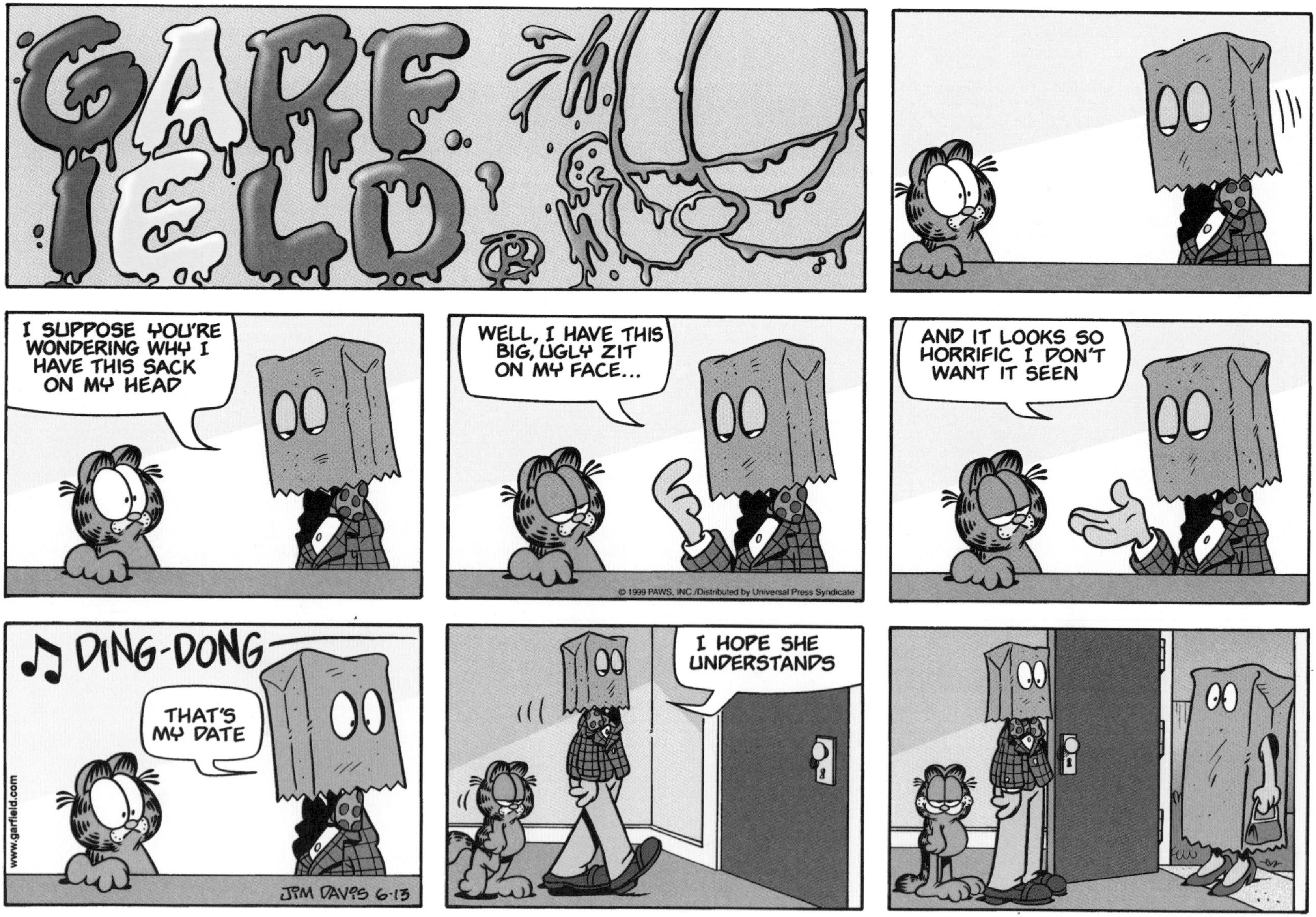
GARFIELD
I SUPPOSE YOU'RE WONDERING WHY I HAVE THIS SACK ON MY HEAD
WELL, I HAVE THIS BIG, UGLY ZIT ON MY FACE...
AND IT LOOKS SO HORRIFIC I DON'T WANT IT SEEN
© 1999 PAWS, INC./Distributed by Universal Press Syndicate
DING-DONG
THAT'S MY DATE
www.garfield.com
JIM DAVIS 6-13
I HOPE SHE UNDERSTANDS

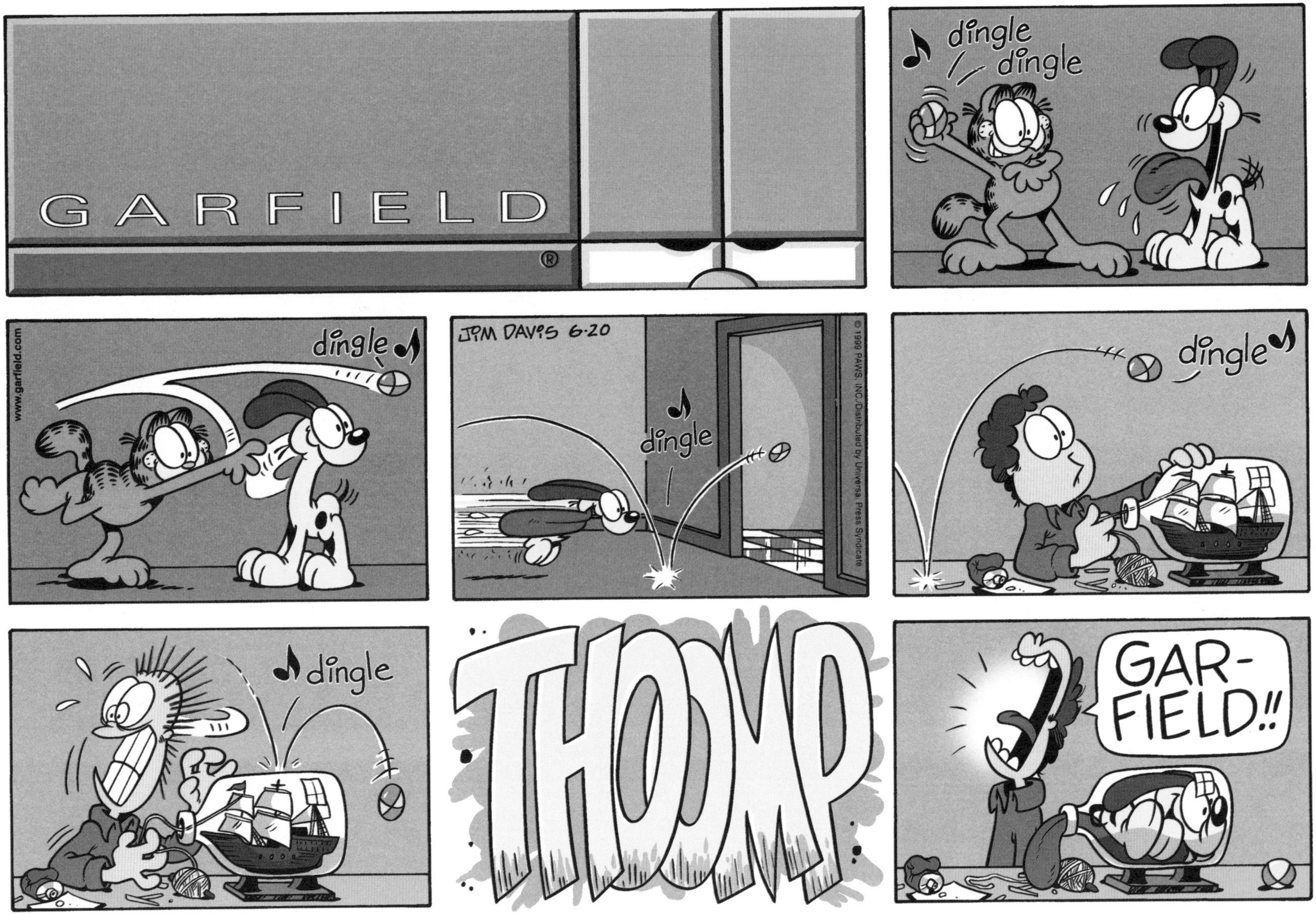
GARFIELD®
dingle dingle
www.garfield.com
dingle
JIM DAVIS 6-20
© 1999 PAWS, INC./Distributed by Universal Press Syndicate
dingle
dingle
dingle
THOOMP
GAR-FIELD!!

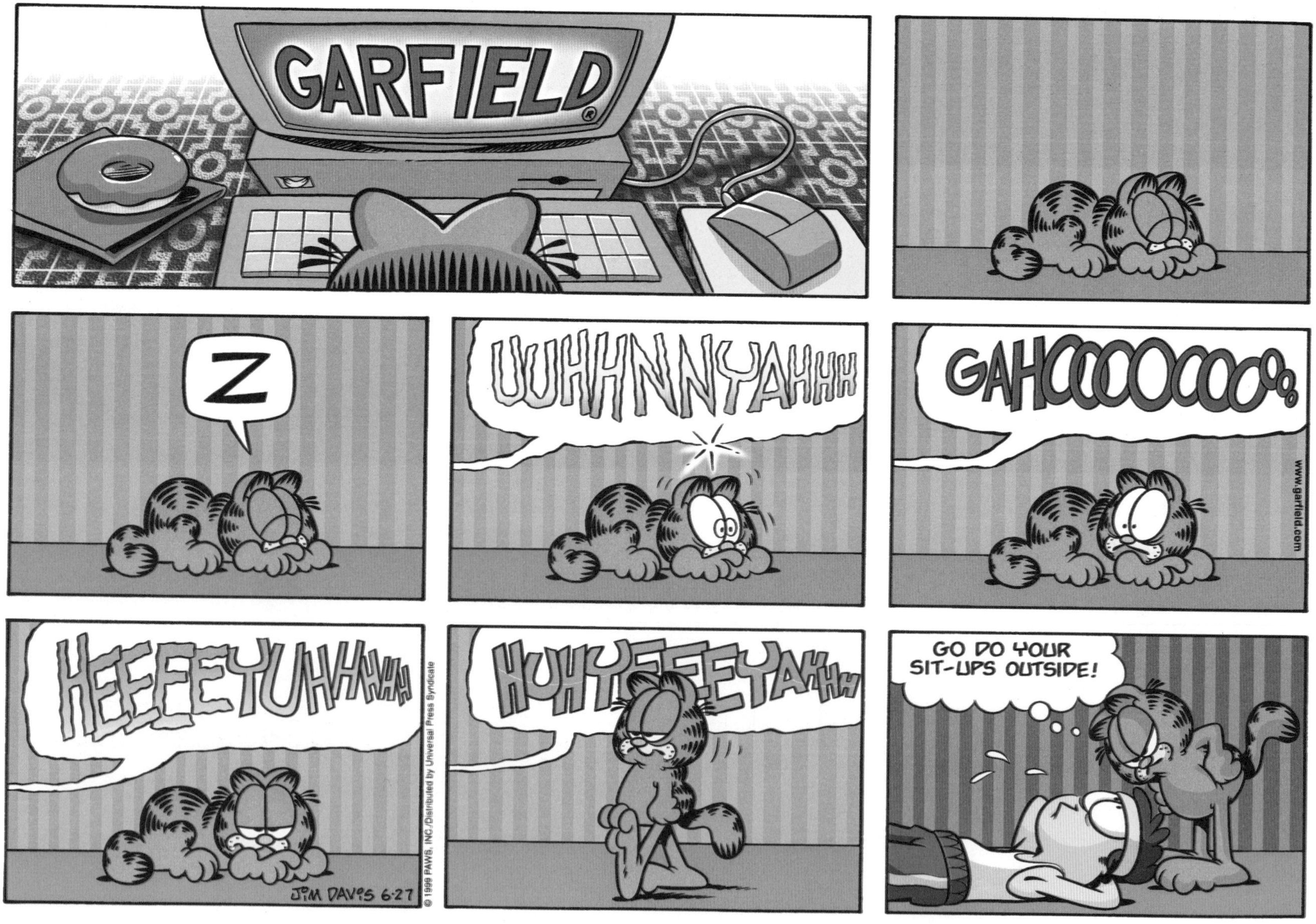
GARFIELD®
Z
UUHHNNYAHHHH
GAHOOOOOOOOoo
HEEEEEYUHHHHHH
HUHYEEEYAHHH
GO DO YOUR SIT-UPS OUTSIDE!
JIM DAVIS 6-27
© 1999 PAWS, INC./Distributed by Universal Press Syndicate
www.garfield.com

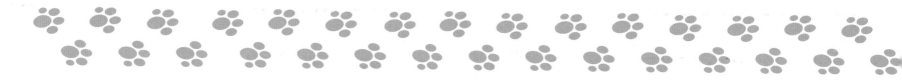

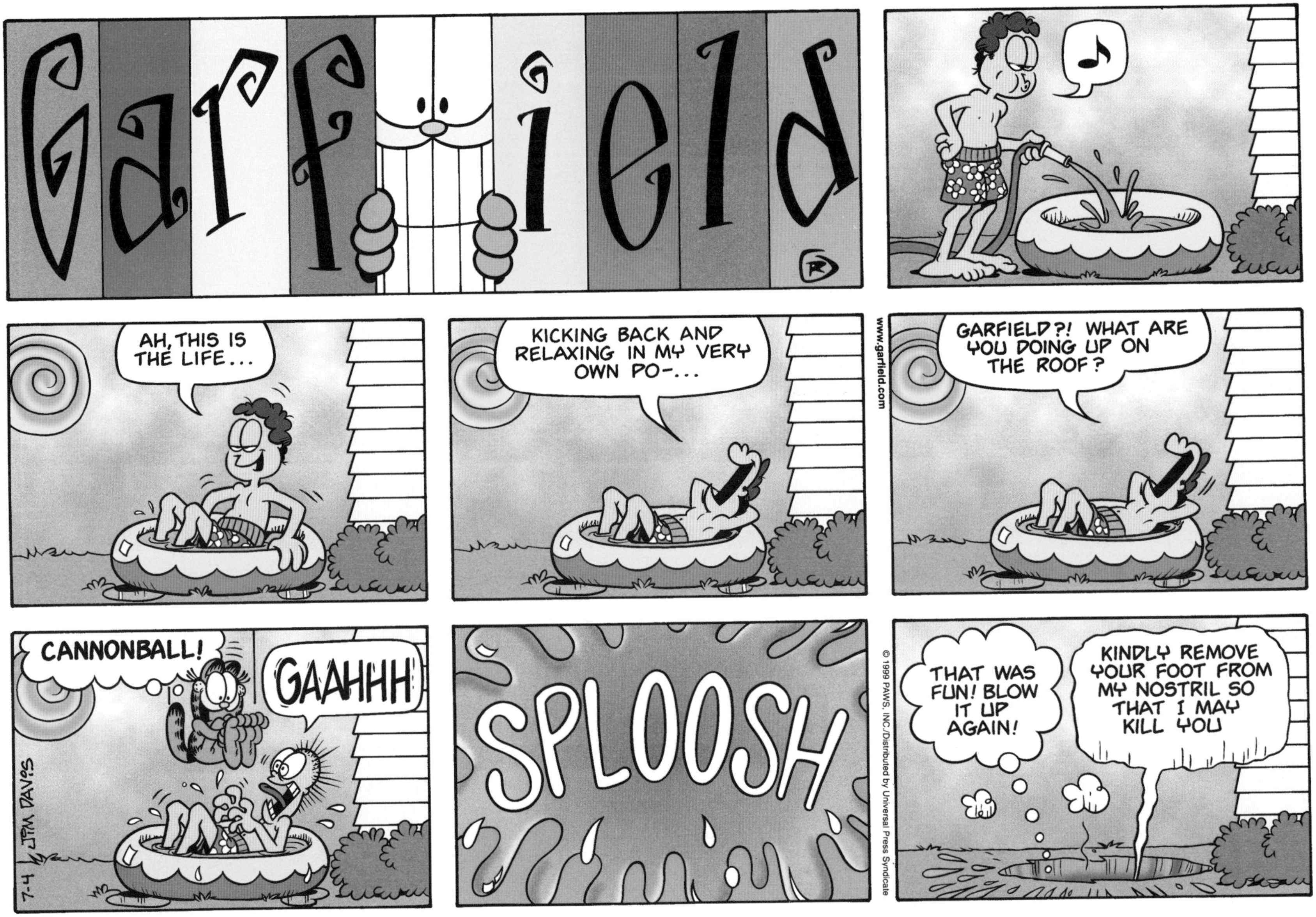

Garfield
♪
AH, THIS IS THE LIFE...
KICKING BACK AND RELAXING IN MY VERY OWN PO-...
GARFIELD?! WHAT ARE YOU DOING UP ON THE ROOF?
CANNONBALL!
GAAHHH
SPLOOSH
THAT WAS FUN! BLOW IT UP AGAIN!
KINDLY REMOVE YOUR FOOT FROM MY NOSTRIL SO THAT I MAY KILL YOU
JPM DAVIS 7-4
www.garfield.com
© 1999 PAWS, INC./Distributed by Universal Press Syndicate

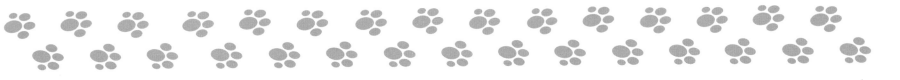

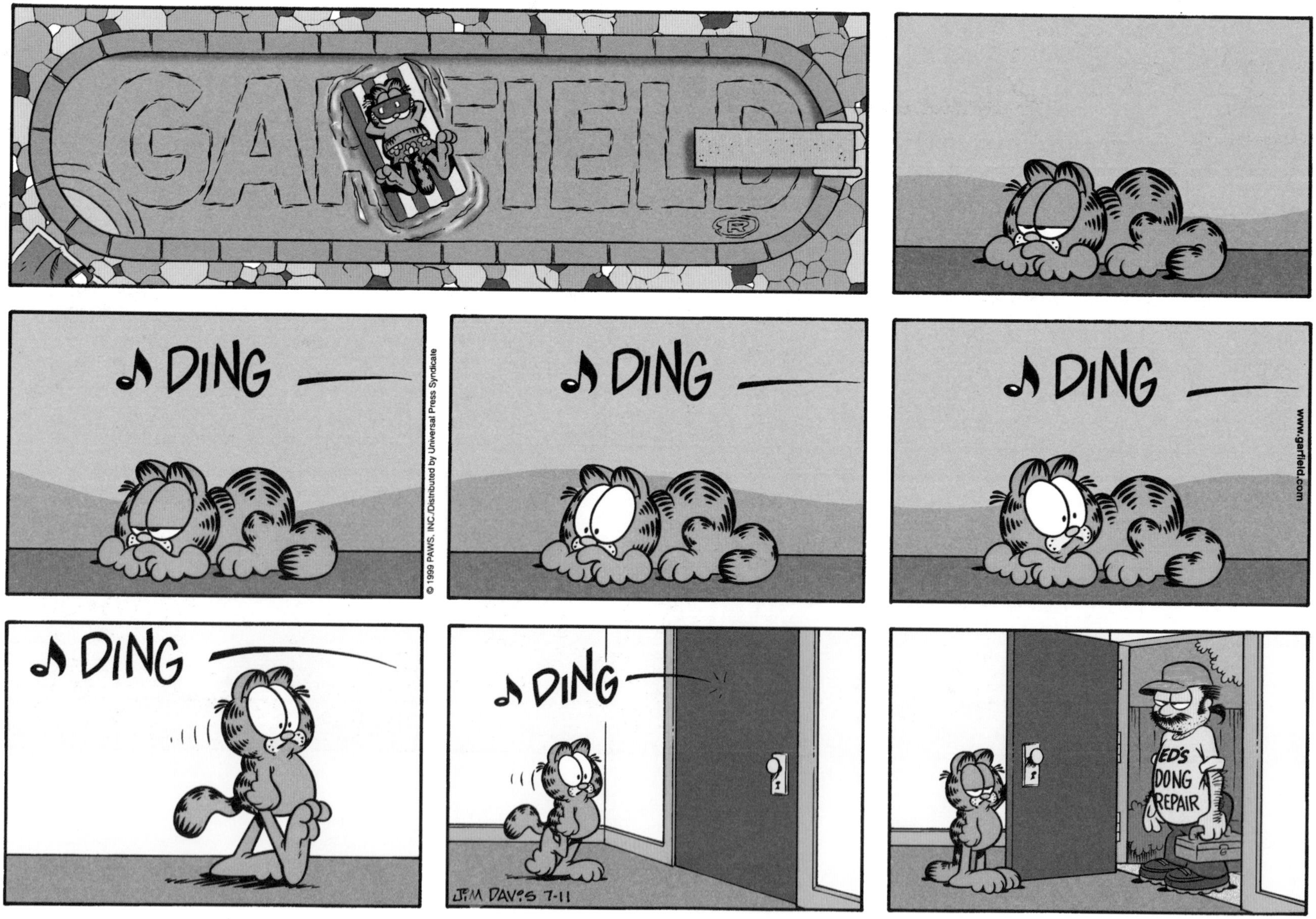
GARFIELD
DING
DING
DING
DING
DING
JIM DAVIS 7-11
ED'S DONG REPAIR
© 1999 PAWS, INC./Distributed by Universal Press Syndicate
www.garfield.com

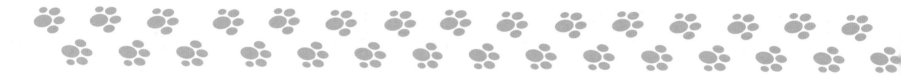

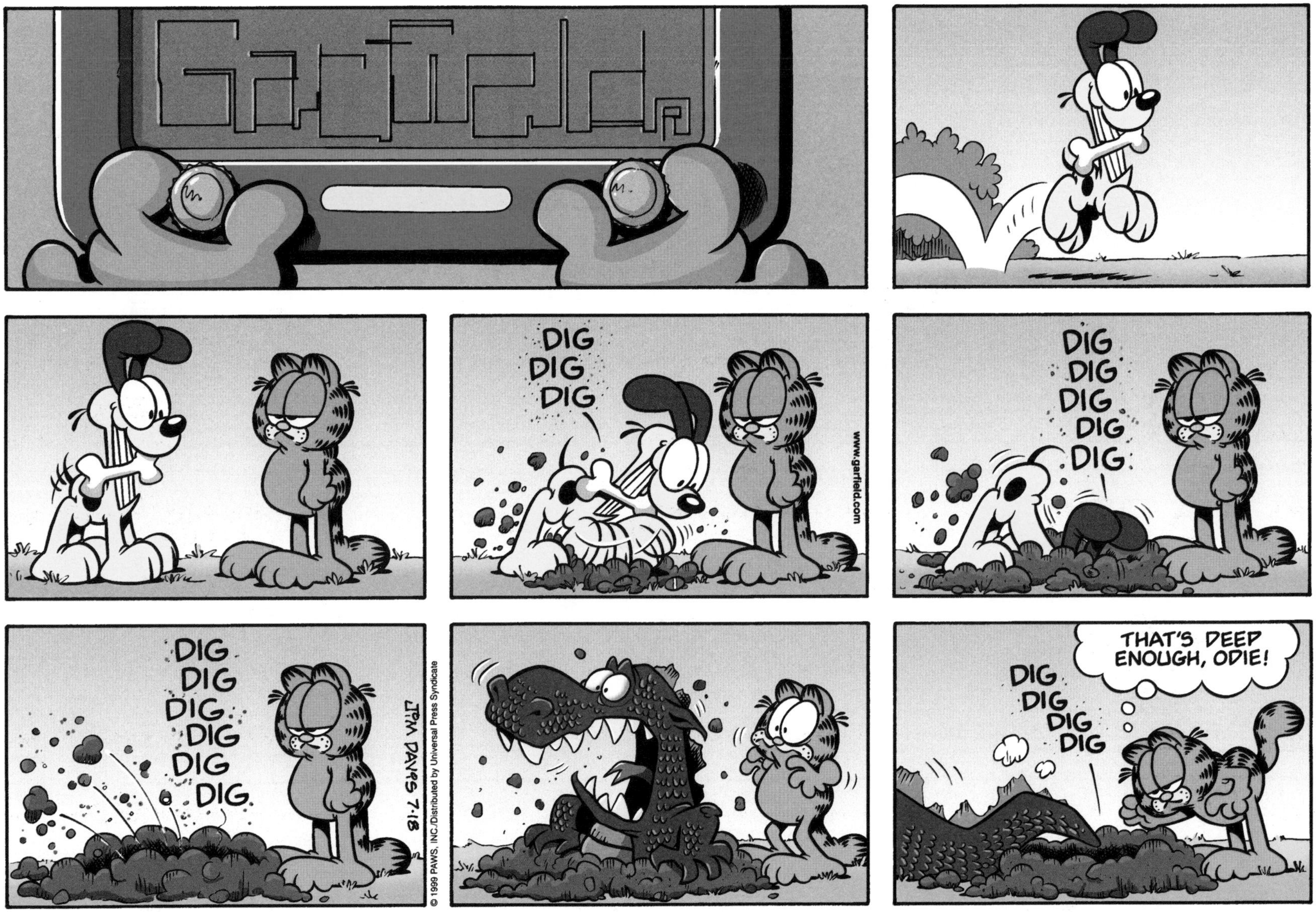
Garfield
DIG DIG DIG
www.garfield.com
DIG DIG DIG DIG DIG
DIG DIG DIG DIG DIG DIG
JPM DAVIS 7-18
© 1999 PAWS, INC./Distributed by Universal Press Syndicate
DIG DIG DIG DIG
THAT'S DEEP ENOUGH, ODIE!

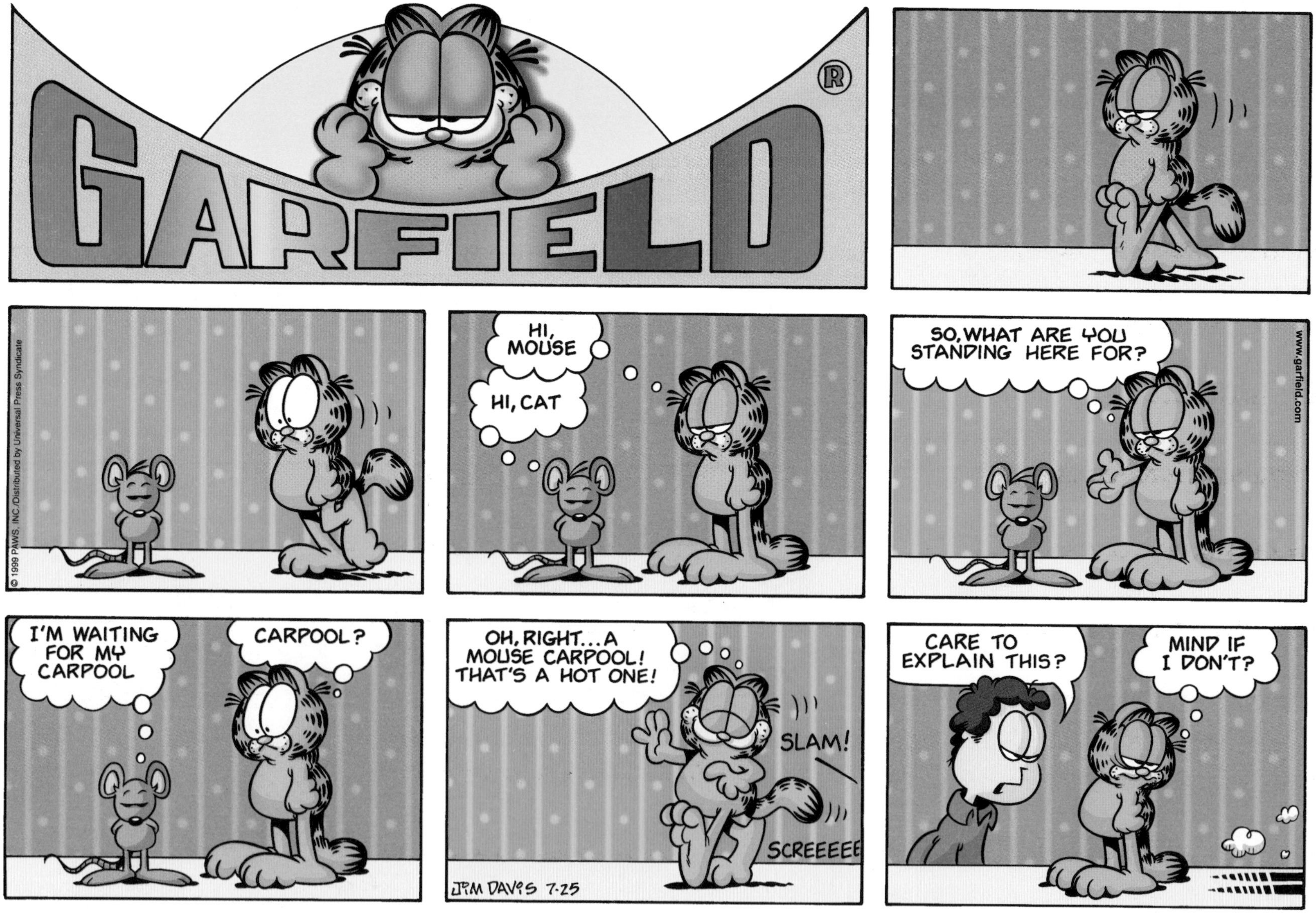
GARFIELD
© 1999 PAWS, INC./Distributed by Universal Press Syndicate
HI, MOUSE
HI, CAT
SO, WHAT ARE YOU STANDING HERE FOR?
www.garfield.com
I'M WAITING FOR MY CARPOOL
CARPOOL?
OH, RIGHT... A MOUSE CARPOOL! THAT'S A HOT ONE!
SLAM!
SCREEEEE
JIM DAVIS 7-25
CARE TO EXPLAIN THIS?
MIND IF I DON'T?

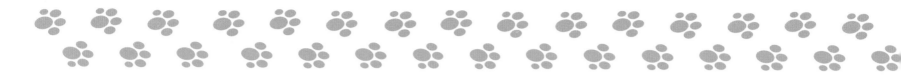

Garfield's Wacky World Tour

Buckingham'n'Cheese Palace

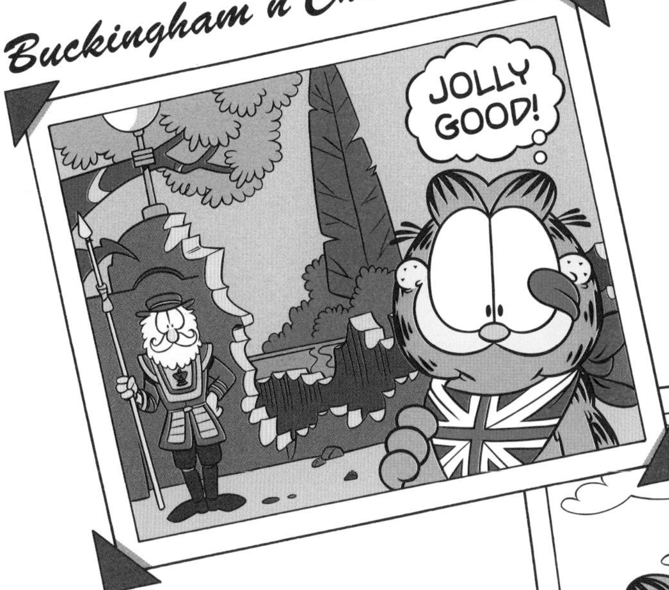
JOLLY GOOD!

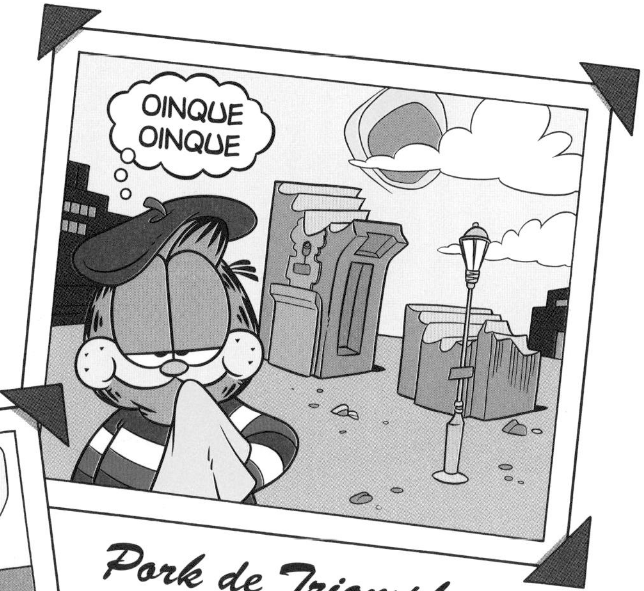
OINQUE OINQUE

Pork de Triomphe

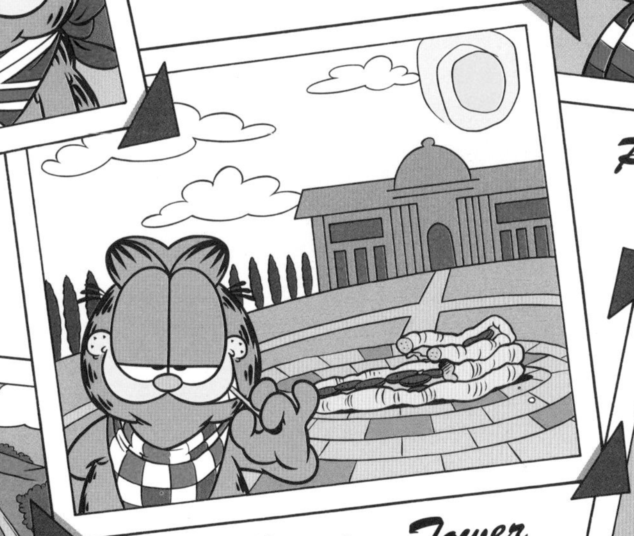

The Leaning Tower of Pizzas

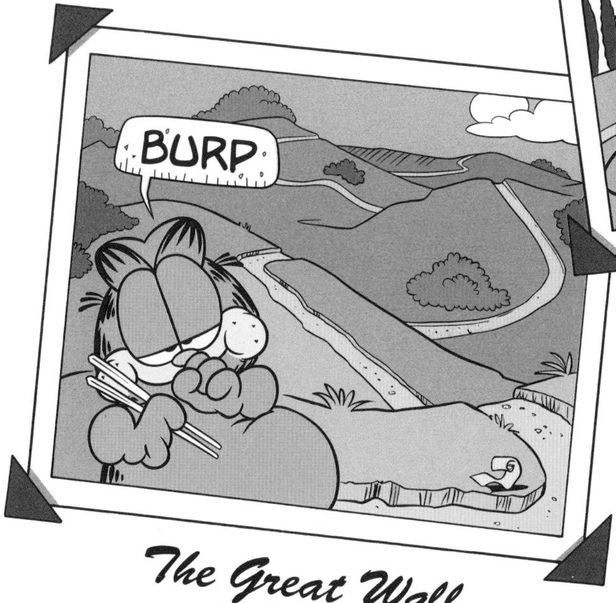
BURP

The Great Wall of Lasagna

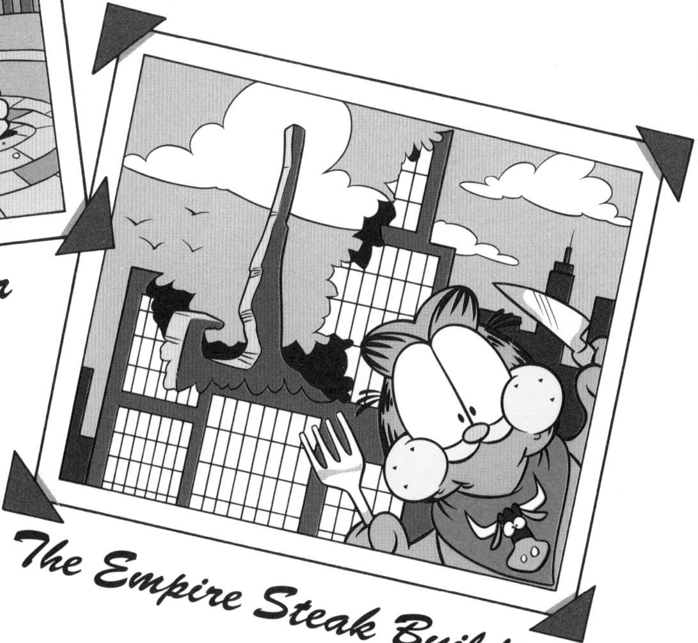

The Empire Steak Building

Like to get a **COOL CAT**alog stuffed with great **GARFIELD** products? Then just write down the information below, stuff it in an envelope and mail it back to us...or you can fill in the card on our website - **HTTP://www.GARFIELD.com.** We'll get one out to you in two shakes of a cat's tail!

Name:
Address:
City:
State:
Zip:
Phone:
Date of Birth:
Sex:

Please mail your information to:

**Garfield Stuff Catalog
Dept.2BB38A
5804 Churchman By-Pass
Indianapolis, IN 46203-6109**

© PAWS

STRIPS, SPECIALS, OR BESTSELLING BOOKS . . .
GARFIELD'S ON EVERYONE'S MENU
Don't miss even one episode in the Tubby Tabby's hilarious series!

__GARFIELD AT LARGE (#1)   32013/$6.95
__GARFIELD GAINS WEIGHT (#2)   32008/$6.95
__GARFIELD BIGGER THAN LIFE (#3)   32007/$6.95
__GARFIELD WEIGHS IN (#4)   32010/$6.95
__GARFIELD TAKES THE CAKE (#5)   32009/$6.95
__GARFIELD EATS HIS HEART OUT (#6)   32018/$6.95
__GARFIELD SITS AROUND THE HOUSE (#7)   32011/$6.95
__GARFIELD TIPS THE SCALES (#8)   33580/$6.95
__GARFIELD LOSES HIS FEET (#9)   31805/$6.95
__GARFIELD MAKES IT BIG (#10)   31928/$6.95
__GARFIELD ROLLS ON (#11)   32634/$6.95
__GARFIELD OUT TO LUNCH (#12)   33118/$6.95
__GARFIELD FOOD FOR THOUGHT (#13)   34129/$6.95
__GARFIELD SWALLOWS HIS PRIDE (#14)   34725/$6.95
__GARFIELD WORLDWIDE (#15)   35158/$6.95
__GARFIELD ROUNDS OUT (#16)   35388/$6.95
__GARFIELD CHEWS THE FAT (#17)   35956/$6.95
__GARFIELD GOES TO WAIST (#18)   36430/$6.95
__GARFIELD HANGS OUT (#19)   36835/$6.95
__GARFIELD TAKES UP SPACE (#20)   37029/$6.95
__GARFIELD SAYS A MOUTHFUL (#21)   37368/$6.95
__GARFIELD BY THE POUND (#22)   37579/$6.95

__GARFIELD KEEPS HIS CHINS UP (#23)   37959/$6.95
__GARFIELD TAKES HIS LICKS (#24)   38170/$6.95
__GARFIELD HITS THE BIG TIME (#25)   38332/$6.95
__GARFIELD PULLS HIS WEIGHT (#26)   38666/$6.95
__GARFIELD DISHES IT OUT (#27)   39287/$6.95
__GARFIELD LIFE IN THE FAT LANE (#28)   39776/$6.95
__GARFIELD TONS OF FUN (#29)   40386/$6.95
__GARFIELD BIGGER AND BETTER (#30)   40770/$6.95
__GARFIELD HAMS IT UP (#31)   41241/$6.95
__GARFIELD THINKS BIG (#32)   41671/$6.95
__GARFIELD THROWS HIS WEIGHT AROUND (#33)   42749/$6.95
__GARFIELD LIFE TO THE FULLEST (#34)   43239/$6.95
__GARFIELD FEEDS THE KITTY (#35)   43673-/$6.95

GARFIELD AT HIS SUNDAY BEST!
__GARFIELD TREASURY   32106/$11.95
__THE SECOND GARFIELD TREASURY   33276/$10.95
__THE THIRD GARFIELD TREASURY   32635/$11.00
__THE FOURTH GARFIELD TREASURY   34726/$10.95
__THE FIFTH GARFIELD TREASURY   36268/$12.00
__THE SIXTH GARFIELD TREASURY   37367/$10.95
__THE SEVENTH GARFIELD TREASURY   38427/$10.95
__THE EIGHTH GARFIELD TREASURY   39778/$12.00
__THE NINTH GARFIELD TREASURY   41670/$12.50
__THE TENTH GARFIELD TREASURY   43674/$12.50

AND DON'T MISS...
__GARFIELD'S TWENTIETH ANNIVERSARY COLLECTION!
42126/$14.95

Please send me the BALLANTINE BOOKS I have checked above. I am enclosing $_____. (Please add $2.00 for the first book and $.50 for each additional book for postage and handling and include the appropriate state sales tax.) Send check or money order (no cash or C.O.D.'s) to Ballantine Mail Sales Dept. TA, 400 Hahn Road, Westminster, MD 21157.

To order by phone, call 1-800-733-3000 and use your major credit card.

Prices and numbers are subject to change without notice. Valid in the U.S. only. All orders are subject to availability.

Name_____

Address_____

City_____ State_____ Zip_____

BIRTHDAYS, HOLIDAYS, OR ANY DAY . . .

Keep GARFIELD on your calendar all year 'round!

GARFIELD TV SPECIALS
__BABES & BULLETS   36339/$5.95
__GARFIELD GOES HOLLYWOOD   34580/$6.95
__GARFIELD'S HALLOWEEN ADVENTURE   33045/$6.95
  (formerly GARFIELD IN DISGUISE)
__GARFIELD'S FELINE FANTASY   36902/$6.95
__GARFIELD IN PARADISE   33796/$6.95
__GARFIELD IN THE ROUGH   32242/$6.95
__GARFIELD ON THE TOWN   31542/$6.95
__GARFIELD'S THANKSGIVING   35650/$6.95
__HERE COMES GARFIELD   32021/$6.95
__GARFIELD GETS A LIFE   37375/$6.95
__A GARFIELD CHRISTMAS   35368/$5.95

Please send me the BALLANTINE BOOKS I have checked above. I am enclosing $_____. (Please add $2.00 for the first book and $.50 for each additional book for postage and handling and include the appropriate state sales tax.) Send check or money order (no cash or C.O.D.'s) to Ballantine Mail Sales Dept. TA, 400 Hahn Road, Westminster, MD 21157.

To order by phone, call 1-800-733-3000 and use your major credit card.

Prices and numbers are subject to change without notice. Valid in the U.S. only. All orders are subject to availability.

GREETINGS FROM GARFIELD!
GARFIELD POSTCARD BOOKS FOR ALL OCCASIONS.
__GARFIELD THINKING OF YOU   36516/$6.95
__GARFIELD WORDS TO LIVE BY   36679/$6.95
__GARFIELD BIRTHDAY GREETINGS   36771/$7.95
__GARFIELD BE MY VALENTINE   37121/$7.95
__GARFIELD SEASON'S GREETINGS   37435/$8.95
__GARFIELD VACATION GREETINGS   37774/$10.00
__GARFIELD'S THANK YOU POSTCARD BOOK   37893/$10.00
ALSO FROM GARFIELD:
__GARFIELD: HIS NINE LIVES   32061/$9.95
__THE GARFIELD BOOK OF CAT NAMES   35082/$5.95
__THE GARFIELD TRIVIA BOOK   33771/$6.95
__THE UNABRIDGED UNCENSORED
  UNBELIEVABLE GARFIELD   33772/$5.95
__GARFIELD: THE ME BOOK   36545/$7.95
__GARFIELD'S JUDGMENT DAY   36755/$6.95
__THE TRUTH ABOUT CATS   37226/$6.95

Name_____

Address_____

City_____ State_____ Zip_____

Allow at least 4 weeks for delivery   7/93 TA-267